I found this compelling reading, almost more a novel than a memoir. AJ does a great job of getting her readers to keep turning pages, because they cannot wait to find out what is going to happen next.

—Bill Worth--Editor, and Author of the novels "House of the Sun: A Metaphysical Novel of Maui," and "The Hidden Life of Jesus Christ: A Memoir;" and the Author of non-fiction book exploring his 28-year journey with multiple sclerosis: "Outwitting Multiple Sclerosis: How Forgiveness Helped Me Heal My Brain By Changing My Mind."

Gardening With Guns

A Memoir

by AJ Wootton

Gardening With Guns
A Memoir
by AJ (aka Amber) Wootton

Published by

Tom Bird Retreats, Inc.

For permissions:

AJ Wootton
authorajwootton@gmail.com
ajwootton.com

ISBN 978-1-62747-314-9 (paperback)
ISBN 978-1-62747-315-6 (eBook)

Prologue

Sitting in the parking lot of Michaelson Industries collecting myself, I was grateful for the cushion I had built into my travel time. I was 30 minutes ahead of my 3:00 p.m. interview.

My stomach tingled. Despite the fact I was being referred by a former colleague, I was nervous. Avery and I had worked together for almost three years before he joined Michaelson. After only 18 months, he was already being promoted to a new job and was recommending me to backfill his job. Having the endorsement of someone on the inside at Michaelson gave me a huge advantage, and my track record with interviews was good -- but the stakes were higher here. This was a vice-president role, the top human resources job within one of the company's five business units, a level I had yet to attain in my 22-year career.

This job not only offered a promotion in terms of title, it provided a pathway back to the world I loved most -- dealing with the inherent conflicts that arose between employees and their leadership in the workplace.

It had been 10 years since I'd held a similar role, having diverted my focus instead to the niche area of compensation and benefits. This factor posed the biggest risk of my being selected for the job, as people from business segments typically frowned on corporate office types. In their estimation we were overpaid, spent our time kissing up to top management, and added no value. While I liked to think none of those attributes applied to me, I had held nothing but corporate roles for nearly a decade. I fully expected to be probed mercilessly on my ability to transition back to the "real world," the part of the company that was responsible for making profits, not sucking them up.

Flipping my auto sun visor down, I inspected my make-up and hair in its mirror. Satisfied, I returned it to its upward position, reached for my handbag, and opened the door of my black Nissan Murano. I smoothed my jacket and adjusted the waistband of my slacks before retrieving my briefcase from the back seat. If I had it my way I would go into the interview void of any baggage other than my handbag. But experience had taught me that my interviewers would be watching my every move in an effort to assess my engagement and interest in the job. Eye contact and asking insightful questions were, in my view, the best ways to convey interest, but I also knew that many a potential boss expected candidates to take notes.

In addition to a portfolio for recording noteworthy commentary regarding the company and the job, my briefcase also contained extra copies of my resume and a list of questions I had generated the night before. I doubted I would need to refer to my hand-written questions, and knew for a fact I would never again look at any notes I took during the interview, but it was all part of the dance.

It was early May and the Houston weather could not have been more agreeable. The sun warmed me as I walked across the parking lot toward the office entrance. The building that served as both a manufacturing facility and the division headquarters was situated in the middle of a large industrial park at the intersection of two major highways. High above me a steady stream of vehicles snaked their way along the elevated ramps that joined Beltway 8 and Highway 290. The air was tinged with the scent of heated metal and something else I couldn't identify, some sort of plastic or polymer maybe.

I still had 25 minutes to kill before my interview, maybe more. Having been on the other side of the desk countless times in my career, I knew the interview had a far better chance of starting late than early. Executives hoarded time like an urchin hoards food. But if things went well the interview could extend beyond its scheduled conclusion. That would be a good sign.

Seated in the waiting room, I scanned the walls, scattered with posters showcasing various pieces of Michaelson equipment. A three-dimensional version of a compressor, encased in glass, stood in the middle of the seating area. The lobby, which I found rather impressive, posed a contrast to the building's modest exterior. The metal chairs lining the perimeter of the seating area looked new and were complemented by sleek white tables placed intermittently between them. The room was well-lit and inviting. Having spent my entire career in the manufacturing sector, I had seen my fair share of manufacturing facilities. This one looked better than most, likely because it housed the senior leadership of the division. It probably didn't hurt that this facility was also located in Houston, instead of some remote town no one had ever heard of in the middle of nowhere.

Prior to moving to Houston, I had visited countless manufacturing facilities sprinkled across a half-dozen different northern states. Tiny towns in Michigan, Indiana, Illinois, and Tennessee came to mind. My current job with Dynamo Electronics required travel, but most of it was by air as none of the company's manufacturing facilities was within driving distance. I felt fortunate that the business travel requirements of my career had always been reasonable. Even now, as I weighed the pluses and minuses of my current employer, I could not complain about the travel. Generally, I loved my colleagues, from my administrative assistant, to my peers, to the senior leadership team. Sure, some of them were quirky and demanding, but each was intelligent, committed, and sincere in his or her own way. I had developed a true sense of camaraderie with the team in the four years I worked for Dynamo, a rare occurrence in the business world.

So why was I considering leaving for another job at a different company? It boiled down to one issue -- workload. The company, which had moved from private ownership to a publicly traded entity just months before I joined, had a seemingly endless list of processes, programs, and plans that needed significant upgrading. The work was challenging and rewarding. Each morning, as I plopped down in front of my computer, I told myself I would get out the door by 5:00, or 5:30 p.m. at the latest. But with meetings, impromptu calls, and countless crises du jour, I found the only time I could get any real work done was between the hours of 4:30 and 7:30 p.m.

When that wasn't enough, I began supplementing by working either at the office or at home on the weekends. I told myself it would be temporary, that after this project or that deliverable was completed, I could cut back to a normal eight-to-five routine. But now, four years later, the end to the backlog was still nowhere in sight. While much improvement had been achieved, the company's growth was multiplying the already long list of demands. Dynamo's CEO was determined to keep overheads low, making the addition of staff a virtual impossibility. I was not alone. All of Dynamo's employees wore multiple hats and worked hard and fast, just like me.

I willfully retrained my thoughts on the present. In an effort to maintain focus I got up and walked over to the model of the compressor. Inspecting it closely, I quickly concluded that I had no idea what it did or how it worked; not a clue. My preoccupation with trying to figure out exactly what the thing was used for was interrupted when Deanna, the receptionist, called to me from across the room.

"Annette will be right down for you."

I glanced at my watch. Impressive, five minutes ahead of 3:00 p.m. Annette was the pleasant, dark-haired assistant assigned to the division's president and his executive team. She was attractive, mid-forties and spoke with a charming Texas twang. By the time we reached the conference room I felt as if I had known her my whole life. After stopping at the break room, where she fortified me with bottled water, she opened the door and I saw four men, all late-forties to mid-sixties, seated around a large, oval-shaped table. They all stood when I walked through the door, each extending a hand and offering his name and position as he handed me his business card.

I had been told to expect a panel interview and was not put off by being outnumbered four to one. I rarely practiced for interviews, as I had always done best by simply answering questions honestly and in the moment. My preparation encompassed researching the company and running through my resume, in the process reminding myself of my accomplishments and each of the job's key responsibilities. After all, it had been more than 20 years since I started my career and it wasn't often that I reflected backward in time.

I was directed to a chair at the center of the table. The four of them settled back into their seats, flanking the two ends of the table and intermittent seats across from me. I made a mental note that I would need to remember to turn my head in alternating directions while speaking, in order to give adequate address to each of them.

Wayne, the Vice President of Supply Chain, started off.

"Well, there's four of us and one of you, but hopefully that doesn't make you nervous. I think you'll find us to be a pretty easy-going bunch. I know you met our President, Bob Walters, last week. You must have impressed him, or you wouldn't be here. He wants his team to work well together and that is why he leaves the final decision to us, the ones you will be working with each day. We're here together because it saves us time if we do this in one meeting versus four. So, if you don't mind, we're going to ask you some questions first, and then if you have any for us, we'll take those at the end."

He spoke with an undeniably Texan accent. His height was obvious even when he was seated. Broad shoulders were evident beneath the confines of his starched white, Polo button-down shirt. A natural smile illuminated his entire face, and his eyes were animated and friendly. He projected an air of easy charm that put me immediately at ease.

The questioning ensued, most of the focus devoted to how I had handled people situations in my former roles. All three executives asked questions, but Wayne dominated the process, often referring to notes he had written next to items on his copy of my resume. I could tell he had put some thought into his questions. There was no hint of an attempt to trip me up or catch me off-guard. His down-to-earth manner made me feel more like I was conversing rather than being interviewed.

Could I contrast and compare the balance between hiring externally and promoting from within? What was my philosophy regarding career development? Could I give him some examples of how I had helped my own employees develop? The four alternated with questions for 45 minutes until Dave, the Vice President of Sales, dropped the bomb that many men think, but rarely say, while interviewing a female candidate.

"So have you worked with an all-male team in your past?"

Before I could answer, Wayne cut in.

"You know she's in HR, right Dave? What kind of question is that?"

He was smiling, but I could tell he was embarrassed. Smirks twitched on the mouths of the other two interviewers. I guessed it wasn't the first time Dave had committed an interview faux pas. The air stiffened, so I rushed to answer before things became even more awkward.

"No, it's fine, I will certainly comment on that. I have to say I have worked with predominantly male teams throughout my career. Most of my bosses have been male, and a good majority of my colleagues as well. I have never felt any concern about this, nor have I really noticed the difference between working with a man versus a woman. People have told me I work well with others and I am a good team player. I enjoy interacting with people of all backgrounds. I guess that is what drew me away from my early career in finance toward my first HR role almost 20 years ago."

My answer killed two birds with one stone. They hadn't yet gotten around to asking the question of what prompted my move into human resources. My degree was in finance and I had spent the first four years of my career in accounting and financial analysis roles. My answer seemed to alleviate the mild tension Dave's question had created. Wayne, who by now had established himself as the clear leader of the process, invited me to ask my questions of them. I spent the remaining 15 minutes probing them on the company culture, the reputation of HR within the division, and their expectations of me as their colleague, should I be offered the job.

At the conclusion, I gathered up the business cards each of them had provided, shook their hands, and followed Wayne back to Annette, who escorted me to the lobby.

Overall, I felt it had gone well. I had to admit I did get a bit of an "old world" vibe from the exchange. Dave's question took me back a good 10 years. I knew if I got the job I would have to be prepared for his attitude to pervade the culture of the division, but that didn't scare me. I had not only dealt with far worse, I had succeeded in changing that stereotype in several of my past roles.

Several weeks ago, when Avery contacted me to assess my interest in making a job change, he had espoused to me the advantages of working for Michaelson. Having now spent 18 months with the company he could attest that the culture was very different from Dynamo. The demands and expectations were much more reasonable. He worked between 40 and 50 hours a week and felt valued here, as if the company genuinely cared about him and his well-being. As I melded Avery's description with my interview experience, I felt myself moving from skeptical to hopeful.

Yes, I decided as I pulled out of the parking lot, I wanted this job. Now all I had to do was get the offer.

Contents

Chapter 1

Independence Day

I admired the view above me as my raft drifted gently in the pool. The sun gleamed high and bright against a backdrop of blue sky. Intermittent white cotton clouds drifted in the forefront. Lowering my gaze to the horizon, I could see nothing but lush, green landscape. Trees reached tall in the distance and grass carpeted the foreground. Bronze-colored pots, profuse with red geraniums, green ivy and white petunias, flanked each corner of the textured, cream-colored, cement rectangle that bordered the pool. The temperature was impeccable. Drenched in warmth from head to toe, sufficient to counter the coolness of the water that collected in the curve of my back, but not enough to make me sweat, I was in my element. I could not imagine a more ideal backdrop for celebrating Independence Day.

A light breeze caught the hairs on my arms, creating a momentary tingling sensation before it died away only to be replaced once again by the penetrating warmth of the sun. Sunglasses shielded my eyes, permitting me to take in the panorama surrounding me without squinting. Squeezing my eyelids at this moment would have been punishing, serving only to exaggerate the pain that already coursed behind my eye sockets, stretching from temple to temple, and upward to the crown of my head. The shakiness in my stomach deemed the scent of chlorine, faint as it was, a further assault on my physical self.

My first sensation upon awakening earlier that morning was of my head being squeezed between the two ends of a vice grip. My affliction seemed to intensify as my mind journeyed toward full wakefulness. When the fog lifted from my sleepy brain, I tried to think what the cause of my headache could be. Drinking too much?

The events of the night before came slowly back to me. Yes, I drank some wine. I couldn't remember how many glasses, but I didn't think it was a lot, certainly not enough to cause the relentless throbbing I now felt. I did a quick inventory, confirming that I could recall all the prior evening's events, right down to the last act of brushing my teeth. I hadn't felt drunk. In fact, I felt pretty sober when I got into bed last night.

Suddenly I remembered running into Jules last night. A frequent fixture of our former social life, she and I easily picked up a conversation that bridged the gap in time since we had last seen one another. I readily accepted her offer of a cigarette and smoked it with her behind the big pine tree, out of sight of the kids. Maybe the nicotine was the culprit. But then again, I wasn't exactly a stranger to the act of sneaking cigarettes. I couldn't recall a single time when smoking had made me feel this awful the next day. Maybe I still hadn't caught up on my sleep? I suppose that would make sense. The past few days had been harried, between getting ready for our trip and the long drive.

Our family landed at my sister-in-law, Jill's, house yesterday afternoon around 5:00 p.m. The only interruptions we permitted ourselves on the way were bathroom, gas, and food breaks. Our frenzied pace was fueled both by the anticipation of seeing our extended families and the reality of the limited amount of time we would actually have to spend with them. We had a week, nine days if you count both weekends, but two full days would be dedicated to driving. Before our move to Houston our lives had revolved almost exclusively around our relatives, nearly all of whom were deeply rooted in northwest Ohio. Every holiday, birthday, anniversary, and countless random weekends were celebrated with a swarm of family that included parents, siblings, nieces, and nephews.

Now, the combined obstacles of distance, limited time off, and the hectic schedules of our three children permitted a maximum of two vacations per year, usually taken at Christmas and in the summer. Each trip seemed to turn into a marathon, as we attempted to pack six months of interaction into one week. This trip was no different. After unloading our luggage and exchanging hugs and greetings with Jill and her family, we shook off our road fatigue and headed straight to a barbecue in honor of the July Fourth Holiday.

Many of our northwest Ohio friends lived just as we had, outside of the town limits. The hosts of last night's party were no exception. Subdivisions had been popping up in the area for many years, but there was still a healthy population who bought or built a house in the middle of a good-sized lot and enjoyed the surrounding peace, quiet and privacy.

Four years ago, my husband Matt and I made the decision to trade our two-acre wooded lot, on a street full of farmland near the tiny town of Whitehouse, Ohio for a suburban house in Houston. The kids missed their big yard in Whitehouse, but loved their new pool and the year-round warm weather in Houston.

Overall, I had to say the move had been great for our whole family, but even after four years our Houston home still felt new. The sights, the sounds, even the smells of northwest Ohio reminded us of all that was good in our lives when we lived here, and all that we missed about it. The fresh country air, clear skies, and the 20-degree cooler and less humid temperature worked their magic last night. Eating and drinking with friends and family whom we hadn't seen in months, or even years, chatting about our jobs, what our kids were into now or which college they were headed to next fall, made for a spectacular first night in town. Maybe I drank more than I remember?

While the precise cause of my current state was still unclear, the regret I felt was distinct. The Ibuprofen and numerous glasses of water I downed earlier had yet to provide relief. I sighed, resigning myself to feeling sub-par for the better part of the day. Oh well, I could be much worse off. I was, after all, on vacation, today marking just the second of nine glorious days away from work. More so, sunning and floating were two of my all-time favorite activities.

I also knew the pain I was experiencing was temporary. By the end of the day, or worst-case scenario, by tomorrow, I would be back to my old self. In the flurry of activity planned for the week ahead, today's affliction would soon become a distant memory.

The analysis of my current discomfort conjured an inkling of something unpleasant. Fleeting as it was, a half memory of something troubling was ducking in and out of my consciousness. Rather than attempting to dismiss it, I grasped for it, feeling around for the elusive thread that hovered in the back of my mind.

What was it? Not the kids. Not work.

Dad. Yep, that was it. Dad.

Concern seeped over me as I considered the source of my angst. Despite my efforts to shelve my uneasiness, it had resurfaced numerous times in the last 12 hours, preoccupying me last night during the fireworks, earlier this morning, and now, here in the pool. Just seconds ago, I was firmly committed to the task of relaxing, but I gave in to the urge to once again pick through the conversation that had taken place on the heels of our arrival the night before.

I had pored over our telephone conversation at least four or five times already, but had yet to identify anything that would allow me to dismiss the nagging feeling that something wasn't right with him. If I hadn't felt so lousy when I woke up this morning I would have called him. But I found myself unable to use my mobile phone for the first hour, unable to bear the thought of focusing my eyes on the small print of my iPhone's contact list long enough to locate his number and press the button. I had laid there for what felt like two hours trying to go back to sleep in the hope I would reawaken with a new head.

By the time I forced myself out of bed and into the shower, Matt reported that our friends, Rob and Sally Simon, had invited us to a pool party at their house. It was already approaching noon and I knew the drive to their place would take an hour. Unlike me, Matt had awakened refreshed and rested and had already been up for hours. Knowing everyone was waiting on me, I hurried to get ready. We packed ourselves into our rented minivan and headed to Rob and Sally's house.

The fray of our morning's activities had distracted me from my mission. I resolved to call my father as soon as I got out of the pool.

Chapter 2

Dad

For as long as I could remember, I had talked to Dad at least once a week. This routine became even more important to me when we moved to Houston, as our calls became the means by which we remained present in each other's lives. It was how I kept him up to date on the kids, my job, and the timing of plans for our next visit. He shared the details of his life, what car project he was currently working on, what the Ohio weather was doing. The topic of weather received extra play in the winter, when he described the frigid temperatures and snowstorms that I became exempt from when we moved south. I had considerably less contact with my brothers than with him, so Dad always filled me in on what they were up to.

My dad was not a fan of travel in general and he hated to fly. He managed to put aside these inclinations when he and his wife, Doris, visited us in Houston two years ago. It was March, the month of both my son, Cameron's, and my birthdays. I was thrilled that his visit would enable us to celebrate together, a cherished annual tradition when we lived in Ohio.

The mood was festive and lighthearted. We visited the gulf shore and feasted on seafood. Matt and I showed off as much of our new city as time permitted. Unlike me, my father didn't gravitate to the sun and water. In spite of this fact, he

spent hours in the pool with the kids that week. Visions of
my daughter, Rachel, diving off of his shoulders into the deep
end still brought a smile to my face. He had been comfortable
and completely at ease. He broke with tradition that year
and bought me a birthday gift, a necklace bearing a delicate
pendant with five tiny diamonds -- *one for each of my children,
Matt and me.* He beamed when I opened the box.

My father was a good six years into his retirement and
living on a fixed income, so we had stopped exchanging gifts
years ago. I knew the necklace was expensive, but pushed aside
my guilt when I saw how happy he was to give it to me. He
told me countless times during that visit how proud he was of
me. It wasn't easy, he had said, to pick up and leave everything
familiar behind and take a job with a company so far away and
in a city I had never even visited before. The kids seemed so
happy, so well adjusted, he said, and we (meaning Matt and
me) were doing something right. I reminded him, as I often
did, about his role in my success. Not only had he financed my
college tuition, he encouraged me every step of the way. I knew
with complete assurance there was no request I could have
made of him that he would have refused if it were in his power
to grant.

The demeanor he projected over the phone last night stood
in sharp contrast to his temperament when he visited Houston
two years ago. The benefit of hindsight now helped me to
see that the changes in him had not happened overnight. Our
family had visited for Christmas, just six months ago. He was
fine, and as much like the father I knew and loved as he had
ever been. There was nothing I could recall that seemed out
of place or abnormal. It was after that, in the early months
of the new year, that I began to notice deviations from his
formerly predictable and reliable behaviors. The frequency of
our conversations began to fall off. This past March he forgot
to call Cameron on his birthday, something he had never done

before. I picked up the slack, trying to keep our weekly rhythm humming along.

I sensed something was amiss, but I believed the blip was temporary, and that it would right itself. I reasoned that he was still mourning the loss of his mother, Gramma Millie, who had passed away the previous October. My father had always been close to his mother. His own father abandoned their family when Dad was just a boy. I also knew that Dad was frustrated by the contract jobs that took him out of town for weeks at a time. Throughout his entire life my father had often worked two or three jobs at a time. After being forced into early retirement, he had yet to find what he deemed to be an adequate income replacement. The contract jobs paid well, but he hated being away from home.

I observed in that moment, as I had so many times before, how much our relationship had changed over the years. My father was a virtual stranger to me when I was a young girl. The stormy landscape of my childhood left me expecting little from my parents. The blossoming of my relationship with my dad when I was 18 was something I never imagined, let alone hoped for. He wanted me to have opportunities he didn't have as a young adult. He wanted me to go to college. I could live with him, he explained to me when I was in high school, and commute to the local university. He would pay my tuition, so long as I kept my grades up. It would be affordable, because I wouldn't have room and board expenses. Taking him up on his proposal turned out to be one of the best decisions I ever made. In my adult years, he became a trusted confidant, an enthusiastic grandfather to my three children, and the person in my life who most adored me.

As my raft turned with the gentle current created by the pump that hummed softly in the background, the group sitting poolside came into view, comfortably lounging in cushioned patio chairs, sipping drinks and talking. Bits of conversation and laughter floated upward toward the light breeze that caught them and delivered them to me in the form of dull murmurs. Our friendship with our hosts, Rob and Sally, had begun before we moved to Houston. Even though we were now separated by hundreds of miles, we still found a way to get together whenever vacation time and travel plans permitted. We always made a point of seeing them during our visits, and they had made several trips to visit us in Houston.

My serenity was momentarily interrupted by a hearty gust of laughter, unmistakably my husband's. Matt had a big laugh, not unpleasant but contagious. His voice was surprisingly deep for someone of his small stature. I listened harder and discerned that he was telling the story about our trip from Houston and how Cameron, during his late-night driving shift, had missed the turn onto Interstate 57, taking us off course. Meanwhile, Matt and I were catching a few much-needed winks in the back of the van. Luckily, I awoke in time to right the mistake before we strayed too far off course. Fortunately, the diversion ended up adding only a few extra hours to our travel time.

I smiled at the thought of Cameron, known to us simply as "Cam," being not only old enough to shoulder some of the responsibility for the 24-hour drive from Houston, but to also be college bound in the fall. How quickly 18 years had passed! Cam's childhood friend, Jake, picked him up shortly after we arrived last night. Jake's grandparents own a cottage on a nearby lake, so by now they too were probably floating on rafts, driving jet skis or fishing. After spending the weekend with Jake, Cam would have two days with the family before we headed to his freshman orientation at Michigan State University on Wednesday. I felt a twinge of anticipation on his behalf. I had a feeling he was going to have a great experience this week.

I knew many a mother who shuddered at the thought of their children leaving the nest. There was no doubt I would miss Cam terribly, but I was far more excited than saddened. My college years changed me dramatically, and unlike my primary school years, left me with only fond memories. I found the courage to dip my toe into the sea of college social life and was rewarded with greater confidence, and friendships that endured the two decades that followed. And there was the additional perk of meeting Matt during our senior year in college. Cam had loads more confidence than I had at his age, but I knew college would change him too, hone him more keenly into the person he was meant to be. I looked forward to watching him step into his own, transforming from boy to man, and establishing his own set of beliefs and opinions.

Chapter 3

Hair of the Dog

I winced as a spasm shot across my forehead. Upon our arrival at the Simon's home just 30 minutes before, Rob offered me a drink, which I declined, believing it might actually make me throw up. I assessed my situation as I lay floating on the raft and decided I had nothing to lose by having a little "hair of the dog." Worst case scenario, if I did throw up, maybe I would finally feel better.

I called to Matt, "Hey, honey?"

"Yeah?" he said, turning from his poolside conversation and looking my way.

"Could you get me a glass of wine? Please?"

"I thought you weren't drinking today," he responded with a smile, flashing his perfect white teeth.

"Well, you know what they say about the old hairy dog. Might as well have a little more of what made me feel so bad this morning."

Matt got out of his chair and Rob rose to follow him. I watched them walk toward the house and was struck once again by the contrast between Matt's slight, just under 5-feet-8 inches and Rob's towering 6-feet-3-inches height. Both fitness enthusiasts, they were in excellent shape. It had been their somewhat twisted and sarcastic senses of humor that had attracted them to one another when they met at the gym some six years before. They bantered back and forth on their way into the house, Matt gesturing all the while with his free hand, the other holding his drink.

My husband definitely had a flair for drama, especially when telling a story. Copious waving of his arms, gesturing with his hands and embellishing the details were all essential elements of his technique, which became more pronounced with the introduction of alcohol. The vision walking toward the house was no exception. I laughed to myself at the sight of them.

A few minutes later Matt returned, handed me a glass of wine and said with a mischievous smile, "Don't hurt yourself now."

"Believe me, that objective is foremost in my mind," I said, taking the glass and carefully sitting myself upright on the raft as he made his way back to his chair. I tried a sip and swallowed slowly. When I was certain it was not going to produce the retching I had feared, I took another, then set the glass on the side of the pool and once again admired the beautiful day. I could not recall a more perfect Independence Day in all the years I had lived in northwest Ohio. I reclined again on my raft and became fixated on a small cloud that looked like a four-leaf clover, when Rob got into the pool and immediately started hammering me.

"So, you had a bit too much to drink last night, huh? I guess Houston is making you soft. Back when you guys lived here and hung out with us on a regular basis, you didn't seem to have any problem holding your liquor," he said.

"Actually, I did have a problem. It's known as over-indulging," I said.

I drifted closer to him, taking a few more verbal jibes as I recalled ski trips, festivals, and charity fundraisers we had attended with the Simons that frequently turned into wild affairs, often involving pitching food and beverages at unsuspecting victims. During a New Year's Eve party a few years back, Matt managed to duck his head a split second before being hit by a flying cheese ball. We had all laughed hysterically when it smashed into the wall behind him. On other occasions, pitchers of water were emptied on unsuspecting heads. I had learned to keep my guard up when partying with this couple.

Part of the allure of hanging out with the Simons was indeed Rob's completely over-the-top sense of humor. Whatever the occasion, we were always assured of lots of laughs at both his antics and his edgy and embarrassingly inappropriate sense of humor. Rob explained his zest for fun as being a necessary outlet for his profession as a mortician.

"Just remember, the first three letters of the word funeral are F-U-N," he often said.

Rob's sense of humor and affability enabled me to grudgingly let go of the resentment I had first felt toward him for stealing my former workout buddy from me. Matt and I had exercised together from the very onset of our relationship. Initially we joined the same health club and dedicated ourselves to going each day after work. After the children came we could no longer justify the time away from our young family and shifted to working out together at home. Later, when on the heels of a corporate layoff Matt decided to start his own construction business, the flexibility of his schedule permitted him to go to the gym during the day when the crowds were light. He began a practice of daily gym workouts and met Rob, who maintained a similar routine.

Meanwhile, my eight-to-five schedule remained fixed and my home workouts became solitary. Feeling a key element of our relationship slipping away, I tried to revive it by inviting Matt to work out with me on the weekends, but there was already more to do on the weekends than those precious two days allowed. I eventually conceded to let go of that part of our relationship.

Things change, I reminded myself. Matt came from a long line of builders, his father and grandfather having also been in the business. He had a passion for beautiful homes, and kept a mental list of all the high-dollar properties in the area that were located in the most prestigious parts of town. He could cite on cue facts and figures such as square footage and lot acreage. He could even tell you the number of fireplaces, whether they were constructed of white marble or black granite, whether the flooring was honey-colored oak or dark cherry, the width of the crown moldings and the style in which they were carved. He knew with complete accuracy the price the home last sold for. His passion was contagious, and I threw myself enthusiastically behind him, convinced he could not only make a decent income, but that the flexibility of his new career would alleviate some of the pressure of the growing demands of our family.

Within two years the bottom fell out of the northwestern Ohio housing market. All that remained of his venture was his fit, toned body, and a newly formed group of friends he had accumulated by visiting the same coffee shop each morning. He built and sold two homes in two years, making a good profit on each. The amount he netted from those two homes was less than his corporate salary would have delivered, but we had expected that. We didn't, however, anticipate his earning potential completely evaporating. The prospects for another contract became grim as the housing market remained stubbornly in the tank.

I reminded myself that I had supported his decision to start his business, in spite of the known risks. I also reminded myself for the umpteenth time that he did shoulder more responsibility at home, shuttling kids to and from appointments and activities, thereby alleviating most of our daycare expenses. I welcomed and appreciated the savings, but it didn't make up for the complete loss of his former income.

I worked harder in hopes of positioning myself for a promotion. I hinted to Matt that maybe he should consider returning to the corporate world. He never outright refused, but he also didn't put any effort into trying to find a job. By now he had established a network of high-quality craftsmen, from roofers to plumbers to finish carpenters. He was invested in his business and believed we just needed to wait out the slump. It would take time, but it would come back. It always did, he said.

Meanwhile, he continued his daily workouts with Rob. The subjects of money, the disparity in our schedules, and his seemingly endless supply of leisure time blended together to create one huge sore spot for me. My frustration prompted nasty arguments between us. I was resentful of his lack of focus on finding work while he seemed to have plenty of time to enjoy himself during the day. He said I was being a nag. I was growing increasingly concerned about our household income. We couldn't live this way long-term, I told him. He told me he was well aware of the fact, I didn't need to keep reminding him.

I had put aside my lifelong dream to live in a big city after my relationship with Matt got serious in our senior year of college. He made it clear that he wanted to remain within close distance of his family. Looking ahead to our future, I, too, saw the appeal of having our then unborn children grow up amidst grandparents, cousins, aunts, and uncles. By the time Matt proposed marriage, I had firmly committed myself to staying in northwest Ohio. It was, after all, my home too. We bought

Matt's family home from his parents when they were ready to downsize.

Matt's sister, Jill, later moved into the house next to us. Her children provided a constant source of companionship and our combined lots provided four acres upon which our children could freely roam. Playing in the tree fort that was eventually erected near the creek, sledding, jumping in piles of dry autumn leaves and endless games of tag and hide-and-go-seek dominated the landscape of their childhood. The cocoon of love and support would forever deem Whitehouse home in our hearts.

Idyllic as our life was, I continued to question the financial viability of remaining in northwest Ohio. I knew that once the housing market recovered, there would be a delay in bringing cash in through Matt's business. The time span between signing a contract and finishing a house, including the punch list, was upwards of a year or more. It may be three or four years before we saw any money from a contract. Meanwhile, my employer was teetering on the brink of bankruptcy.

My childhood dream of moving to a big city bubbled up and eventually I could no longer contain it. I pitched the idea to Matt, asserting that if I expanded my job search outside of northwest Ohio, I had a far better chance of garnering a promotion and a bigger salary. We could sell our house, pay off the equity loan we had borrowed for the kitchen addition, and get ourselves into something more affordable. And the kicker was that in a larger city with a thriving economy, he would have much better prospects for restarting his business or finding corporate work.

To my surprise, Matt put aside his resistance to leaving our families and the world in which he had lived all his life. He agreed, and within six months we were headed to Houston. The move was a success on all counts -- except for the part about Matt finding a job. Four years later he was still going to the gym every day and still unemployed. But, I countered myself, I had only started my new job at Michaelson two weeks ago. Matt believed that my recent workload was as much due to my own drive as it was the demands of my former employer. I knew I would have to prove to him that I was capable of limiting my input to a 40-hour week.

To be fair, I also needed to test the theory that my new job would in fact be less demanding than my last one. But, assuming this proved out and I started being more present at home, there was no reason for him not to return to work. I began contemplating how long I should give it before raising the topic again. One month? Two?

Just then I became aware of my rising blood pressure. Moments ago, I was floating in a state of complete relaxation. And now I was ruining it. Stop thinking about it, you're on vacation, I told myself, willing my mind back to the here and now.

Chapter 4

Unthinkable

"On the note of overindulging, may I top up your glass?" Rob asked.

"No, I think I'll hold for a while," I answered.

As I continued to float aimlessly, the group on the deck came into view. I noticed Matt walking toward the foot of the pool, away from the party clustered in lounge chairs. He was looking my way and my eyes caught his. He motioned me toward him with his arm. I mouthed "What?" to him, at which point he repeated the arm sweep, this time adding head movement and saying, "Come over here."

My first thought was that one of the kids had done something, broken a window with a baseball or somehow violated something in the neighbor's yard, and he wanted to consult on the remedy, or perhaps the discipline.

Rachel and Austin, our two youngest children, had accompanied us to the pool party. Probably due to the closeness in their ages, 13 and 12, it seemed that when one got into trouble the other was not far behind. And anything was possible when they were playing with the two Simon kids, who were almost identical in age. I tried to imagine what trouble they had found as I propelled myself toward the side of the pool.

By now Matt was standing behind the diving board waiting for me. Rob gave my raft a final push toward the edge and I heaved myself onto the side of the pool, my concern growing as I focused in on my husband's face, which bore the same serious look it had since he began beckoning to me just moments ago.

"Is it the kids? Did they get in trouble?" I asked, feeling anxious now.

"Just come over here," he replied.

Leading me to the side of the house where we were completely out of view of the others, Matt finally stopped and faced me. I was in a full-on state of panic by now.

"What? What, for God's sake!" I demanded.

"It's your dad."

He stopped, as if trying to frame the words he would speak next. Seeming unable to find whatever approach his mind sought, he pushed on.

"I don't know how to say this."

Another pause.

"He's gone, Amber."

"Gone?" I repeated, feeling my heart rate elevate at an uncomfortably fast rate, staring hard into his chocolate-brown eyes, searching for an answer I could not yet comprehend.

"He's dead."

His eyes were full of sadness and he spoke quietly and carefully, knowing that the last phrase carried the impact of a sledgehammer, so much more powerful and damaging than the imaginary one that had pounded my head earlier that morning.

My voice was something just above a whisper as I said slowly, mechanically, with my eyes fully fixated on his face, "What? What happened? How?"

I watched him suck in a deep breath before he said, "Suicide. He shot himself."

The corners of his mouth were now turned downward as if he were about to cry.

"No one had your number since you just changed phones, so your cousin got a hold of my cousin, who called me."

I froze as I absorbed his words, my breath suspended in my chest. Finally, my mouth opened.

"No," I pleaded, "no."

But even as I asserted my denial over and over, I knew it must be true. No one would ever make a mistake or joke about something so awful.

"I can't ... I don't ... believe it."

I felt my legs turning to jelly and myself falling and feeling sick to my stomach all at once. My hangover was a distant memory. In slow motion, I saw Matt's arm extend and catch me as I slumped forward. He pulled me into him as my body, unwilling to hold itself upright, buckled. I shook uncontrollably as my mind struggled to comprehend. It seemed like we were there for hours, my head hanging over his shoulder, arms limply wrapped around his neck.

I was vaguely aware of moisture trickling down my arms, forming droplets and falling from the tips of my quivering fingers. Were those my tears, I wondered absent-mindedly? Had I cried that much? Then I remembered I was still wet from the pool.

I stared at the ground, not seeing it. Instead, I saw my father's face and the only word my mind could form was, "Why?"

Chapter 5

The Party's Over

The next thing I knew I was being surrounded, steadied and led inside. Sally handed me a towel that I used to blot my dripping arms and legs before I collapsed into a chair. My body was resistant to sitting up, so I leaned forward, elbows on thighs, my head in my hands.

After an indefinite lapse of time, I said, "I need to call my brothers."

I had yet to circulate my new work cell phone number. I knew that my brothers and my father's wife would have already tried, probably numerous times, to reach me on my old number. I was angry with myself for the second time that day, this time for being inaccessible. Instead of hearing the news directly, the horrific headline had traveled to me on a fragmented path. My cousin and Matt's cousin had been best friends since high school. How long, I wondered, had it taken them to figure out the formula that succeeded in reaching me?

Matt handed me my phone and I fumbled to find the number for my brother, Kirk. Seeing my shaking hands, Matt took the phone, located his contact and pressed the call button. The phone rang six times and then went to voicemail.

"He's not picking up," I said. "I'll try Jay."

Again, Matt performed the mechanics and handed the phone back. My brother, Jay, answered on the second ring.

"Is it true? Is he dead?" I asked, fresh tears rising in my throat and making my words hard even for me to understand. "Did he really *kill* himself?"

"Yeah, it's true," he said, pausing for a moment, "Amber, I hated that we couldn't reach you. We weren't sure if you were here yet or still on the road."

"What happened?" I asked.

After clearing his throat and sucking in a long breath, he began.

"He did it out back, on the far edge of the property. With a shotgun. They found him this morning."

Jay paused, letting me digest. His words etched the beginning of a picture my mind's paintbrush began to fill in. The centerpiece was the same bright yellow sun that so generously bathed me in warmth just moments ago, glaring down from the cloudless sea of morning sky. I pictured the butterscotch colored, aluminum sided structure Dad referred to as "the barn," its three gaping brown doors hanging closed in silence. He would have had to walk past it to make his way to the far edge of his ten-acre property.

He most likely had on a racing t-shirt, probably something with Dale Earnhardt on it. I imagined him wearing either khaki or denim shorts. This being the peak of summer, his face and arms would be a light brown, the skin on his smooth cheeks rosy from the sun, but his legs stubbornly pale. He would be wearing his staple white crew socks and white tennis shoes. The air was laced with the scent of dry leaves and pine. As he made his way through the woods the light from the intermittent sunbeams danced through his silky white hair. Twig, branch, and vine crunched and sighed with every step as he walked, shotgun propped against his right shoulder, barrel pointing behind him, to the far side of his property. I pictured him walking resolutely, staring straight ahead, his face fixed in a firm expression, absent even the slightest hint of a smile.

I paused, allowing the mental scene I had just created to sink in. What did he do once he reached the spot? Did he hesitate, arguing with himself as to whether this was really how he wanted to end it? Did he have any last-minute second thoughts? No, I decided. He would never have gone that far, weapon in hand, unless his mind was firmly made up.

Did he say his final, mental goodbyes, I couldn't help but wonder? Did he pray? He wasn't religious, but on the cusp of the action he was preparing to take, he may have found faith. Or was he so consumed with the task at hand that there was no room for any thought other than pulling the trigger?

Did he feel fear? Fear of the pain he was about to inflict on himself? Or perhaps fear of leaving all that he knew behind as he jumped feet forward into the abyss of death?

The lonely scene I pictured, and the questions my mind relentlessly fired at me regarding what he must have been feeling in those final minutes, left me heartsick.

I reluctantly decided that he plunged ahead with no fear or regrets, and without saying any final, mental goodbyes. I wanted to think otherwise, to believe that leaving this world was agonizing for him, but knowing my father as I did, I doubted there was any second-guessing.

How could he do this? I asked myself this over and over again. I couldn't comprehend taking my own life for so many reasons. I could never bear to leave my children behind. Even worse, I couldn't bear the thought of the pain my decision would inflict on them. It was incomprehensible.

The nagging worry that I could not seem to shake the day before returned front and center: Was he depressed? I could see no other explanation. His life had to have lost every shred of joy in order for him to do such a thing. This notion, the thought of my father in a state of such extreme misery that his only relief was death, caused my lip to quiver and like a switch, I released another bout of tears.

I reached for the tissue Matt handed me as I willed myself to finish the scene, to see it through to its conclusion. Why, I did not know. Perhaps it was some form of sympathetic expression, a way to help me understand what could have driven him to this end. A way to go with him, if only in my heart.

I squeezed my eyes shut. The blast of the shotgun echoed through the woods, sending flocks of quietly nesting birds into frenzied flight. Forest creatures of every variety -- coon, rabbit, mouse, and possum -- startled at the sound. Sitting upright, they would have been on high alert for danger. Tiny hearts pounded, ears and noses were fully engaged in the task of identifying the nature of the intrusion into their peaceful world.

My father lay motionless on the ground. The force of the blast had sent him reeling backwards. He would have landed face up I guessed, the gun somewhere at his side. Would the impact have knocked the glasses off his face? How long, I wondered, had his lifeless body lay among the dry leaves and ferns, utterly alone and eternally still, before he was discovered?

I dragged my focus away from the theater of my mind's eye and back to Jay.

"But *why*? Was there something going on with him?" I asked my brother, knowing he and my father saw each other almost daily.

"I don't know, Amber. I am just as shocked as you and everyone else."

Jay released a long breath and I imagined him in deep thought, probing his brain for the answer I sought. Finally, he asked, "Did you know he got a DUI Friday night?"

"Yeah, I talked to him last night," I said.

I relayed the conversation I had had with Dad just after we arrived in town the night before. The one I would forever classify as 'the last time I talked to him.' The lack of animation in his voice when he answered my call had planted the seed of worry in my mind. Instead of his usual, "Hi there, honey," it was simply, "Hello," emphasis on the first syllable. His voice spoke to me slowly, deliberately, in a volume barely above a whisper, telling me he had gotten a DUI on his way home from my brother, Kirk's, the night before. His pain came through in the delivery of each word.

"It was a dumb-ass thing to do. I know better," he said with a heavy sigh. I pictured his face, his blue eyes uncharacteristically hard and steely, his mouth drawn in a tight line. If I were standing in front of him he would be looking off to his right instead of directly at me. I would honor his silence as he cycled through his options.

"You always gotta have a plan," he so often said.

His despair was rooted in the fact that he was now part of a plan of another one's making. His arraignment would take place early in the upcoming week. At that time the presiding judge would assign a court date. There was no avoiding conviction, he said with complete resignation. There was no escaping the system in which he found himself trapped, and no effect whatsoever he could instill upon his fate. The desire for control over his destiny had driven my father his whole life. It was the cornerstone of his very existence. On the heels of an admittedly bad decision he now found himself powerless, a feeling he had never been able to abide. Not in his entire life.

He continued his self-admonishment, saying he would not be able to look his grandchildren in the eyes after this. How could he, he asked me? I was frustrated at my inability to conjure up some means of comforting him.

"Dad," I said, "everyone makes mistakes. We all do things we aren't proud of. Things we regret. Stop worrying about how we will view you. We would never judge you or look at you any differently. You're Dad, Grampa, and awesome all in one, and we love you so much."

Trying to lighten things up a bit, I added, "Besides, you have been through much worse than this."

My attempt at humor only seemed to make him feel worse, as he reminded me that this was not his first DUI. I grudgingly accepted his words as fuzzy acknowledgement formed in my head. I vaguely remembered he had gotten a DUI before. But that had been more than 20 years ago. I suddenly realized how long it had been since I had thought about that topic.

My attention quickly snapped back to the situation at hand. We hadn't seen each other since Christmas and my only concern about the current DUI was how it was affecting his state of mind. The purpose of my call was to let him know we had arrived and to organize our visit with him around one of the several days that remained available the following week. After hearing his story and the defeat in his voice, I went into high alert mode. I wanted to see him right away. I told him I would drive out to his place. He declined, saying he was tired, and promised we would see each other later in the week. He would know more about his availability after his arraignment. We would make plans then.

I was tempted to insist, believing that if I could just see his face my worry would subside. He would feel better after a hug, a talk, and a beer. I could take his mind off his troubles by catching him up on the recent goings-on in my life. I debated for a minute after we hung up. I knew my father to be more negative than positive at times, someone who could get down about things, but I had never known it to last for long. Throughout the many challenges his life had thrown him, he had always endured and eventually overcome. I finally allowed myself to give in to his wishes.

He needed to get some rest, I told myself. I resolved to call again the next day, and if he did not seem better I would not take no for an answer. I would get in the car and go over there. How I now regretted not listening to myself. My presence may have done nothing to alter his plans, but at least I would have seen him one last time.

My worries had continued to poke holes in my thoughts last night at the barbeque, and today as I floated in the pool. But suicide? The thought had never once occurred to me. Not my father. It was unthinkable. Could he have really felt bad enough about a DUI to plan such a morbid end to his life?

Was there something else? I thought again about his change in demeanor over the past few months. I became increasingly convinced that there had to be something else, something bigger and more threatening than a DUI. Maybe he was sick? Having always enjoyed good health, he staved off regular doctor visits. He had little patience with maintenance, swearing off the cholesterol medication that was prescribed in his thirties, saying he would live his life and take his chances. Could his lack of annual physicals have allowed some serious illness to go undetected for so long it was now beyond repair? Like cancer?

"The DUI is the only explanation I have been able to come up with, but it doesn't make sense. This isn't something Dad would do," Jay said.

"Where was Doris when all this happened?" I asked.

"Dad got up early this morning, like he usually does, and went out to the barn. He was out there a couple of hours when Doris went out to tell him she was going to church. She couldn't find him. His truck was in the driveway but there was no sign of him anywhere. She called Uncle Bob and he came over. When Bob couldn't find him either, he called me and asked if I had seen him. After that he phoned the sheriff, who showed up with another officer and a K-9. The dog led them to Dad's body."

"What time was that?" I asked.

"Bob called the sheriff around 10:30 am, so he did it sometime before then," Jay said quietly.

I could not help but think of that morning. Was the eviscerating pain I had experienced upon awakening the result of some sort of subconscious sympathetic reaction? Had my soul somehow connected with my father's across the dimensions of space, time, and physical matter? The possibility was strangely comforting. I knew I was grasping, desperately clinging to any little part of him that may still remain, cosmic or otherwise.

If I let go he would be gone forever.

"Did he leave a note?" I asked.

"I'm at Dad's right now. Doris has been surrounded since I got here so I haven't had a chance to ask her," he said. "Can you come over?"

"Is Kirk there?" I asked.

"No. You know him. He probably won't come over here," Jay said.

I understood precisely what Jay meant. Kirk was a pillar of stormy quiet and this news would take him on a deep inward dive. He was not the type to participate in the group mourning session that was currently under way at Dad's house. Nope, I decided, he wouldn't step foot anywhere near that place right now. There was little doubt in my mind that he was alone at this very moment.

"Yes, I do know him and you're right. OK, we will head your way shortly. I'll see you soon. Love you," I said, ending the call.

I felt an instinctive need to co-process the unbelievable news I had just learned with both of my brothers at my side. As much as I craved the fortification that I would derive from such an experience, I knew it was not to be. The only way I was going to see Kirk was to go to him. But first things first. I needed some answers. My thoughts turned to Doris. I considered calling her, and then quickly dismissed the notion, reflecting on Jay's comment that Dad's house was swarming with people. Best to see her in person.

While I was on the phone with Jay, Matt had gone to round up the kids. I looked up to see him enter the living room where I still sat, followed by Rachel and Austin. I had no preparation for the task of telling my children the life-altering news that I myself had learned less than 20 minutes earlier. My swollen, tear-streaked face alerted them to danger as they entered the room. I was not by nature a crier, so the mere sight of me put them on edge. I took a deep breath and launched full bore into the facts. Poppie had died. Having no stomach for sugar-coating the facts, I went on to tell them he had committed suicide with a gun. I watched their faces, blank at first, not comprehending.

The pages of a mental photo album turned in my mind. I flipped through the most memorable pictures of Rachel and Dad, struck as always by their identical blue eyes. Like the marbles I played with as a child, the color attracted attention, but the sparkle held it. My father holding her, smiling from ear to ear as he gazed into the mass of swaddling that encased her just moments after she entered the world. She, driving his golf cart recklessly, swerving between the trees, and he gently reminding her to be careful and to stay in the clear and open areas of the yard. Sitting in his lap as he drove his tractor, swimming in his pond, eating a cookie out of his hand, patting his face when she was just a few months old.

Finally, Rachel asked, "Why, Mommy?"

"I don't know honey. I want to understand that too, but right now I don't," I answered her.

I turned to Austin, who had spent countless hours traipsing around my dad's property, doing what the two of them came to refer to as "jobs," running errands together, and enjoying a juice box while his Poppie drank a beer. Visions of Austin wearing his *Bob the Builder* tool belt, waving to me from the cab of Dad's dump truck, watching the two of them hunt for frogs in the pond, and marveling at Dad's ability to hold his attention last summer when he taught him how to shoot a gun for the first time. I could not help but wonder if my father had used that very same gun to end his life. God, I hoped not. As Austin seemed to struggle for comprehension, his dark brown eyes brimmed with tears, "You mean we won't see him anymore?"

"No, sweetie, we won't see him anymore."

Chapter 6

Reality

Exhaling, I paused to let the news sink into my son's innocent heart. I cringed inwardly at the recognition that my children were also going to suffer. Our family had been blissfully sheltered from the tragedy of death. Until now. Rachel and Austin were still so young, it would take time for them to fully comprehend the implications of their grandfather's departure from this world.

I braced myself for the unpredictability of the mourning process, something I had virtually no experience with. Sadness was a given. As the reality of his death settled over them, would the fact that it was brought about by his own hand create fear in them? Would they have nightmares?

Although I had no idea what to expect in the weeks and months to come, I knew I could count on Matt to help keep a watchful eye on them. We were equally adept at perceiving changes in their moods. I was overcome with a wave of appreciation for him, his commitment to his children, his loyalty to our family, and his love for us. I reminded myself how good my life was. We would get through this together, I told myself.

As much as I dreaded it, I knew I needed to call Cam next and deliver the news to him. I debated letting him have the weekend, allowing him to remain oblivious to the life-changing event I was still trying to digest myself. But that didn't feel right. Knowing my son, he would want to be told immediately and he would want to be with his family.

I hated giving him the news over the phone, but there was no excuse I could think of that would require him to return from the lake. He had been there less than one day. I could not imagine a means of getting him in front of me that would not raise suspicion and concern. In this situation I could think of no alternative to ripping off the bandage and getting it over with. I looked at Matt, and as if reading my mind, he nodded slightly, once again placed a call, this time to my son, and handed me my phone.

Cam listened quietly. I imagined his mind and heart cycling through the same process his siblings had gone through just moments before. First disbelief, as emotion attempted to shield his heart from the reality that he would never see his grandfather again. Then sadness, as the emotion conveyed by my words convinced him that it was true.

Cam, the oldest of my children by five years, had spent more time with my dad than Rachel and Austin had. Cam's memories would center around the pond, the half-days spent one-on-one with his Poppie after kindergarten, before Rachel and Austin were born, the Pinewood Derby cars, riding on his lap as Dad zig-zagged the tractor across acres of grass in need of cutting, admiring his knife collection, and shooting a gun for the first time. While his age might enable him to comprehend my father's death more quickly, it would by no means make it any easier for him.

I ended the call. The sobering task of telling the kids now complete, we gathered our things in preparation to leave. Our leisurely pool day was terminated in less than two hours. Rob and Sally hugged me, asking if there was anything they could do for me. I could think of nothing. They told me to call if I needed anything, anything at all. I was warmed by the sincerity of their care and concern.

I could recall only a few times I had witnessed a friend experiencing the agony of loss. And like Rob and Sally, I was desperate to help, to provide even the slightest bit of comfort. I remember feeling useless, as if my words meant nothing, did nothing, changed nothing. But now I understood. Their words, and the words and thoughts of others, would be essential to staying afloat, to getting through the minutes, hours, and days ahead as the reality of my loss set in.

The four of us said our goodbyes and climbed mechanically into the van, silent and stone-faced. The sounds of the engine starting and the radio were welcome intrusions, filling the noiseless void and creating a momentary distraction. I listened to the words of the song that was playing in an effort to divert my mind, soaking in the lyrics, *"I could really use a wish right now."*

What I wouldn't give for a wish right now. I would bring him back. I vacillated between denial and a compulsive need for understanding.

The notion of my father taking his own life was ludicrous. It was unthinkable. Had I not just been told that very news I would have laughed out loud at the thought of it. I allowed my weary body to slump sideways as Matt backed the van out of the driveway, wondering if I would ever laugh at anything again.

Chapter 7

The Three Fingers of Justice

I sagged in the passenger seat, my head pressed against the window, eyes closed, mind trying to process, forcing myself to consider the implications of my father's death.

Visiting him would be forever absent from our Ohio itinerary. He would never again make the drive to Houston to see us. I would never again toast him with a Bloody Mary on Christmas morning, kiss his cheek or watch him blow out the candles on his birthday cake. We would never again eat Mexican food together. I would never hear him tell me how proud I made him, or smile to myself as I watched his delight in my children. We would never again have one of our long conversations about life.

I felt the sting of life's injustice as I recalled the many years that my father had been lost to me. My mother firmly stewarded my childhood years, while Dad often worked the equivalent of two full-time jobs, between overtime at the factory and contract work he did on the side. My brothers and I only began to really know him during our scheduled Sunday visits after his first of two divorces from our mother. Even then, having witnessed so many incriminating conflicts between the two of them, I remember being very wary of him. Initially, this presented challenges to our bonding process.

Later, other obstacles surfaced. Obstacles I helped create. The guilt, hot and sharp, swept over me at the thought of the part I had played in alienating my father from my brothers and me.

I wasn't quite 10 years old. My mother and I had just arrived home from my private appointment with the family court judge. My mother's new boyfriend, Glen, was anxiously awaiting our return and immediately began peppering me with questions.

"What did you tell him?" Glen asked.

"I just answered his questions," I said.

"So, you told him that your father takes you to a bowling alley every week during his visits with you?"

"Yes," I paused for a moment, then said weakly, "but we like doing that. We ask him to take us there."

"If you asked to go to a cockfight, do you think your dad should take you to see one?" he asked. His mouth was pulled into a tight, thin line and his eyes bore into mine as the question hung in the air. I didn't know what a cockfight entailed, but I knew the answer I was expected to give and replied with an obedient, "no."

"Bowling alleys serve alcohol. It's not a place for children. Did you tell the judge you volunteered to talk to him about this, that it was your idea?" he asked.

"Yes," I answered. And this part made me feel squeamish.

Mom and Glen told me I should talk to the judge because it would help my mother's divorce case against my father. It was the second time that my parents had decided to sever their marital ties from one another. And I was pretty sure that this time would be their last. Naturally, I wanted to help my mother, but I worried that based on the scorn Glen attached to our choice of entertainment, the judge may also frown upon it. It didn't feel right to help my mother at my father's expense. I didn't say yes immediately, but I also didn't say no.

Thus, before I knew it, my lack of conviction somehow became a commitment and I found myself in the car with my mother on our way to the Wood County Courthouse. Our drive was carried out in silence. My mother and Glen had already rehearsed with me what I needed to tell the judge. I was to tell the truth, of course, and in the process not divulge the fact that they had prepped me for the conversation.

We arrived at the courthouse ahead of our appointed time. The sand-colored stone building occupied the better part of one city block. I admired the clock tower, which stood in the center of the building, while I waited for my mother to put coins in the parking meter. The clock's four faces were visible from each corner of town, its tower standing almost twice as high as the three-story wings that flanked it on two opposing sides. My mother took my hand and we walked toward the main entrance, directly beneath the massive clock tower, and up the granite steps. I counted each step, focusing on placing my foot perfectly in the center of each tread in an effort to take my mind off the task before me.

As we stepped through the double glass doors, a vast open space awaited us, encompassing the entire main floor. I could see all the way across the expansive room to the windows on the opposite end of the building. The floor was covered in gray and white marble. Light filtered down through the tower windows three stories above us. As we made our way across the room, the sound of our footsteps carried upward and echoed throughout the immense space above. Landings lined each side of the three floors above, leading to doorways spaced evenly along each of the four walls. The reflection of light and color on the marble floor drew my eyes upward as we walked toward the elevator and I saw stained-glass panels above me.

Had I been less nervous, I would have found more enjoyment in the beauty of the building. Instead, it seemed severe and quiet. I felt the urge to whisper as I asked my mother which button to push upon entering the elevator. She pressed the button with a two on it in response.

We exited onto the second floor, turned left and walked along the landing, passing door after door adorned with names and titles of clerks, judges, and other court-related positions. I glanced downward through the slats in the open brass railing that bordered our walkway. I could see just one group of three people standing in the huge space below. Strange, I thought, for such a big place there were so few people around. That explained the deathly quiet. We turned the corner and upon reaching the second door, its glass panel painted in black with the words, Judge Orson L. Swartz, my mother stopped, turned the handle, and we walked through.

The interior office was appointed with burgundy-leather stuffed chairs, a matching sofa, and dark walnut paneled walls. An oversized Oriental rug covered most of the floor, exposing only a sliver of the marble beneath it. The furniture was much nicer than anything in our house. A woman sat behind a desk across the room. She was neither young, nor old, wore cat-eye glasses, and smiled pleasantly at us as we approached her. Her sandy brown hair was swept up into a loose bun, she wore soft pink lipstick and had a powder-blue cardigan draped over her white blouse. The nameplate on her desk read, Janet Delaney.

"Do you have an appointment with Judge Swartz?" she asked.

My mother indicated that we did, and after giving her name to Janet we situated ourselves on the leather sofa. I began searching for an issue of *Highlights* magazine from the stack on the side table. After a few minutes I noticed Janet pick up the telephone on her desk and murmur something into it that I could not hear. She replaced the receiver, got up and walked toward me. When she was just inches from me she bent over so as to look me in the eyes and said, "Judge Swartz is ready for you."

I rose and looked at my mother one last time. After being gratified with a faint smile, I followed Janet through another glass-paneled door, down a carpeted hallway lined with a few smaller office spaces along its way, and through yet another door at the end of the hallway. She held the door, motioned me through, then closed it behind me. The sound of the latch clicking echoed in the office where I now stood. Judge Swartz was sitting behind a massive cherry-colored wooden desk. He rose when I entered, walked around his desk and extended his hand, "You must be Amber."

I nodded, and he invited me to sit in the chair across from his desk. I eased myself into it and watched him walk back to his side of the desk. He was tall and stern looking. He had a very long face with a pronounced chin, a wide straight mouth and thin lips. His full head of gray and white-streaked hair was parted on one side. He smiled, which made a very pleasant difference in his face, and looked intently at me with small, dark eyes.

"I don't want you to be nervous or afraid. I am just going to ask you some questions and all you have to do is answer them honestly. There are no right or wrong answers. I want you to answer the way that seems right to you. Do you understand?"

I nodded again. His desk bore a nameplate, a fancy-looking pen holder and a telephone. In front of him was a pad of yellow, lined paper. A pen was positioned in perfect parallel with the long side of the tablet. Bookshelves lined every wall. Eager to divert my mind, I began scanning the shelves, looking for an open space. When I found none I started over, this time looking more closely, my eyes moving more slowly around the perimeter of the room. Nope, not a single spot for another book. Did he already have every book he would ever need, I wondered? Or did he just remove an old one every time he got a new one? Heavy gold draperies adorned the floor-to-ceiling windows that flanked the bookshelf immediately behind his desk.

He picked up the pen and got right down to business, easing into the questioning by asking first about our family, my brothers, their ages, what I liked to do for fun, and my favorite subject in school. I answered readily, the uncontroversial topics serving to relax me somewhat.

He seemed to sense my nervousness subsiding and began drilling down to the real purpose of our meeting. How did I feel about my parents getting divorced? Did I enjoy my visits with my father? Where did he take us during our Sunday visits and what did we do?

"Well," I said, "we do lots of things. Sometimes he takes us to Gramma Millie's, or we go to our cousins' house and play in the woods. Sometimes we go to the movies. At Christmas, Daddy took us to see *Santa and the Three Bears*."

"Has your father ever taken you to the bowling alley?" he asked, staring directly into my eyes.

"Yes, sometimes," I said, "but we don't bowl so much as play pool. I think it's fun and so do my brothers." The truth was Jay didn't actually play much pool. He was just turning four and spent most of his time running around the place. If a nearby table was available, he would roll the balls around on it and pretend the cue stick was a guitar. He loved the rock songs that played on the radio and would turn anything he could find into a pretend guitar. That was another reason we liked the bowling alley, come to think of it; there was always good music playing.

This answer seemed to neither satisfy, nor to dissatisfy him. He then asked me if my father ever brought other women around us. I answered that no, he had not. Then the judge asked if anyone, for example, my mother, had told me what to say to him today. I sat silently long enough for him to next ask me directly if my Mother had put me up to it. To this I answered no. He asked me if I had volunteered to speak with him and I again sat silently. I could not point the finger at my mother, but at the same time I could not find it within myself to say it had been my idea.

Throughout our meeting Judge Swartz remained pleasant, never showing any emotion, and speaking to me in quiet, even tones. In between his questions, while he was taking notes, I tried to count the books on each shelf without losing my place. This proved to be challenging, given the sheer volume of spines stacked on the shelves on each wall of his office. When he exhausted all of his questions he walked me to the outer door where my mother was still sitting. She rose to retrieve me. He thanked her and told her he would be in touch with her attorney. We left the waiting room and walked the short distance to the elevator. By the time my mother pushed the button to summon the carriage that would return us to the first floor I had relaxed considerably. The fluttering in my stomach had all but subsided. Whether I had done well or not, it was over.

As we waited, my eyes wandered toward a glass-enclosed display case adjacent to the elevator door. Taking a few steps toward it, I could see framed black-and-white photos of judges and lawyers on the shelf slightly above me. Another shelf housed some old knives and pistols. My focus came to rest on the shelf directly in front of me. A jar containing some shriveled carrot-shaped things, grayish-brown in color, was displayed in the very center. I looked more closely and counted three of the carrot-shaped things inside the jar. They could have been ancient, dried up cigars, but for the lighter colored crescent shaped sections on one end of each of them. My curiosity piqued.

*What **are** these things?*

I shifted my focus to the placard to the right of the jar as I continued to ponder the question. It was an invitation to the public hanging of Carl Bach, in the year 1883, for the crime of butchering his wife in cold blood.

Eww. Looking to the left of the placard I saw a rusty-bladed knife and a noose.

By now my morbid curiosity was at its peak. I read the placard below the knife and the noose, labeled *A* and *B* respectively. I quickly ascertained that the knife was the murder weapon and the noose the means by which Carl met his end. The placard continued with a notation for *C* that read, "Three of his deceased wife, Mary's, fingers were collected from the crime scene and preserved as evidence."

My mind connected the dots at last. The carrot-cigar-looking things in the jar were fingers. The brown, decayed fingers of Mary Bach, chopped off her hand by her murderous husband. Forcing my gaze away from the jar's contents, I turned my back on the case, my hand involuntarily rising to cover my mouth.

Why on earth would someone feel the need to preserve the poor dead woman's fingers?

Was the noose, the knife, and the written description not a graphic enough means of memorializing the story? At that moment I wanted nothing more than to get out of that place. I made my way back to my mother's side just as the elevator door opened.

All the way home, I thought about my conversation with the judge and the creepy courthouse fingers. Was the purpose of showcasing them intended as a warning to would-be offenders, so that people understood the consequences of bad behavior?

My father was no murderer, but I didn't like the associations my mind was making between the heightening tension surrounding my parents' pending divorce and the fingers in the jar. The nervousness I had felt for the past two days was once again peaking instead of subsiding, in spite of the fact that the act I had so dreaded was now complete.

The instinctive distrust I felt when Mom and Glen first asked me to talk to the judge, and the guilt that plagued me afterward, were validated when the judge made his final custody ruling, deeming my father to be unfit. The conditions of their final divorce allowed my father to see us for just five hours every other Sunday. He was given holiday visitations at my mother's discretion. The outcome caused me a great deal of angst and I could not help but feel I had contributed to it by talking to the judge. I regretted not speaking up for my dad. What if I had done more than just answer the judge's questions? If I had volunteered that my brothers and I loved our father and liked seeing him every Sunday, maybe things would have turned out differently.

I didn't know it at the time, but within two years we would become physically separated from our father by five states and 1,500 miles. His presence in our lives would be reduced to a voice on the telephone every Sunday night and a week at Christmas and in the summer.

All those years lost and now no way to make them up.

Chapter 8

Mom

I resurrected my old game, attempting to count the endless rows of green stalks as the expressway cut through cornfield after cornfield, the monotony of the scenery broken up by an occasional pond or soybean field.

As Matt slowed to exit the freeway a whiff of manure meandered into my nostrils. Although unpleasant, it was a sure indication of a nearby chicken farm, a hallmark of the northwest Ohio countryside. My nose wrinkled involuntarily as I inhaled deeply and waited for the scent to shake loose some old memory from the many years I had spent in this part of the world. I hoped to take my mind off the news I had just received, even if for only a few moments.

Rolling through the possible explanations for my father's sudden and deliberate departure had already become exhausting. Looking forward was painful as I considered my life without him, so instead I turned my focus backward in time with the help of an old familiar smell, sifting through memories, trying to elicit something pleasant to focus on.

The memory of a family photograph we had taken for the church directory surfaced. I was six years old at the time. We were all wearing our Sunday clothes, my father in a brown plaid suit with a yellow shirt that matched both my mother's lemon-colored dress and the oversized bow in my hair. Kirk was in a three-piece, blue plaid suit and Jay, barely able to sit up on his own at the time, wore a butter-colored romper. I wore a dress my mother had made for me. I could still remember wearing it to church and fiddling with the crescent shaped tufts that adorned the white fabric during the boring parts of the service, which now that I thought about it, was most of it. My mother's dark hair was teased, stacked and sprayed into a pillar atop her head. Ringlets cascaded downward from the space next to each of her ears. She was smiling broadly, exposing her straight white teeth, and her eyes were shining. She looked genuinely happy.

I imagined my mother at the time the photo was taken, young, in love and still hopeful her marriage and our family would survive. She had just given birth to my brother Jay, her third child. I suspected she may have believed that his arrival would help to ensure my father's fidelity and redirect his attention to his family. The photo would have been taken before their first divorce and almost three years before their second, and final, divorce from each other. I couldn't help but feel sorry for my mother, who at 18 years old and fresh out of high school, married my father and had two children within two years. Whatever ideal image she envisioned at the onset of marriage was shattered into a million pieces by the time her relationship with my father ended some 10 years later.

As if reading my mind, Matt asked, "What do you think your Mom will make of this?"

"Funny, I was just thinking about her. I can't imagine she wouldn't be as shocked as we are. My dad was anything but suicidal, especially during their days together. If anything, her complaint would have been that he lived life a bit too large, if you know what I mean. So, yes, I expect the news will have her scratching her head like the rest of us. But I doubt I will get the chance to confirm that," I said, my voice trailing off.

"You never know," Matt said, "she might decide to call you. This is pretty major."

"Yeah, it is," I said, "but she moved on a long time ago. You know her. When she's done she's done, no looking back. And on top of that, there's that huge, gaping hole that sits between us. It's been almost three years since I've heard from her. She's not going to call me, and I made the decision the last time she walked out of my life that I wasn't going to reach out to her again."

I paused, reflecting on the words I had just spoken.

"It sounds so childish when I say it out loud," I shook my head, "but I just don't have the will to keep repeating the same pattern. Didn't some famous person say that the definition of insanity is doing the same thing over and over again and expecting a different outcome? If I extend the olive branch, sure, she might take it. Then, we'll experience some period of normalcy as long as I keep it going, you know, call her regularly, pretty much take the burden of the relationship onto my shoulders. And it's not even that I mind doing that part. I've done it lots of times before. So yes, I could do that again, but I know if I do it will just be a matter of time before she pulls the rug out from under me. It's that prospect that holds me back. No matter how much I brace for it, it still cuts deeper every time."

"I know," he said, reaching across the space between our seats and touching my knee gently.

"It's so frustrating. I tried to pretend it didn't hurt every year when my birthday came and went without a call or a card, or so much as an acknowledgement of the anniversary of my entry into this world. I told myself I was an adult now, I shouldn't need my mother to acknowledge my birthday. Just focus on your behavior, be a good daughter, and she will come around. I tried. I really did. But as you well know, she next began ignoring the kids' birthdays. Now that I think about it, I guess she did sort of ease into it. She didn't kick our whole family out of her life at once. There was some lead-up to my excommunication. I guess I was stupid for not seeing it coming."

Now I was on a roll. Matt had opened the door and damned if I didn't walk right through it.

"And just like when I was a kid, there's no discussing anything with her, certainly not anything controversial. You remember the few times I gathered the courage to ask her, after months had passed since we had spoken, why I hadn't heard from her. She would tell me in that terse, unemotional tone of hers that 'the road runs both ways.' Nope, I've resigned myself to the fact that she's closed her heart to all that involves me. But I still don't get it. Even grandparents who have no use for their own children seem to gravitate to their grandchildren, putting their difference with their own children aside in the process, but not her," I said, at last pausing for a breath.

I had listened to more than one friend complain about an overbearing and controlling mother. Others demeaned their daughters, tearing away at their self-confidence. I had no such grievances against my mother. She had always encouraged me and had demonstrated no interest in making me into some ideal. I always felt free to be myself. We developed an especially close bond during my high-school years. Before I got my own car she willingly drove my friends and I around, taking us out for a Coke, or just indulging our endless desire to check out who was out "dragging Main" in downtown Cody, Wyoming.

We even worked together at the IGA, she as a cashier and me as a carry-out. We were in constant contact with one another. She listened to my music, laughed with my friends and me, and entertained our endless chatter about which boy we liked at that moment. She was like a girlfriend. And on top of all of that, I was given pretty much free reign to come and go as I pleased. She issued me a curfew, but I learned that violating it brought no consequences. I was envied for having such a cool mother.

That period marked the peak of our relationship. The years that followed saw its gradual decline. Throughout the low periods our relationship endured over the years, I pondered the nature of our problem, picking away at it like a stubborn remnant of Scotch tape. Each time I thought I had peeled it away, I would run my finger across the surface only to feel the roughness still present. How, I asked myself, could a mother be so indifferent to her own child? What had I done to alienate her?

Now, after years of chasing the string, I believed I had finally unwound the ball of yarn. It was just a theory and I knew I would probably never get the opportunity to confirm my conclusion with her. She would never have it. She would never engage in a conversation about something so sensitive, so dark, so shameful. Something she had tucked away in some dark corner of her mind. If she were open to discussing such a heady topic, I doubt we would be in the predicament we were in.

Having thumbed through the book of our shared past until the corners of the pages were bent and worn, I finally isolated what I believed to be the source of the unspoken conflict that haunted us...

Chapter 9

Fox in the Henhouse

In the weeks following my testimony regarding my father, Glen treated me with unusual mildness. His uncharacteristic behavior puzzled me. In the short time I had known him I had come to understand the near impossibility of pleasing him. He came into our lives like a tornado, blustering and blowing, cleansing the landscape of all that was familiar and comfortable and setting in its place his military style of command.

He was a stickler to the point of being fanatical about cleanliness and order. He pointed to deficiencies in both the upbringing and character of my mother's three children, believing fervently that his redirections were imparting rare and precious wisdom that would alter our lives for the better.

We were weak and spoiled, and he saw only one means of raising our standards -- hard work, responsibility, and a steady stream of criticism.

Tasks we completed were inspected and the deficiencies pointed out. Every job, he explained, could be done better, more thoroughly, or more quickly. His critiques were a means of helping us improve ourselves. We needed to apply ourselves more and resist our lazy tendencies. Positive reinforcement was a term foreign to the vocabulary of his soul. He could not risk the potential setback a compliment may impose on the progress

AJ WOOTTON

he had achieved with us. He needed to be vigilant, keeping his eyes focused keenly on us, if we were to be salvaged.

My preoccupation with the task of talking to Judge Swartz had me focused exclusively on my father and how he would be affected. It never occurred to me that I would come into Glen's good graces by doing his bidding. Yet, I could think of no other explanation for his change in attitude toward me. In spite of the discomfort I still felt regarding my meeting with the judge, I wondered if in fact I had done something good. If it made my life easier with Glen, if he yelled less, demanded less, and was actually nice to me at times, maybe it was worth it.

Even though my parents were not yet divorced, Glen had already taken up residence in our house. His favorite possession, a black vinyl recliner, was placed squarely in front of the television in our living room. He would settle himself into the recliner after supper, pull the handle to extend the footrest, and dictate from his roost for the duration of the evening. Anything he happened to need -- fingernail clippers, a Kleenex, a glass of water -- was fetched by whichever one of us kids was closest to him. On one particular evening he called upon my brothers to do his bidding, allowing me to watch TV uninterrupted. With each request I fully expected my turn would be next, but it never came.

At bedtime, I headed toward the bathroom to brush my teeth. As I passed by his chair, Glen called me over. I felt instinctive apprehension and wondered what I had done wrong this time. I walked back and stood in front of his recliner. His voice lacked the tone of irritation that typically preceded a lecture, but I was still wary. He released the handle of the recliner, snapping the footrest down and returning the chair to its upright position. As I stood in front of him, my face was level with his. He looked at me through his thick-lensed glasses and I noticed his eyes were uncharacteristically soft, a half smile playing at the corners of his mouth.

He put his arm around me and pulled me into his lap.

"I want you to know how proud I am of you," he said. "You showed a lot of maturity talking to the judge the other day. I think we're going to get along just fine. You are easygoing, not like Kirk, who's stubborn and angry all of the time."

I felt a simultaneous wave of relief and a pang of concern. Not only was I not being reprimanded, he actually said something nice to me. On the other hand, he was trash-talking my brother in front of me. Something about his comment made me uncomfortable. It was true, Kirk was completely resistant to Glen. The truth was, I often envied my brother's unwavering stance. I, on the other hand, engaged in a full-on inward struggle whenever I felt anyone might be angry with me. No matter how justified I felt, the stress of letting someone down, of disappointing them, always tore at my resolve and eventually brought me into compliance.

So great was my dislike for conflict that even my brother's unwillingness to acquiesce to Glen, something I had no control over, caused me anxiety. I pushed the concern to the back of my mind and for the first time allowed myself to consider the possibility that Glen had begun to care about me. Maybe, I thought, having him as a second father wouldn't be so bad.

The universe of laps that I had graced in my young life was limited to those of my parents and my grandparents. Sitting on Glen's lap was unfamiliar and a little uncomfortable, but it still felt nice. I thought back to the times I had crept out of bed, long after my bedtime, to see my father when I heard him come home from work. He always let me sit on his lap for a few minutes before carrying me to my room and depositing me back in my bed. That practice dated back a few years to the days before I had any fear of my parents splitting up.

It was one of the few untainted memories from the days before their conflict began. I had tucked it neatly away for safekeeping, saving it for resurrection when once again I felt free to look upon my father fondly, when their divorce and the tension that permeated our house had subsided. But sitting here now, the comfort and security I felt in my father's lap came flooding back, creating an irresistible urge to duplicate it. I felt my face smiling as hope for a new beginning surged through me.

"Will you carry me to bed?" I asked.

"Sure," he said, the half-smile now fully formed and illuminating his face.

He stood up with me still in his lap, adjusted his arms so one was under my neck and the other under the crook of my knee, and carried me down the hall and into my room. He laid me on the bed and I pulled up the covers as he turned toward the door.

"Good-night," I said, thinking he was leaving.

Instead, he closed my door, very quietly.

Walking over to my bed, he knelt beside it.

He took my hands in his, placed them on the covers atop my stomach and looked into my eyes in a way that made me feel uncomfortable.

"You know, you shouldn't be wearing this see-through nightgown around me. I can see your nipples."

His mouth was twisted upward at the corners, his eyes shining, magnified through pop-bottle lenses. Fear seeped upward through my stomach and into my throat, constricting it. I yanked one hand free and started scooting myself toward the opposite edge of my bed.

How can he see through my nightgown?

He let go of my other hand, but before I could move an inch he pulled the covers off me with one hand and grabbed the hem of my nightgown with the other. I clenched my legs tight, jerked my knees up and rolled away from him so that my back was toward him. *What was he doing?*

"Hey, hey now," he said in a loud whisper, sounding out of breath.

"I'm just being affectionate. You aren't used to that are you? You know your mother wasn't either, but she really likes it now, if you know what I mean," he said, chuckling.

By now he had gotten up onto my bed and was lying behind me, pressing himself into my backside, one arm was thrown across me, imprisoning me. I squirmed and jerked my shoulders, but the bulk of him was like a dead weight pressing on my shoulder and side.

He reached across me and with his free hand flipped me face up. He hiked up my nightgown, grabbed my underpants and pulled them down to my knees. I was completely exposed to him from the waist down.

My eyes were squeezed tightly shut. I couldn't bear the thought of seeing myself this way. I instinctively squeezed my legs together and continued to try and jerk my body away from him.

"Stop it, stop it!" I said as forcefully as possible.

"Come on now, I just want to touch it, just for a minute," he said, freeing his grip just enough for me to turn to my side, then catching me in the cage of one arm before I could squirm away.

His free hand found my now exposed pubic area and began rubbing lightly at first, then harder as he rhythmically ground himself into my side. The scent of Old Spice filtered into my nostrils as his pace quickened, along with his ragged breathing.

AJ WOOTTON

Finally, he pushed into me so hard I almost fell off the bed, with him groaning into my ear as he finally went still beside me.

I wanted to run out of my room, but the fear of encountering my mother kept me frozen in place. I pulled up my underpants as soon as his grip relaxed. Wanting to get as far away as possible, I jumped off the bed and stood facing my closet with my back to him, praying he would get out of my room.

His joy-ride now complete, he got up from the other side of the bed. He was still breathing hard when he walked around to where I stood; he finished pulling down his white t-shirt that had hiked up during all of his grinding, once again covering his blubbery, white stomach.

Looking down at me, he cupped my chin in his hand and said, "You have a body just like your mother's."

My gaze was focused firmly on the floor, my stomach turning at his unthinkable comparison between my mother and her nine-year old daughter.

He yanked my face upward, and before I could squeeze my eyes shut I could see he was still wearing that sick smile. Tiny beads of sweat peppered his forehead.

"I can't wait until you get a little bit older. Oh, I'll make sure you like it before I do it, but if you're anything like your mother that won't be a problem."

With that, he turned and walked out of my room.

Chapter 10

Parentless

The impact of the van bumping across railroad tracks jolted me back to the present, releasing me from the memory. I felt the tension in my body and tried to relax. I suspected that, in spite of the fact that I was the victim, my mother could not forgive me for telling her. Once the words were spoken she could no longer pretend that what I revealed to her had never happened. But, I had reasoned with myself time and time again, it took me five years to get the nerve to tell her.

At times I still found myself at odds with that girl who didn't have the courage to defend herself, to put her foot down. Perhaps it was also the source of my mother's disgust? Whatever the precise reason, my eventual confession inflicted a wound that festered over the years, its toxic core growing and spreading with the passage of time. Like many unattended afflictions, ours eventually became inoperable.

I was not blameless in our predicament. I entertained my fair share of anger and resentment toward her over the years. These bouts became most pronounced after I became a mother. In the 15 or so years after Glen exited my life, any blame I felt the need to lay was placed firmly at his feet, but having children of my own caused me to view the world through a different filter. The perfect, innocent faces of my children created in me a protective fury toward anyone or anything that would ever dare to harm them. I began to subconsciously draw comparisons between the passion I had for protecting my own children and the ruin of my own perfect innocence.

True, Glen had been my abuser, but it was she who had invited him into our lives. I was nine years old at the time. Did I not, at the very least, deserve protection? I had no choice but to debate myself, and depending on my mood or the situation, I would judge her either accomplice or victim. It would have been healthy for us to talk about it, we might both have been able to heal our wounds. But, history had taught me that discussing something this big and ugly with my mother was out of the question.

Her reaction to my eventual confession about Glen's abuse taught me a great lesson about my mother's reaction to topics she wished to avoid, and the result was that I avoided broaching any subject with her that she may deem controversial. I made an exception to this rule just once and had not found the courage to do it since. After high school I made the decision to delay college for a year. I planned to live with her, work and save as much money as I could, then head to the University of Wyoming with my boyfriend the following year. Admittedly my rationale was completely unsound and was motivated more by my unwillingness to leave my boyfriend than by the goal to save money.

My mother was less than enthusiastic about my decision, and demanded that I pay her rent to continue living in her house. I debated, knowing all too well the extent of the financial woes that had plagued her since Glen's departure several years before. She worked a full-time job but made just above minimum wage. My father was still paying child support, but according to her it didn't make a dent in our expenses. I knew better than to believe that Glen was giving her any financial support. Even if he had been ordered to do so, knowing him, he would find a way around it. On several occasions when our refrigerator held little more than margarine and condiments I bought groceries for our family. Somehow, we got by.

Things had improved since then. She had recently gotten engaged to Bruce, who would become her third husband and had already moved in with us, so I imagined he was helping her with expenses. Even though she was no longer financially desperate, I knew her demand wasn't unreasonable. She was asking for $100 a month and I had to admit it was not an exorbitant amount of money.

What bothered me was that I sensed that the rent was less about the money and more about getting me out of her house. I had viewed myself as an asset to her, a supporter, someone who asked little and gave much. I got my first job in the fifth-grade delivering newspapers, and since that time had paid for pretty much all my own expenses. I hadn't asked for so much as a pair of shoes from her since seventh-grade. I wasn't actually costing her anything more to live under her roof. It was the principle of the situation that nagged me.

I found myself unable to let go of it and decided to talk to her about it. I didn't expect her to embrace my point of view, but I felt if she listened I might be able to get her to see my side. Feeling a wave of courage one afternoon when she walked in from work, I launched into the topic, telling her how unfair I thought her request was considering the financial self-sufficiency I had demonstrated for so many years.

As if not hearing a word I said, she responded by telling me that I was free to move out if I didn't like the terms she was imposing. I reiterated my belief that her request was unfair. Her face had turned progressively darker as our exchange continued. We were standing in the living room, just a few steps from the front door, when she put her hands on my shoulders and began pushing me toward the door.

Somehow, we got out the door. I reached out to steady myself, grabbing onto whatever I could reach, which happened to be a column of lace that adorned the blouse she was wearing. The fabric ripped, tearing the lace clean off the front of her shirt. I was still holding it in my hand when I landed on the ground.

I stayed with my boyfriend for the next week, until I was eventually invited back to my house by her fiancé, Bruce. She didn't speak to me for another week, even when she walked past me at the IGA where we both worked. Then one day she took up with me again as if nothing had happened. She never brought up the topic of rent again, but her actions conveyed her intended message. First, I knew that whether or not I chose to go to college, I would need to move on before the end of the next summer. Second, my instincts about raising sensitive or controversial topics with her had been spot-on. It was taboo.

My mother had hoarded her emotions all her life. My teenage ego dared to believe I could draw her out. The ugly residue from our tussle served as a permanent reminder of the consequences of pursuing conversations on sensitive topics with her, and soured me on the notion of ever trying again. Instead, I was left to debate myself about the issues that separated us, mulling over possible causes and potential remedies. The turmoil created by the one-sided conflict eventually got the best of me and I sought counseling. I was able to let go of my own anger and get off my high horse. She had done the best she could. I not only survived those years, I was thriving. My adult life was better than I ever imagined it would be. I eventually forgave her and empathized with her own victimization. It was a relief to be free from the intrusion of those memories on my day-to-day life and to feel neutral at last.

I believed I had finally pinpointed the root cause of our issue and worked past my own anger and judgment, while at the same time theorizing that she hadn't done the same. How could someone work past something they refused to acknowledge? Furthermore, at some point, being around me, perhaps even the mere sight of my face and sound of my voice, became a reminder of a time in her life she wanted to forget. I couldn't help but think it would be easier to hire a therapist and purge herself once and for all of the pain she suffered so many years ago. That, I finally concluded, was simply not her way of dealing with things.

The jolt of the van turning brought my focus back to my physical surroundings. I could see that we were now on the road where my father's house stood. I couldn't help but shudder at the thought of entering his house knowing that he wouldn't be there today, or ever again. Matt was driving silently, knowing the rant about my mother had been rhetorical. Sitting up straighter, I thought about all the times he had listened to me go on about my past. He knew every last line of my story and could probably recite all of the details. I had blabbered on and on about it on countless Friday nights over more glasses of wine than I cared to remember. He also knew better than anyone what a blow my father's death had dealt me.

I was now parentless. I couldn't imagine going through the loss of my father without Matt. He was being so supportive, so patient, so compassionate. As I turned to look at Rachel and Austin, who were just waking up from their motion-induced naps, gratitude washed over me, baptizing me and renewing me. This family, my family, was so much more than I ever hoped for. In that moment all my doubts and frustrations about Matt, about us, which had wormed their way into my subconscious over the past few months, evaporated into thin air.

Chapter 11

Copse of Death

The tires crunched across the gravel as we turned into Dad's driveway. I counted at least 10 vehicles parked helter-skelter, some in the grass, some along the road, others lining the edges of the drive. We managed to find an open space to park near the barn. As we got out of the van I spotted my brother, Jay, standing on the back deck.

"Why don't you two go in and find Gramma Doris. Dad and I will be right behind you," I suggested to Rachel and Austin. They hesitated, still sleepy, as they eyed the large crowd of people scattered between the back yard and the mouth of the garage, some in lawn chairs, others standing and talking. I took the opportunity to give them each a quick squeeze before they wove their way through the crowd and into the house.

I scanned the faces, recognizing many as members of Doris' substantial family. Waving, I mouthed hello to a few whom I recognized as Jay and I made our way to each other. I hugged him hard, and as I leaned on his shoulder my gaze met the serene beauty of my father's yard.

The scene was exactly as my mind had painted it earlier. A carpet of tender green flanked by trees on all sides, their bark a deeply textured brown-black and their tops full and leafy, whispering in the light breeze. It was hard to believe this peaceful sanctuary had served as the stage upon which my father performed the final, violent act of his life. It would have been so much more fitting if his death had taken place in a dark alley or some weed-infested, abandoned city lot. The bright, cheery weather continued to contradict my mood. Shouldn't the skies be thunderously dark and pouring sheets of rain?

"I still can't believe this is happening," I said, releasing my hold on Jay.

"Yeah, this is the last thing I ever expected," Jay said as he turned to greet Matt. His face was composed, but I could see moisture rimming his blue eyes, which were the exact color of our father's. Jay, now 40, still had a full head of thick hair, the color a mix of gray and white. *Just like Dad's.* For years my father's thick, wavy hair was the color of salt and pepper. It was not until he reached his sixties that his hair turned a silky, snow white. My brothers and I were all dark-haired until our late thirties. At 46, I still sported dark roots, thanks entirely to a regular hair-color regimen.

I had always been told that I favored my mother. Kirk was the spitting image of our father, while Jay, I decided, was a mixture. All three of us had my father's square jawline and my mother's pointed chin. Jay and I had both inherited my father's full face, which was more pronounced in our younger years, before gravity and the aging process exposed the underlying cheekbones. I always joked with Jay that he got the best nose and the cutest ears, both of which were petite and, well, cute. Jay had an easy smile, somehow missing out on the expressionless look of intense seriousness that both Kirk and I wore unconsciously most of the time. Throughout my life, I endured complete strangers telling me to smile or asking me if everything was all right. The interventions always struck me as presumptuous and rude, prompting the opposite of their intended reaction.

"I can't stop thinking about my conversation with Dad last night. My gut was telling me something was wrong. I mean, I know he got a DUI and yes, that is serious. I couldn't take it lightly if it happened to me either, I get that. I also get that you are going to feel like shit for a while, maybe even weeks or months. But to lose all hope? Not to even give yourself a chance to get back up again? That's the part I can't understand. He just seemed so down, so defeated. I can't remember ever seeing him like that before. I felt like I should come out and see him, like, right then. But he was so resistant and said he was just tired and he'd see me later this week, so I talked myself out of it.

"I really regret it now," I sighed heavily.

"You know how he was, Amber. He has always done things his way. Once he made up his mind about something, that was it. He never made snap decisions and I never really knew him to back down or change his mind. I'm not sure there is anything any of us could have done," Jay responded.

"But I would at least have gotten to see him again," I said.

Matt squeeze my hand and said, "I can't say I've had a lot of experience with suicide, but of all the people I know in the whole world, I would've placed your Dad very last on a list of people likely to do something like this. I can picture him fighting someone to the death, or getting shot because he refused to hand over his wallet or get out of his truck, but no way does this seem like something he would do."

"I know. That's why this is so hard," I said, gripping his hand tightly.

I turned to my brother and said, "Start from the beginning. Tell me everything you know."

Jay nodded, looked downward briefly, then began.

"Dad called me yesterday. He told me he got pulled over by the police on his way home from Kirk's on Friday night and that he had to spend the night in jail. Doris had already brought him home when he called me. After they arrested him they towed his truck. He asked if I would go get it and bring it to the house. I told him of course I would. Then I called Kirk to help me. Kirk picked me up and we went and got Dad's truck. I drove Dad's truck and Kirk followed me," Jay said.

"Did you talk to Dad when you dropped off his truck?" I asked.

"Yes, but just for a few minutes. He wasn't really in a social mood," Jay said.

"How was he?" I asked.

"The same way you described him. He was tired. He'd just gotten back from a two-week contract job in Dayton. He'd stopped by Kirk's on his way home, and as we now know, ended up in a jail cell instead of his house. He didn't get any sleep. He wanted to get some rest, so we didn't stick around. I didn't talk to him for very long, but I could tell he was really upset about what happened, embarrassed you know, mad at himself. He said Doris was really pissed at him. I didn't talk to him again after that," he said, pausing for a long time.

"And then this morning, around 11:00, I got the call from Uncle Bob."

I could not stop myself from resurrecting the mental scene I had created while talking to Jay earlier on the phone.

"So, he took the shotgun from the barn, walked to the far edge of his property and shot himself?" I asked.

Jay nodded his head almost imperceptibly, pausing for several seconds before going on, "But it seems odd to me that he would have used a shotgun. He owned a half-dozen pistols."

"What's odd about it?" I asked, having little understanding of the varying characteristics of firearms.

"Well, the mechanics of a shotgun make it an awkward choice for a suicide. Think about how long the barrel is. He would've had to rest the butt of the gun on the ground and then use a stick or something long to reach the trigger, keeping it pointed at his head at the same time," Jay said. "He couldn't have reached it with his finger. A pistol is much easier to control and carries a greater certainty of instant death," he said, wincing slightly, as he dropped his head and stared at the ground to the side of his chair.

Had my father brought some sort of implement from the garage or did he forage around in the woods for a stick of the perfect size and dimension to execute his plan? My father was a man of vision who didn't stop until his concept of the moment became reality. He tinkered and tested and tried until his idea came to life. Every job he held in his life -- gas station mechanic, electrician, laborer -- all had one common thread. They all involved making something work, bringing something inanimate or malfunctioning to life. How ironic that his final design was a contrivance to supplement a less-than-ideal weapon, an artificial trigger finger that he used to end his own life.

The skills he didn't learn on the job he taught himself. Driven by curiosity, he was always applying his skills in new and untested ways. I smiled, remembering the one-of-a-kind motorized bicycle he created. I had listened intently as he described his accomplishment to me during one of our long-distance telephone conversations. His sense of pride and amusement was dampened only by the fact that he ran out of gas on his maiden voyage and had to call Doris to bring him the gas can. I could never forget the time, energy, and passion he put into Cam's Pinewood Derby cars in preparation for the annual Cub Scout competition. Good was not good enough. He set up a track in his garage and countless trials were run before the big race.

But his love affair with all things that moved through mechanics and the forces of nature began long before the bicycle and Cam's Pinewood Derby competitions. It all started in the garage of the first home I could remember. The creative process that yielded his first combination of street machine and showpiece, the blue '57 Chevy Bellaire, infected him with a passion that he spent the rest of his life feeding. Each project started with the barest assortment of components that he patiently and lovingly set about fashioning into a one-of-a-kind work of art. I ran through my mental list. The first one, the '57, would always live largest in my mind, but there were countless others. I remembered a burgundy Pontiac GTO, a Chevy El Camino, and a circa 1950's Chevy truck.

His choices evolved in stride with his life. Corvettes dominated his interest when he was in his thirties. I recalled at least three of these, all early 1960s models. His most recent fixation was the Chevy Nova. I had lost count of the number of these that had rolled out of his garage in the past decade. In between working on his own mechanical undertakings, he had also managed to engage both of his sons in building their own dream machines. A red '68 Camaro was kept under protective cover in Kirk's garage and Jay's garage was home to a black 1975 Monte Carlo.

I recounted the numerous conversations my father and I had had over the years about the car he would build for me. I was fond of Kirk's Camaro, and in particular liked the convertible feature. We discussed the merits of a variety of models that ranged from a Mustang to the Corvette. He was clearly in his element as he described this feature or that feature, commenting on the pluses and minuses of each. I felt a sting as the realization sunk in that the architect of my future car would never again conceptualize or build anything. The creative genius that was but one part of my father was forever extinguished.

"Why? Why do you think he chose the shotgun over a pistol?" I asked my brother.

"I don't know. It doesn't make sense," Jay said, then continued with his story as if trying not to linger over the unanswered question.

"Kirk tried to get him to stay over that night. But you know Dad. He was anxious to get home and sleep in his own bed after being gone for two weeks. He said he felt fine. Yesterday when I talked to him he told me he took all the back roads. He was within a mile of being home when they stopped him. Not surprising I guess, considering it's a holiday weekend."

"He should have stayed at Kirk's. This wasn't his first DUI. It was actually his third offense. He kept saying that he would now be classified as a felon. I don't know the details, but I do know that the other two happened years ago – like 25 or more years ago. I tried to tell him that in light of how much time had passed, the other offenses might not even factor into this case. But he wouldn't listen. It was like he had already given himself the maximum sentence," Jay said, shaking his head in a gesture of hopeless acceptance.

Chapter 12

The Note

Jay's comment took me back in time. So much had changed in the past 20 years. My father had settled down, seeming at last to satisfy his need for change and his thirst to keep moving on to that next new and better thing.

I pictured my father in a hospital bed. He had arrived by ambulance after being pulled from his truck, having attempted to skirt the dropped railroad crossing arms a split second too late. The oncoming train caught the tail of his pickup truck, sending it into a ditch. If just one more split second had passed before he crossed the tracks, he and his truck would have been smashed to bits or dragged for miles by the speeding locomotive. In either scenario, death would have been a certainty.

I arrived at the hospital to find my stepmother, Jennie, at his bedside, holding his hand. She was leaning over him and listening as he spoke quietly, his voice filled with emotion, expressing the gratitude of someone who knew he had just succeeded in cheating death. I leaned down to hug him, and he held me for a very long time and told me he loved me. His voice was ragged, as if he were fighting back tears. His emotion and my extreme happiness in learning he had sustained no major injuries dominated my memory of that incident. Had alcohol been involved then, I wondered?

I hadn't thought about the railroad accident for years. I began to see the parallels in his behavior during our conversation yesterday and after his accident 25 years earlier. The DUI he received two nights ago was a huge step backward for him. If only he would have stayed at Kirk's for just two more hours, long enough for his body to absorb the three or four beers he had likely consumed. But that just wasn't my dad. Like Jay said, he did things his way, on his terms. His entire life had been purposed around the objective of self-sufficiency. He told me on more than one occasion that he would rather be dead than be debilitated in some nursing home. He had no intention of burdening anyone with caring for him when he got older.

I remember assuring him that I would gladly take care of him. At the same time, I was completely incapable of imagining him ever being debilitated, no matter his age. If that were to happen I had a plan. I assumed such a time was far in the future, and that by then Matt and I would be empty nesters. I would have flexibility. I could take a job near him for a period of time, or I could negotiate with my employer to allow me to commute back and forth. I would figure it out. It would be my pleasure to care for him, especially after all he had done for me.

"Hi, honey," said a voice behind me.

I turned to see my father's wife, Doris, wad of tissue in hand, eyes red and watery, standing with her arms open.

"Doris," I said, turning to hug her. As we embraced she let loose a long, sob-induced moan, followed by several more. I held her, rubbing her back in an effort to comfort her. When we finally pulled away from each other, I said, "This is unbelievable. How could he have done this?"

"I don't know," she said, still sobbing, "I just don't know."

She continued to cry, alternating between wiping her eyes and moaning. I backed away to give her some space and Matt stepped in, arms extended.

After a few minutes she collected herself, blowing her nose into her handful of tissues. My mind and emotions wrestled. I was as devastated by the news as she was and respected her need to grieve, but I was desperate for an explanation. I debated whether now was the time. Oh, screw it, I thought, and plunged ahead with the question that had been burning inside me since I first heard the news.

"Did he leave a note?"

"He left something on the computer," she answered, still wiping her face.

"What, a note? What did it say? Can I see it?" I asked, my heart pounding.

"I'll show you later, after everyone leaves," she said, looking straight into my eyes before blowing into her wad of tissues again.

"I've got to go and say goodbye to a few people right now," she motioned toward two people walking to their car, "be sure to get something to eat. Everyone brought food and there's beer and drinks in the coolers in the garage." She dabbed at her eyes one last time and turned toward the driveway.

"OK," I said, trying to hide my disappointment.

As I watched her walk away, I turned to Jay and asked, "Have you seen the note?"

"No. This is the first I've heard of it. I talked to her right after we got here, but she's been surrounded by people the whole time and I was trying to give her space," he said.

"Well, I would have thought she would have already told you that he left a note and shown it to you. Like the minute you walked in the door today. I know it just happened a few hours ago -- but he's our Dad. It's driving me nuts trying to understand why he would have done this," I said, trying to imagine the motivation for her evasiveness.

"I think it's weird."

"Yeah, it is," Jay said, looking away. Following his gaze, I saw his wife, Glynis, coming toward us. After exchanging hugs and another round of, "I-can't-believe-this-is-happenings," the four of us found chairs and sat down.

"Oh, the kids! I told them we would be in," I said, having momentarily lost track of the present.

"They're fine. Don't worry. I saw them inside. They said they were coming out here after they finish eating," Glynis said.

"OK, good," I sighed. Glynis sat next to Jay, extracted a pack of cigarettes from her purse and after taking one out, offered one to my brother. Their actions were always in unison. An unspoken symbiosis existed between them, conveyed by their physical proximity to each other, their similar soft-spoken and quiet natures, and the way they looked at one another. The corners of my mouth spontaneously turned upward as I watched them. They were cohesive. Happy. And that made me happy.

I curbed my urge to bum a cigarette. This was one of those times when smoking seemed not only appropriate, but also necessary. I reminded myself that I would surely get caught. Rachel and Austin were milling about and would most certainly bust me if I lit up. As much as I enjoyed an occasional smoke, I couldn't bring myself to do it in front of them.

"You know what I remember the most?" Jay said.

"I remember those blue coveralls I would wear when I helped Dad in the garage. I couldn't have been more than four or five years old. I wasn't in school yet and he must have been working third shift because he was around a lot during the day. I would hang out with Dad while he worked on whatever car he was building at the time."

"Good idea, let's talk about something happy," I said in support of the change in subject. "And oh, yes, I remember those coveralls. You looked so cute in them," I smiled.

"Dad was always working on something. He could do anything with his hands," Jay said.

"Yes, he could," I said in agreement. I pictured my father's hands; broad and big-knuckled, veins protruding to the surface of his skin. His nails were always dark, not dirty, but stained from their ceaseless interaction with engine oil, grease, and metal. He was in his forties before he transitioned from his blue-collar roots to management. Prior to that his hands were essential to his ability to earn. He would often hold them up and say, "As long as I have these I can do anything I need to do."

Damn it, why hadn't he kept "doing?"

Why did he stop fighting?

Some of my earliest memories of my father were centered around the many things he did with those hands. My thoughts drifted back to the '57. The body had appeared in the garage first. I couldn't have been more than five years old. Absent any discernible paint color, fenders, tires, hood, engine, and interior, the heap of metal in the middle of the garage bore no resemblance to a car. Gradually, manufactured appendages appeared and began to flesh out the body, and my inexperienced self could begin to imagine the finished product. My father sought and secured parts from a variety of sources, ranging from junkyards to newspaper advertisements, to his car-enthusiast network.

The lifeless, disjointed pieces finally began to look like a car. Next, an engine block appeared, to which my father applied numerous and mysterious ministrations. Then one day its jagged roar practically jolted me out of my chair as I sat watching television in the living room. I ran to the garage, my hands clapped over my ears, to see my father standing next to his creation, grinning from ear to ear. The finishing touches included a set of chrome wheels surrounded by fat tires and a metallic blue paint job. His name, painted in chunky, bronze-flecked letters, adorned each of the car's sides, rendering it unmistakably his creation.

"I was thinking about the '57, but you probably don't remember it, do you?" I asked, trying to recall the exact timing and if it was before or after Jay was born.

"No. I was too young to remember, but I've seen pictures. I have my Monte Carlo, though. That was a big project. I loved that car from day one. And now, I'll love it even more. All those hours we spent working on the car together were really good times. Great times, actually. We talked, drank beer, and planned how we were going to finish it. What color to paint it, the seats, the wheels, every last detail. And when we weren't talking about the car he told me stories. Mostly about his younger days. His glory days," Jay said.

"Some of the stories happened before I was born. Listening to him, at the time he was in his sixties, made it hard to imagine him doing some of the stuff he talked about," Jay said, a wide grin spreading across his face.

"He found his way into more than one fight. He told me about one time he and Dave went beer-drinking on the east side of Toledo. Long story short, they woke up in an alley, pretty beat up and their wallets missing. When they got to talking about it the next day, they put together that they were jumped from behind, giving them no chance to fight back. The thugs robbed them and ran off. Dad was pissed. So, he decides they are going to go back and look for the guys who did it. Now mind you, neither of them had seen their attackers' faces so they had no idea who they were looking for. But Dad was determined to get some revenge."

As Jay told the story I imagined the area. Toledo's east side had a reputation for being gritty and potentially dangerous, especially at night. In spite of this fact its bars and nightclubs drew substantial crowds on the weekends. I had made my share of visits to one club in particular, Jason's, during my college years, but always as part of a group. It was well understood that it wasn't safe to venture into certain parts of east Toledo alone.

He continued, "So they go back. Dave's driving and they are cruising the street near where they were jumped. There are lots of people milling about and suddenly Dad tells Dave, 'That's them! Right there!' Dave doesn't even have time to ask how he could know that before Dad starts pulling full beer cans out of a bag and pitching them at this guy. Dad hits him in the back of the head with the first toss and his second pitch meets with a huge glass window in front of one of the bars. It shatters, of course. By now all eyes are on them and the guy he hit is back on his feet and running after the car. Dave floors it and they peel out of there."

I smiled, recounting a few of my own recollections of my father and his best friend, Dave's, antics. They met shortly after my parents married. Their conversation began over what else but a machine, a motorcycle if I remember correctly. Whatever motorcycle Dave was driving at the time attracted Dad's eye, and so began a relationship that endured the rest of my father's life. Knowing that Dave probably knew my father better than anyone else in this world prompted another question.

"I don't suppose you've talked to Dave?" I asked Jay.

"Just for a minute. He is beyond disbelief," Jay said, shaking his head.

"Did he have any wisdom to offer?" I asked. "Any ideas as to what would have driven Dad to do this?"

"No. He can't believe it. You know they were working this last job together. He said Dad didn't act different in any way. For a guy who not only knew him, but was his best friend for the last fifty years, that tells you something," Jay said.

"How could none of us have seen this coming?" I asked.

"It makes me feel like I never knew him at all. I hate to even say this out loud, but is there any way someone else was involved? Could he have been killed?"

Jay began nodding before I finished the question.

"That thought has already occurred to me," Jay said, his smile completely vanishing.

Chapter 13

Jay

I noticed Jay wincing as he stretched his legs out in front of him.

"You doing OK?" I asked.

"Yeah, just stiff," he said.

I watched my brother as we sat in momentary silence, paging through our individual memory books of our father. I paused on an image of Jay and me playing in his bedroom. He was no more than three or four and we were huddled on his bedroom floor playing Matchbox cars. At one point the character driving his Corvette got excited about something, and in the course of acting out the emotion of the scene, Jay raised both arms, the one closest to me smacking me square in the nose on the upswing. I smelled the coppery scent of blood and felt a trickle on my upper lip. I jumped up and ran to the bathroom to get a tissue. I was in no pain. My haste was focused on saving my clothes and his bedroom carpet from stains. When I returned, Jay was curled up on the floor next to his bed, crying.

"What's wrong?" I asked.

"I hurt you," he said.

"No, you didn't. See, I'm smiling! It was an accident. I know you didn't do it on purpose. It's just that your arm hit me just right. It doesn't hurt at all, really. It just looks bad. Don't cry," I said, hugging him.

That scene typified his gentle and sweet nature. My brothers and I all sustained damage from the abuse we suffered at the hands of our stepfather, but I couldn't help but feel that Jay was affected the most, simply because of his age. He was but four years old when the father we barely knew was replaced by one we wished we had never met. Being six years older at the time, I had accumulated enough positive experiences with adults to understand that Glen's tyrannical and perverse parenting style was neither the norm, nor a benchmark I should strive for when I someday became a parent. His goal was to garner complete control over his charges. He achieved this end through intimidation and punishment. Love, positive reinforcement, and encouragement were for sissies. Jay retained only bits and pieces of his pre-toddler years, mere sound bites of memories that preceded Glen, whereas I had an entire library of happy remembrances that characterized my young life.

I was in my forties before I actually did the math and concluded that the evil reign of Glen lasted a brief five years. It was hard to imagine how my vast collection of awful memories of him and those days could possibly be compressed into such a brief time frame. His influence and control over my brothers and I created unique dysfunctions in each of us. Jay's biggest challenge was to build the confidence and self-esteem he had little opportunity to develop in his childhood home.

Kirk and I had reaped the benefits of my grandparent's love and influence during our formative years, basking in the glow of their adoration. My mother's parents, Thelma and Bernard, represented everything that was good about our childhood. By the time Jay came along my beloved grandparents had been demoted from their former status of immediate family to distant relatives, and stripped of their power to positively influence the life of their youngest grandson. Jay retained very few memories of our grandparents. The thought that he had missed out on one of the brightest spots of my childhood always made me feel sad for him. Seeing he and Glynis now and feeling the contentment that emanated from their relationship was tremendously satisfying. *There is such a thing as redemption.*

Jay stood up, flexed, and stretched his legs a few times. I cringed, as I always did, when I looked at the scars that spanned the full length of each calf, sections of which measured a good six inches wide. When he lost control of his pickup truck some seven years ago it had rolled multiple times before coming to rest, ejecting him from the rear window in the process. Fortune smiled when a passing driver witnessed the accident and immediately called for help. The early call and helicopter transport to the hospital were key factors in salvaging not only his legs, but his life.

His rehabilitation spanned a year and involved numerous additional surgeries. As a result, he could no longer do many things he had previously taken for granted. Tasks requiring significant exertion and maneuvering were totally out of the question. Simple activities like sitting and walking presented their own challenges at times. It was not unusual for him to become uncomfortable after sitting for any length of time, as he obviously had just moments ago.

I went with Dad to visit Jay in the hospital shortly after the accident. Both of his legs were suspended above the bed with pulleys. The combination of his injuries, the loss of skin upon impact, and surgical incisions left sections of muscle exposed on each leg. The doctors said it was nothing short of a miracle that he survived, considering the severity of the accident. The rest of his body was surprisingly unscathed. In the early days following his accident his physicians could not assure that he would retain the use of his legs. In spite of the deep scars and his physical limitations, I couldn't help but marvel at how famously he had healed. His accident, ironically, played a big role in solidifying his bond with our father. Dad not only visited him regularly, but also drove him to doctor appointments, surgeries, and eventually to physical therapy sessions. They were tight from then on, in recent years, seeing each other almost daily.

The thought of someone murdering my father played at the corners of my mind. The idea had injected itself into my brain on the drive to my father's house, as I rejected one possible explanation after another as to the cause of my father's decision. Although far more unsettling, foul play made a lot more sense to me than the idea of my father offing himself.

But who?

Who would have hated him enough to kill him? I could think of no one, and if my father had such an ominous enemy, his best friend Dave would surely have known about it, wouldn't he? And yet Dave, like us, couldn't fathom my father committing suicide. I batted the plausibility of both explanations around in my mind, becoming frustrated in the process. I finally resolved to push the murder scenario off for now. Absorbing the reality of my father's death was enough to deal with for the moment. The police were involved. If there were any suspicious factors at play it would come to light, I reasoned.

Sitting back down, Jay complied with my silent decision, changing the subject.

"I guess the funeral is going to be toward the end of the week. Doris told me she isn't sure yet how long it will take the coroner to complete the autopsy and release the body, but right now it's looking like Friday," Jay said.

"This sucks," I said, looking at Matt, "two days ago my biggest concern about this trip was that we were so pressed for time. I was worried we wouldn't be able to squeeze everyone in. My whole reason for calling Dad last night was to pencil in a date to see him, to be sure we would actually be able to get together this week." I sighed deeply.

"I didn't have a clue. No idea. Now, not only won't I see him this week, I will never see him again," I said, shaking my head.

When I spoke with him the night before, had he already resolved to take his own life? When he told me he would see me later this week, could he have been implying that I would see him at his funeral? As I pondered the answer to my own questions, I realized I couldn't come up with an answer. At that moment, the man I thought I knew so well was foreign to me.

Had I ever really known him?

From the vantage point of my lawn chair I could see the house, a ranch style with a walkout basement. While I couldn't see the interior through the window, I could easily picture it. The majority of the downstairs comprised a comfortable room, cozy and large. A party room. A bar complete with two long counters and stools was built into the far-right corner. My father's vision; he, Kirk, and Jay took on the project shortly after he and Doris moved in. Another one of his many ideas brought to life, I thought. The rest of the room was dedicated to comfortable seating, featuring a sectional and several plush chairs. The wall-mounted wide-screen TV was visible from anywhere in the room, virtually always playing the NASCAR channel. The walls were covered with racing paraphernalia. A lit Budweiser sign, his all-time favorite beer, was mounted on the back wall. It was a really great room. A room that served as the backdrop for so many celebrations, Christmases, birthdays, and countless other impromptu gatherings.

That room was where I last saw him when we came for Christmas, just over six months before. One of Matt's sisters and her children were with us. The kids were playing games on the Wii, while the adults sat at the bar visiting and drinking Bloody Mary's, a Christmas tradition.

What had we talked about?

Probably the kids ... Cam's pending college choice, Rachel's dance recital, Austin's football season. *Yes, we would have talked about all of those things.* It was happy and lighthearted, and typical enough that I couldn't remember anything truly specific about it. It was familiar and comfortable, and I had no reason to believe that the same interaction would not repeat itself every year for the foreseeable future. I now realized how completely I had taken that assumption for granted.

I sighed as I expanded my contemplation to the lot upon which the house was situated. My father's property was long and narrow and surrounded by woods on three sides. The house was visible from the road, but the sprinkling of trees and shrubs in the front created a screen of privacy. My father seemed to gravitate to owning property outside the confines of town. I ticked off the five houses he lived in prior to this one and reflected that most of them had indeed included acreage. Part of this desire was to assure adequate room for an oversized garage, or barn as he referred to it, to accommodate his car hobby. But even more so, he valued privacy.

Chapter 14

Garden of Youth

The very first house I could remember, the one we all lived in together, sat on close to an acre of land. It was located within the village limits of Grand Rapids, Ohio but stood at its outermost edge. At first my father made do with the single-car attached garage. After completing the '57 he decided he needed more space. It was then that he erected an aluminum sided, two-car garage in the back yard, and added a gravel driveway to enable access from the street.

That house, the first home of my memory, the one-story, white-sided and black-shuttered house, sat a mere ten steps from the street that happened to be a major east-west artery through our little town. Drivers routinely began ramping up to the 50-mph speed limit in effect just past our house, in spite of the posted 30-mph limit in front of our house. This created what my mother considered to be a very dangerous situation for two young children, and accordingly Kirk and I were strictly forbidden to enter the front yard without supervision. We knew if we did we would be spanked on the spot. No questions asked.

The front of our lot sloped sharply downhill, such that our basement opened directly to the back yard. This was our domain, the place where we spent all of our outdoor time.

Trees dotted our property: apple, spruce, willow, pear, plum, and mulberry. The vegetable garden occupied nearly a quarter of the remaining space. Neighbors lived on either side of us, and our three lots shared access to a pond in the back. Just as the very front of our property was off limits, so was the very back. We didn't yet know how to swim, and our mother was convinced that drowning was a certainty if we set foot anywhere near the banks of the pond. The mulberry tree on the left edge of our yard and the weeping willow on the right marked our boundaries. We knew better than to breach them.

That yard. How many memories did I have of that house and those days? The apple tree, Kirk commandeering it and making it into his clubhouse and mandating it members-only. The password … what was it again? Can't remember. Pink peonies bloomed in the spring, the weight of their showy and fragrant heads bending their stems toward the ground. I imagined the crunch of a rhubarb stalk, sour and juicy in my mouth. The scent of lilacs. The soft, fuzzy tips adorning a pussy willow branch. I smiled as my mind drifted back in time, trying to recreate a specific moment, something involving that place and time. At last my memory cooperated.

I was five, maybe six years old. The June sun had not quite peaked in the sky and it was already hot. I was pulling weeds between the corn plants. The green shoots were tender and barely above the ground. I was taking great care not to pull out a corn plant by mistake. Stooping over what seemed to be an endless sea of weeds was getting old already and I had just begun the task. Kirk was hoeing in the row behind me. Despite the intensifying heat, today had turned out to be a perfect day for this job. The rain over the weekend had left the soil in near perfect condition, not wet enough to make mud pies, but just right.

Dragging the three-pronged cultivator (a "hoe" as defined by my childhood vernacular) through dry, crusty dirt could be a strenuous task. I had found this out the hard way when I helped with the planting earlier in the summer, and my efforts resulted in several painful blisters on my fingers. In spite of the occasional challenges the task brought, I found something very satisfying about the look of a freshly tended garden row, the soil black and rich, and completely free of weeds. I even liked the scent of musty minerals that filled my nose each time the hoe broke through the crust, exposing the softer, underlying dirt to the air.

The superior nature of this task, compared with pulling weeds, created constant tension between my brother and me as to who got which job, and today had been no different. I clearly called, "I get the hoe," and was racing Kirk down the basement stairs in pursuit of it before he had even thought about it. He reached the tool first and grabbed it off the hook on the wall. I tried to wrestle it from him when he said with a satisfied smile, "Too late to call it, I already got it."

He was one year older and bigger than me and I knew I would not win. I grudgingly resigned myself to working between the plants while he worked between the rows. My only consolation was that he would likely finish first, and it was understood that he would help me weed until my task was also completed.

My mother reminded us on our way out to the garden that had we torn ourselves away from the morning line-up of cartoons sooner we would be performing our task in the much cooler morning temperatures. She promised to turn on the sprinkler when we finished, and the thought of this provided adequate motivation to move us through the corn to the peas, string beans, peppers, tomatoes, squash, and eggplant at a rapid pace.

When we finally finished I was sweating, my palms were colored a dingy brown and my fingernails were caked with soil. The garden seemed to have gotten bigger over the winter.

My only responsibility last summer had been helping to pick vegetables, which was considerably easier than pulling weeds and hoeing. Now that I was a year older I was being given a larger role which I had to admit made me feel more important.

We raced our blonde shepherd mix, Tina, to the spigot outside the house and took turns rinsing our hands with the hose. When the water began to feel cool we drank and were rewarded with a refreshing stream of water, just slightly tinged with the taste of rubber. We tried to give Tina a drink, but she just looked at us as if to say, "I will take mine from a bowl, if you please." We wiped our hands in the grass and headed upstairs to put our bathing suits on, pausing to take our shoes off in the garage.

"All done?" my mother asked as we passed through the kitchen.

"Yeah," we said in unison, "can we run through the sprinkler now?"

"In a little bit," she said, "I'm busy right now."

I glanced her way and saw that she had Daddy's clean shirts on the kitchen table and was sprinkling water on them. I knew this routine well. After she sprinkled them she would roll them up and put them into the refrigerator. Later on, she would take them out and iron them until they were smooth and crisp. There were parts of my mother's work that interested and even fascinated me. The transformative nature of ironing had appeal, especially the part involving the use of the hot iron. Watching her drag the appliance over a shirt stretched tightly across the ironing board, leaving a cloud of steam in its wake, and then witnessing the resulting crisp and perfectly unwrinkled sleeve was nothing short of magic in my mind.

I knew better than to pester her when she was busy, so I went to my room and changed into my swimsuit. I then started counting to myself to pass some time, so as not to disturb her and make her impatient with me. I had learned that if she became impatient with my brother or me our sprinkler run could evaporate faster than the steam from her iron. When I reached the limit of numbers I could count to, I opened the drawer that held all of my Sunday school crafts and papers (I never threw any of them away) and began sifting through them, wondering if there were other tasks she planned to complete before turning the sprinkler on for us. I certainly hoped not.

I thought about ironing again, wondering when I would be allowed to try it. I knew better than to ask yet. The iron got really hot and it could burn me. *When I get older she'll let me.* Garden-related tasks seemed to be the only ones that my mother felt were safe enough to assign me. Last summer I had been invited to help her and my Gramma when the vegetables came in. I picked tomatoes and corn, snapped beans and put freshly shelled peas into little white freezer boxes. When I asked to help with blanching or stewing the peaches or tomatoes in preparation for canning I was told no. This was a huge disappointment, as I desperately wanted to learn how to cook. Preparing fruits and vegetables for storage hardly counted as real cooking, but it was a start.

I planned to take another run at this request in a few months when we harvested the garden. Once when I was helping my Gramma in her kitchen, taking a few swipes with the rolling pin and measuring ingredients, she shared with me that she started baking pies when she was nine years old. She told me it was a shame that Mommy was not teaching me, and I fervently agreed. The notion of being able to bake a pie in just a few short years both excited and frustrated me. If I didn't start learning some basic cooking skills soon I was certain I would fall behind and never catch up.

After going through the entire stack of papers and critiquing my coloring skills, my thoughts went immediately back to the sprinkler situation. I decided to engage my brother in a plan to get us outside sooner rather than later. Walking into his room I could hear his voice making a series of "vroom" noises, progressively louder with each repeat, mimicking the acceleration of the Matchbox Mustang he was pushing across the floor of his room.

"Want to play Diane?" he asked me, referring to the make-believe persona I had developed solely for the purpose of playing Matchbox cars, "You can drive the Nova."

"No, I want to go outside and run through the sprinkler. Let's go ask Mommy again."

"She said she was busy," Kirk returned, giving the Mustang a vigorous push.

"I know, but that was a long time ago. I think we should ask her again, just in case she forgot. I asked the last time, so it's your turn now," I said.

"I'm not asking," he said, barely looking up from the Mustang.

"Why? Don't you want to run through the sprinkler?"

"Yeah, but if we bug her, she's gonna say no."

I knew he was right, but I couldn't stop thinking about the perfectly sunny, hot day that awaited us. I also knew that when he said no, he meant it.

"Oh, all right," I said, "I'll ask again. I always have to ask," I said.

"So? You like doing it better than me anyway," Kirk reasoned.

This, I had to agree, was true. Kirk was not exactly known for verbalization. In fact, he generally said as little as possible. Even if I had *hated* asking, I probably still liked it better than he did.

I walked down the hallway, standing just at the edge of
the dining room, within earshot but not within the view of my
mother. I could hear that she was still in the kitchen. I called,
just loudly enough for her to hear me.

"Mommy?"

"What?"

"Can we go outside now?"

I waited for it. Somehow, I felt that if she rejected my
request or became angry, it would be easier to handle if I could
not see her. If she yelled or said no, I would simply turn and
go back into my room and resume the sorting of my Sunday
school papers, or maybe go into Kirk's room and play Diane
and drive the Nova while his rendition of Bob drove the
Mustang. My disappointment would be bitter, but it was better
than just sitting around waiting.

"Yes," she yelled from the kitchen. And with that, I ran to
fetch my brother from his room.

Chapter 15

Numbers One Through Four

"You know what's weird?" I said to Jay, who was returning with a round of beers.

"Mom was so protective when we were little. We couldn't go to the neighbor's house, leave the yard, or step one foot out the front door unless she was with us. She knew our every move. I swear she had eyes in the back of her head. You weren't born yet, but trust me, she was tough. I used to try everything to avoid going out to the back yard through the basement, especially in my bare feet. There were always dead spiders and God knows what live bugs lurking in the shadows. But no matter what reason I gave her, no matter how hard I tried to convince her, she never, ever let us go into the front yard without her. The street in front was too dangerous, she always said."

My memories of those days were now flowing freely. I thought of the extremely eccentric neighbors who lived next to us for a short time.

"Do you remember the Grimes?" I asked.

"No, they had already moved out by the time I was born," Jay replied.

"Yeah, I guess that's right. By the time you were born, the Danners had moved in," I confirmed.

"I remember them being really nice, but they always kept to themselves," Jay said.

"True. They were not nearly as exciting as the Grimes. Kirk and I were so excited when the Grimes moved in and we learned that they had kids close to us in age. I remember the first time we went to their house -- actually, it was also the last time we went to their house," I said, laughing as I launched into the story.

Not too long after the Grimes family moved in, Valerie and her brother, Darryl, came over and asked if we could play. Kirk and I stood behind my mother, trying to catch a glimpse of our new neighbors as she talked to them through our front door screen. I could only see the top of Valerie's strawberry-blonde head, but I was immediately enthralled. At this stage in my life, my social interactions were limited to Sunday school and I had yet to encounter someone with such an exotic hair color.

My mother didn't say yes to their invitation to play at their house, nor did she invite them into ours, but she did concede to allowing them to play with us in our back yard. This way she could occasionally check on us through the back window. After directing our two neighbors to the back yard, Mom shooed Kirk and I down the basement steps. Our glorious new neighbors were waiting outside the door when we got downstairs.

We walked into the yard where I beheld Valerie. Pale skin and a sprinkling of freckles complemented her silky red hair. Already nine years old, she stood a full head and a half taller than me. Our age difference elevated my delight even further as my mind constructed endless play scenarios in which she could play the adult and I could be the child. Darryl was two years older than Kirk and had similar hair and skin color as Valerie.

During the summer months our badminton net was a permanent fixture in our yard, and to our great surprise Valerie and Darryl had never played. We explained the rules, demonstrated proper serving and returning techniques, identified the boundaries and commenced playing. It seemed as though only moments had passed when my mother called us in. In response to our complaints she told us that we had been outside for over two hours and that Valerie and Darryl could come back and play again on another day.

We made several subsequent attempts to convince her to let us play next door or to invite our new friends inside of our house, but she remained firm, denying our request to play anywhere but in our back yard. Kirk and I had pretty much abandoned the prospect of ever changing her mind when one day my mother relented and allowed us to accompany Valerie and Darryl next door.

"I want you back in an hour," she said.

Theirs was an old house made of red brick, sort of gingerbread-looking. Our house was old too, but our father had done a lot of remodeling to make it seem newer. The Grimes' place had stood empty for as long as I could remember. The house sat on the far edge of their property. On the edge closest to us stood an old, dilapidated red barn. The side of the barn was close enough to our property line that we could touch it while standing in our yard. More than once we peeked between the slats of siding where gaps existed, trying to see what was inside.

The darkness within illuminated nothing, leaving the nature of its contents to our imaginations. Depending on the theme of our play at the time, Kirk and I imagined countless scenarios, which ranged from secret treasure chests to dead bodies. Without question, we decided spiders and all kinds of other creepy-crawly things lived there, probably some bats and other small animals too.

We were shocked at being granted permission to go next door, and at the same time fearful that our mother would change her mind at any given moment. We raced across our yard in an effort to reach their house before she could call us back. Kirk and I both slowed our pace as we rounded the corner in front of the barn, knowing that even though it sat farther from the road than our front yard, we had best keep ourselves as far from the street as possible. We hugged the front of the barn, our eyes scouring its surface, looking for a crack or missing board through which we could peek. To our disappointment, the boards in the front were tightly fitted and the two large doors bolted closed.

My curiosity got the best of me and I yelled to Valerie, who was a good distance ahead of me by now.

"Hey, Valerie!"

When she stopped and turned I went on with my question, "What's in the barn?"

"Um, I think my dad has an old car in there, but we never go inside so I don't really know," she said.

What a letdown, I thought to myself, as we made our way past the barn and up the worn pathway to their house. As we entered the main room the first thing I noticed was the high ceiling. It made the room seem huge. Bringing my focus downward and into the living area I saw a mismatched couch and chairs. They sat upon a bare wood floor that looked old, maybe as old as the house. Wadded up clothing, a cereal bowl, tattered magazines and some potato chip bags littered the surfaces of both the furniture and floor. I didn't see a television set anywhere. I noticed a faint unpleasant odor that seemed not to belong in a living room, something between socks that had gotten wet and sat for too long and another scent I couldn't place, something sharper and stronger, like ammonia.

"Come on," Valerie said, "let's go upstairs and I'll show you my room."

Following her to the stairway across the room, I noticed movement out of my right eye. I turned my head toward it, but saw nothing. We reached the staircase that curved around the far side of the room and led upward to the second floor. Its banisters were solid wood, and while it looked very old, it was sturdy almost to the point of being imposing. As we began our ascent I noticed movement again, this time from a different direction. I stopped, turning my body to look more closely. Valerie saw me and followed my gaze.

"Oh," she said, "that's Fluffy, one of our rabbits."

Pointing in the opposite direction, she said, "And Thomas is over there. They had babies a few weeks ago and they are in the kitchen."

"Wow, you have pet rabbits?" I exclaimed, wide-eyed.

Right about then, Kirk had wisened to the existence of the rabbits and was on his hands and knees with Darryl trying to catch one of the males, Thomas, who was trying unsuccessfully to hide underneath one of the mismatched chairs. He spread himself out on his belly and lunged beneath a side table.

I heard a disgusted, "Aww!" escape his mouth. He got up off his hands and knees, closely inspecting his palms and then the knees of his jeans. From where I stood I could see the black smears on his pants.

"I think it's rabbit poop," he said.

"Oh, yeah, you gotta watch for that," Darryl said.

We had a dog of our own and were therefore no strangers to animal feces. However, the concept of pets doing their business indoors was, well, unheard of, to say the very least.

"How often do you let them out of their cage?" I asked.

"Oh, they don't have a cage. They just live inside the house here with us," Valerie said nonchalantly.

At that point my brother was laser-focused on one thing and one thing only, ridding himself of the rabbit droppings.

"Come on, let's go," he said to me.

I picked my way very carefully down the stairs and across the room, all the while scanning the floor for black droppings and skirting a few here and there. I felt very thankful that I had not had the misfortune of stepping in any earlier.

The odor I noticed upon entry to the house now made perfect sense. If these rabbits were pooping on the floor they were also peeing on the floor. *Gross!* As we cleared the side door from which we had entered, Valerie was behind me asking if we would come right back after Kirk changed his clothes. I said we probably would, knowing full well that once my mother got a load of the situation in that house we would never be back again.

Our brief visit was a huge disappointment. As I expected, that day marked the end of our interactions with the Grimes kids. Later, Valerie and Darryl's mother would break into the Cook's house across the street and steal a bottle of liquor. Their father would prop his extension ladder up against the back of our house and peek into the bathroom window while our mother brushed her teeth one night before bed. My mother's early protective instincts had proven to be correct. At the time we found her strict nature to be a frustration and could not see beyond the limitations it imposed on us. We could not appreciate being protected when we had never felt danger.

"Yeah," Jay said, "I don't remember her being that way, but then I don't remember much of anything before Glen."

"How could a person change so drastically?" I wondered out loud.

"I don't know," Jay said. "It's a good question. One thing's for sure, we could all have benefitted from protection from Glen. He was way more dangerous than pooping rabbits, speeding cars, and the pond combined."

"I suppose that's the key. He was dangerous, and he treated her as badly as he treated us. There's probably stuff we don't even know about. It's hard to protect anyone else, even your kids, when you are a victim yourself. You know that saying, 'If you stick your neck out too far, it may get cut off,'" I mused.

Changing the subject, he asked, "Have you talked to Jennie or Shelly?"

"No," I said, wondering how quickly the news of my father's death would travel. I was still in college when Dad and Jennie divorced, but she and I remained close. Even though we spoke only a few times a year, picking up the thread of our relationship was always effortless. She never stopped treating me like her own daughter, even when her 10-year relationship with Dad came to an end. She had moved to Florida several years ago, but most of her very large family was still scattered across northwest Ohio.

Shelly, his most recent ex-wife, was still resident in northwest Ohio, having also been born and raised in the area. At the time my father brought Shelly into my life I was still reeling from his divorce from my beloved Jennie. Even though several years had passed, I had hung onto a stubborn hope that he and Jennie might reunite. Shelly, like Jennie, possessed a kind and loving demeanor. I found it easy to welcome her into my life. She, also like Jennie, was a hairdresser, and we bonded immediately over hair and fashion. Her fun-loving nature elevated birthdays and holidays to a new level of festivity. Being an adult at the time Shelly and I were introduced, she and I developed more of a sisterly relationship than the mother-daughter relationship I had forged with Jennie. I quickly realized that I had the best of both worlds.

The end of my father's marriage to Shelly created one of the few rifts that ever came between my father and me. Matt and I were married the day before Dad and Shelly's first wedding anniversary. By the time Matt and I celebrated our first anniversary they had already separated. Unlike my father, Shelly had never before been married. A first-time bride in her thirties, she had waited for her one true love. She could conceive of nothing less than "till death do us part." She was in love with him, deeply committed to him and wanted to make it work. He cited their 15-year age difference and the fact that they had nothing in common as justification for the divorce.

At that point, even I was not naive enough to think that my father was beyond getting another divorce. It wasn't even his quick change of heart that troubled me. What I struggled with was his indifference, his lack of compassion for the pain his decision was inflicting on her. Could he not, I asked him, have waited to take up with Doris until *after* he wrapped things up with Shelly? As Shelly fought to accept the reality that her two-year marriage to the man she had regarded as "the one" was over, he was already barreling at breakneck speed to wife number four.

I was no keener to let Shelly go than I was to let Jennie go. I disliked the trend I was witnessing and chastised my father for the way he was treating Shelly. At one point he and I stopped speaking, but eventually I gave in. I couldn't make him love her and I realized that boycotting our relationship wasn't good for anyone. I grudgingly welcomed Doris into my life and added one more to my collection of stepmothers.

Having lived in the same area his whole life, my father knew and was known by many people. Given the nature of his death, it would be gossip-worthy news in many circles.

Considering small town connectivity, it would not take long for the news to get to the families of both Jennie and Shelly, and then to them.

"They are both going to be shocked," I said, shaking my head as I imagined their responses of disbelief and sadness. "I have already added them to my list of people to call. After I talk to Kirk of course. But knowing them, I wouldn't be surprised if we hear from them first."

Chapter 16

Unanswered Questions

Hearing a loud thump, I turned to see Rachel and Austin tossing horseshoes in the pit near the edge of the yard. *Something else Dad taught them.* I glanced at my watch. It was nearing 6 p.m. It had only been 24 hours since we arrived, but it felt as if five years' worth of events had transpired.

I turned to Matt, "Speaking of Kirk, I think the only way I'm going to get to talk to him is by going over there. And we probably need to get those two back to your sister's house and let them spend some happy time with their cousins," I said, motioning toward the horseshoe pit.

"Yep," he said, "I'll round them up."

After saying our goodbyes to Jay and Glynis I went inside to find Doris. She was standing in the kitchen talking to several of her sisters. Not seeing any of my father's family I noted that they must have already left. I dismissed the momentary guilt I felt at not engaging them as the unpleasant reminder of my father's upcoming funeral surfaced. *I would see them in less than a week.* Doris broke away and came over to me, tissues still in hand, eyes red, but thankfully the bellowing and sobbing were at bay for the moment. I asked her again about the note he left and once again she declined to show it to me, saying she didn't want anyone else to see it.

"Later," she said, she would show it to me later.

Frustrated, I changed the subject to the funeral.

"Do you need help with it?" I asked.

"You know there will be an autopsy," she half stated, half asked.

"Yes, Jay told me," I answered.

"We won't know for sure for a few more days when they'll have that done," she said, "but right now they're saying Friday."

"Do you have a funeral home in mind?" I asked. Matt mentioned the idea of asking Rob to preside over the arrangements during our drive from the pool party. The thought had not occurred to me, as Rob's funeral home was on the opposite side of town, a good 45-minute drive, making it an inconvenient and impractical choice. Matt went on to explain that funeral directors could sometimes arrange to oversee a funeral in another facility. I had to admit I liked the idea of having someone that I both knew and trusted lead me through this unchartered and somewhat terrifying landscape.

"No, why?" she asked.

"I think you have met our friend Rob? He is a funeral director on the other side of town, but he may be able to work out a deal with one of the local funeral homes. I don't know anything about this whole process, but I feel like it would be good to have a trusted friend handling it."

"Sure, I remember him. I don't know anyone in particular so that may be good. Go ahead and talk to him," she said. Pausing for a moment, the tears welling once again in her eyes, she went on, "I'm going to look at caskets tomorrow morning and you're welcome to come."

"I will," I said, before I had time to talk myself out of it. Unpleasant as the task sounded, I wanted to be involved, to help in any small way, knowing that once the funeral was over he would be gone forever. There would never again be a need to do anything for him.

After saying our goodbyes, we climbed back into the van and headed to Jill's house, where we dropped off Rachel and Austin. Mark's sister, Jill, had been our neighbor for more than 10 years. Her two children were close in age to our three. The five of them grew up together, their frequent scampering back and forth wearing a path in the grass between our two houses. I knew that right now there was no better place for my two youngest children to be. Austin was engrossed in a video game with Nate before we were even out the door, and Rachel disappeared into Madison's room and was most likely already trying on her clothes and listening to tales about her latest boyfriend. Let them forget for a while, they need to eke some fun out of this week.

As we pulled out of Jill's driveway, I could not get the suicide note out of my mind. Turning to Matt, I said, "I asked her again about the note Dad left, and once again she put me off."

"That doesn't make any sense," he said. You are his daughter, why wouldn't she give it to you?"

"I don't know. It's driving me nuts. It's almost as if she doesn't want me to see it," I said, the frustration rising in my voice.

Doris and I did not start out on the firmest of footing. My knowledge that she was the reason for my father bringing about such an abrupt end to his marriage with Shelly created tension between us in the beginning. More specifically, it created tension within me *toward* her. I eventually conceded that I had no right to judge either of them. I also had no desire to alienate myself from my father.

In the end I consoled myself by retaining my ties with Shelly, keeping her in my life despite my father's decision to the contrary. I opened my mind to Doris and moved forward. Her relationship with my father had endured for nearly 20 years, the longest in his marital history. He seemed happy, content, and settled in a way he had never been before. That was reason enough for me to accept her. Our families blended after that. She and my father became a constant fixture in my life and my children's lives. There was no issue between us that I was aware of, no reason I could think of for her to put me off.

It just didn't make sense.

Chapter 17

Kirk

Kirk's house was a quick five-minute drive from Jill's. My former commute to work took me past his house each and every morning. The house's age and stately appearance distinguished it from the rest of the aluminum-sided farmhouses scattered along the rural highway. The circa-1800's red brick, two-story was flanked by a detached two-car garage and a large red, aluminum-sided outbuilding that served as the office for his construction business.

Corn fields surrounded his property on three sides. After I passed through a buffer of weeping willow and oak trees, the panorama that unfolded before me brought forth memories of the yard where we spent so much time as children. Peach, apple, and more willow trees dotted the fenced area around the house. In the center of the circular drive, wispy ornamental grass plumed beside a pathway of paving stones that meandered from one side to the other. Black-eyed-Susan, orange day lily and multiple varieties of Hosta adorned the space in front of his office. Two gargoyles, fangs bared, watched through their menacing eyes from atop the fence posts outside the office. An American flag hung on a pole near the door. He had created a sanctuary of his own that boasted both privacy and beauty.

Kirk and I both found satisfaction in cultivating the landscape, a love spawned from our childhood gardening responsibilities. Matt and I kept a vegetable garden for the first few years that we lived together in Whitehouse, but could no longer rationalize the time investment after Cam was born. Our former two-acre yard had hosted six perennial beds that contained lilies in every color, daisies, iris, roses, delphinium, phlox, and a healthy assortment of other plants I couldn't recall. Our yard in Houston was barely big enough to accommodate a few shrubs and a smattering of whatever flower happened to be in season. A few palm trees and a magnolia balanced the trade-off, providing an exotic change from the northern plants we were so familiar to us.

I didn't miss the hours of upkeep required each spring and summer, but I often found myself longing for the therapy that working the soil provided, sifting the rich black silt between my fingers, breathing in the first musty and pungent scent of spring, and the satisfaction that came with planting something beautiful and nurturing it to fruition.

Kirk's house, solid as it was, needed renovation when he bought it. Like our father, he was a man who relied on his hands to make a living. With my father's encouragement, he had started his own construction business almost 20 years ago, utilizing his experience working as a carpenter after he left college. He had a knack for drawing, possessing the ability to render lifelike recreations of his chosen subjects. This talent transcended to crafting creations from wood including shelves, tables, cabinets, and even an occasional rocking horse. He gave Cam a walnut-stained oak rocking horse on his first Christmas. It was corralled in our playroom for years. When the kids outgrew it, I wrapped it in plastic and moved it to the attic, keeping it until some future day when Cam could pass it down to his own children. Between Kirk's talents and experience, a house that needed work was hardly intimidating to him. He had already added a second story to the two-car garage and begun construction of built-in wooden cabinets in the family room of the main house.

Dusk was setting in, the crickets kicking off a chorus. I looked toward the house and seeing no visible activity or lights, decided to head toward the office. As we approached I could hear the mad scrambling and scratching of the beasts on the other side. Alternating black heads popped into view through the window as Kirk's two black labs, Maggie and Mannie, took turns jumping up to see who might be approaching. I turned the knob slowly, testing to see if it was unlocked. When it yielded I turned it fully, and gently pushed into the furry mass of excited paws vying for attention.

A quick scan of the room indicated no sign of my brother. I looked at Matt and motioned my head toward the house as I slowly closed the door, taking care to assure that the two dogs remained inside. We walked across the driveway and through the gated yard to his house.

I banged loudly on the door. Almost immediately my brother's face appeared in the window of the door. He opened it, looking as sullen and grumpy and as much like himself as ever.

"Sis, come on in. Matt, how ya' doing?" he said, hugging me first, then Matt.

I stepped back and eyed him closely. His brow was furrowed, his eyes absent of even the slightest glimmer, and his mouth was drawn in a tight, straight line.

"How are you doing?" I asked.

"Shitty. This sucks," he said, emphasizing the ending "s" sound and turning his face to the side, his eyes boring into the wall as if he could see through it.

Finally, he said, "It sure as hell doesn't seem like something Dad would do and it doesn't make any sense to me. Let's go out back and sit down."

Matt and I followed him back across the driveway to his office-slash-man-cave. Between managing his business and hosting poker parties, this was where he spent most of his time. We walked behind him, giving him time and space to calm the animals and clear a path for our entry. The man-cave portion of the room was appointed with a poker table and chairs, a couch, and two stuffed chairs. The couch was covered in a blanket to protect it from the hair shed by Maggie and Mannie, its two most frequent occupants.

I usually avoided the couch, having been accosted more than once by an exuberant Mannie. I love dogs, but draw the line at face licking. If you got close enough for Mannie to reach you it was only a matter of time until his tongue was all over your face. Instead, I headed for one of the high stools sitting near his drafting table and plopped myself in it. Matt followed suit, selecting the stool next to mine.

Kirk made a beeline to the freezer in the opposite corner, extracting from it a bottle of Crown Royal. After a bit of rummaging, he found three glasses and brought them over to the table. He tipped the bottle, still frosty from the freezer, poured a generous shot into each of the three glasses, and passed one each to Matt and me. Looking directly at me and raising his glass, he said, "To Dad."

I felt the tears stinging my eyes as I drained my glass, the liquid heat searing a path from my throat to my stomach. It occurred to me that I hadn't eaten all day. But why would I have? The thought of food had not been the least bit appealing earlier, nor was it now. But the whiskey tasted damn good. Maybe it would numb some of the pain.

"How was he when you saw him Friday?" I asked.

"Good. We had a great night. Most of the guys from my crew were here. We were drinking beers, shooting off a few fireworks, you know, typical July-Fourth stuff. Dad was in a great mood. He was headed home from a job he and Dave had been doing in Dayton. He stopped by here on his way. It was a really good night," Kirk said, pausing.

"He stayed for a few hours, longer than he planned I think, but we got to talking and we were having a really good time. He was relaxed. Happy. He was Dad at his best. He wasn't worrying about anything. These long jobs on the road were wearing on him. He hated being gone for weeks at a time, but even that didn't seem to be weighing on his mind. He seemed fine, totally sober when he got ready to leave, but I told him to stay over anyway. I reminded him that it's a holiday weekend. He wanted to go, said he wanted to sleep in his own bed."

After a pause and another sideways turn of his head, Kirk finished with, "That's it. Next morning, I get the call from Jay telling me Dad got picked up on his way home and he wanted us to go retrieve his truck that had been towed. That was just yesterday."

My head was in my hands, my elbows leaning on the drafting table.

"Why?" I asked Kirk, still desperate for some neat and tidy explanation, some magic answer that would justify his decision to end his life.

"He didn't want to deal with the whole DUI thing. He's 66 Sis. This was a big deal to him. Sure, he was a bad ass back in the day, but that was a long time ago. He's mellowed out. He's a grandpa now and he takes that seriously. He's proud. And the DUI, it was an embarrassment to him. When I talked to him yesterday he couldn't have acted more opposite to how he was when he left here Friday night. He was down, really down. I've seen him pissed," Kirk said, a momentary smile forming on his lips at the memory of Dad's infrequent yet hotheaded temper. "I just figured he'd get over it, push past it, like he has every other time life kicked him in the ass."

I let Kirk's words sink in, really trying to hear them. I considered for a moment that I hadn't given enough weight to that part of my conversation with my father on Saturday night. He was ashamed and embarrassed, worried about setting a poor example. But still, how could he have built that into something so big and horrible that it drove him to take his own life? He had come so far, achieving the kind of success that many who started life in far better situations could only dream of. How could he think that killing himself was a better solution? I still couldn't comprehend his logic.

"It's a waste. A complete waste. Dad was amazing. He could do anything," Kirk continued, "anything he put his mind to. He started with nothing. Worked his ass off for everything. He got his degree in business while he worked a full-time job at Ford. But that was after he left the union and was promoted to management. Before that, for all of those years, which was most of his working life, he made his living using his hands. You and me, we remember the '57. It was the first one, but you remember how many came after that, the Novas, the Rat Rod, the Corvettes. He made his own knives, for Christ sake, carved pictures of deer into the handles."

Visions of my father's accomplishments danced through my head. My brother clearly inherited his artistic talent from our father. I remembered the first time my father's creative talents benefitted me personally. The image of the large rectangular cardboard boxes that my father transformed into giant dominos flashed before me. Applying black paint and cutting white circles from poster board and affixing them to the outside resulted in Halloween costumes for my brother and me that were the envy of our friends. Granted our nifty costumes limited our dexterity and confounded the act of trick-or-treating, but that fact didn't dampen our pride in the slightest.

"Remember Halloween? Remember the dominoes?" I asked.

"Yeah, but the King and Queen of Hearts were even better," he said.

"Those were the prize winners, right?" I asked.

He nodded slowly and said, "Uh, huh. That was some good shit."

I imagined he was envisioning the playing-card costumes my father had made for us the following year. He and our mother had actually collaborated on the design. As I reflected on that memory, I realized it was one of the few that involved my parents teaming up. *Maybe that was why it remained so fond to me.*

"He was always coming up with ideas, things to do, things to make."

"I'm pretty sure that's why Halloween is one of my favorite holidays," I said, turning to Matt, who rolled his eyes and then broke into a wide grin. My obsession with Halloween was well known. Decorating, costumes, and pumpkin carving were all passions I enthusiastically shared with those close to me. Memories of my dad engineering costumes for my brother and me were the genesis of that love. The year we won a prize for our costumes -- costumes that he designed and created – remained one of my happiest childhood memories.

Kirk stared off into space for a good two minutes. Were it anyone else it would have been just plain awkward, I would be searching my mind for something to say, some way to break the silence. But this was Kirk, He had been quiet his whole life and I was used to it. I figured he was remembering something, so I sat in silence a few minutes longer, letting him savor what I hoped was something happy.

Finally, he said, "I remember when I was little, Mom used to say I was just like him. But she didn't mean it in a good way. It used to bother me, you know, back when we didn't really see much of him, before I really got to know him. But now....now I think it's the best damn thing anyone could ever say to me. He did so much for me. And he knew people. He knew everyone around here. I can't count the times I'd run into someone, bidding a job or just looking for car parts and after I introduced myself they'd immediately recognize the last name and ask, 'You're Jimmy's boy?' All I had to say was yes and I had instant acceptance. Dad gave me my first job, building Shelly's hair salon," he said, referring to the business my father engaged in with Shelly before things fell apart. "After that I suddenly had experience, a finished major project I could point to when I bid on jobs. It was the starting point for my business and I might have still gotten here without his help, but it would have been a hell of a lot harder."

As I absorbed those words, knowing he meant every one of them, I thought about how hard the two of them had worked to reach that point. To quote a former therapist, "A lot of shit had to be cleaned out of the barn," before my father and his eldest son were able to find common ground. I had never given it much thought, but the comparisons my mother drew between the two of them probably contributed to their difficulties. That, on top of typical father-son conflicts that arise when boys become men.

But he was right. I couldn't remember her ever doing it in a complimentary way. My father was more absent than present during the time of his marriage to our mother. His drive to earn was responsible for much of his time away. In the years following their divorce, my mother took to referring to my father as a "good provider", but a poor husband and father.

"I do remember that. She was so bitter about him and given her knack for keeping things bottled up I suppose it was natural that on occasion her true feelings erupted. I guess you, being the oldest, were the likely recipient of her venting. That and the fact that you look like him. You were a walking reminder of him," I said.

As if on cue, filmy memories of my mother lamenting her son's likeness to her unfaithful husband began to surface.

Chapter 18

Where There's Smoke

"Do you remember the smoke-bomb incident?"

"Definitely," Kirk replied, smiling a real smile for the first time that night.

With each passing birthday our mother relaxed her grip a bit more. Initially we were limited to riding our bicycles in front of our grandparents' house under strict supervision. Within a few years we were granted expanded privileges near our own house, on the condition that we would only ride on Third Street, which unlike the street in front of our house was used almost exclusively by its residents, who always drove at the posted speed limit. My mother watched us out the front window as we walked our bikes across our street after looking both ways. Once on the other side we mounted our bikes and took the alley to Third Street. Not only was Third Street void of heavy traffic, it boasted two gigantic hills. A creek that ran toward the river two streets away had cut a valley in between the two rises many years before. The hills flanking the valley served as a beacon that called to us the moment our tires left the gravel of the alley behind and found the smooth pavement of Third Street.

We would ride full tilt toward the downward slope, gaining as much speed as possible on the way, then building even more momentum by pedaling hard all the way down the hill. The challenge was to see how far we could coast up the other side without having to pedal. Running out of speed before reaching the top of the hill meant even harder work getting the rest of the way up. Down one side and up the other we went, over and over, each time striving to make it farther up the hill without pedaling. When we tired of the hills we raced to landmarks and practiced stunts like coasting hands-free and popping wheelies. Sometimes we would park our bikes and Kirk would chase crayfish in the creek. I watched from the bank, having no desire to put my hands on something that not only squirmed but could also pinch me.

We were intent on conquering the hill one summer afternoon, having just reached the farthest rise, when Kirk saw his friends, Kip and Brad Milford, riding in the distance near their house. He immediately took off, pedaling toward them. Our boundary was firmly established at the top of the hill we had just climbed -- and he was blatantly ignoring it.

"That's farther than we're supposed to go!" I yelled at him.

"Come on, you baby!" he turned and replied, still pedaling.

I was reluctant to follow, but he had invited me and that was a rare thing when it came to him and his friends. I suppose it wouldn't hurt, as long as we came right back, I reasoned.

By now he had caught up with his friends and I could see the three of them corralled on the sidewalk, each leaning with one foot on the ground to steady himself over his stationary bike. I began riding toward them but before I could get there they were back up on their seats and pedaling in the opposite direction, even farther past our boundary marker. I pedaled faster, watching as they rode toward the Milford's house, which stood next to some abandoned grain elevators. The three came to a stop in the grassy area in front of the grain elevators and got off their bikes, set their kickstands in place and walked toward one of the structures, disappearing from my sight.

When I finally reached the parked bicycles, my brother and his friends were nowhere to be seen. *Where did they go? What were they up to?*

I parked my bike, dropped my kickstand, and got off my bike. I began walking toward the back side of the grain elevators. Rounding the corner, I saw the three of them standing close together and looking downward.

"Hey, what are you guys doing?" I yelled.

Kirk's head jerked up as he turned around and yelled back to me, "Stay there, I'll be right back!"

He then returned his focus to whatever they were doing, which was still not clear to me. My early excitement at the prospect of an impromptu adventure was turning quickly to anxiety. We were more than halfway across town, at least three blocks past our boundary.

My mother wouldn't be happy if she knew. In fact, I was pretty sure we were now engaged in a spankable offense. I didn't want Kirk to get into trouble, but even more, I didn't want to get myself into trouble. It had been some time since I had felt the wooden paddle on my behind and that was just the way I liked it.

I debated what to do. I would most definitely not tell on him unless I had to. In other words, if given the choice between the paddle on his butt or mine, he would lose. If we got out of there and got back to our end of town fast, there would be no way our mother would know. But we needed to get a move on, the sun was sinking low in the sky and we had strict instructions to be home well in advance of dusk. Ignoring my brother's directive, I walked toward them.

Approaching, I noticed the air was tinged with a strong odor that smelled like eggs, the scent becoming stronger with each step. As I reached the outside of the huddle the closeness of their three bodies had formed, a plume of deep purple smoke appeared in the open space between Kirk and Brad's shoulders, rising upward with force, funneling into the air above them. They were lighting smoke bombs.

Kirk turned around again, saw me, and ordered, "Go back in the front and watch our bikes! I'll be there in a minute."

"We gotta go or we're gonna be in big trouble," I yelled back.

"Stop being a baby," he said without looking at me, while readying a match to light another bomb.

"Kirk! It's getting dark. We gotta go!"

"Get back in front and I'll be there in a minute. Jeez," he said, this time giving me a direct and dirty look.

As I walked back to my bike I thought about threatening to leave, but I knew if I arrived at home without my brother it would be instant trouble. Our mother would demand to know where he was, and I would either have to say I didn't know or that he ran off with his friends. Both scenarios were counter to the deal she had made with us. And there was no way to feign misunderstanding. She reinforced the parameters every time we left the house to ride our bikes. We both knew that one of the requirements upon which our privilege was conditioned was staying together at all times. The other was respecting the boundaries of the farthest hill on Third Street.

Nope, no way I could go home without him. I was stuck. As I waited I began manufacturing the story I would offer to explain our tardiness. It would have to be a really good one. I tried to purge the current facts from my mind, so I could be free to come up with something plausible that didn't involve smoke bombs and matches behind the grain elevators. Telling the whole truth would surely result in a spanking and possible revocation of bike privileges. My brain toiled to come up with a story that wasn't exactly a lie, but also didn't reveal certain incriminating facts. I could take the spanking. All in all, they were usually quick. The sting lasted for a while but was soon forgotten. Giving up our bikes for a week in the summertime would be far more devastating.

Finally, I saw my brother emerge, followed by Kip and Brad. Thank goodness! Kirk picked up his bike, waving goodbye to his partners in crime. He stood up on the pedal to push off, and said, "We're gonna have to ride really fast so try and keep up."

Great. He makes me wait and now I have to break my neck to make it home so I don't get in trouble along with him! The sky was rosy gray when we reached our house. Technically the sun was not down yet, I nervously told myself. In our haste, we didn't have time to discuss a strategy. If our mother started yelling, my plan was to jump in first. This I knew would not be a problem for my brother, who was naturally prone to silence. I planned to opt for the "but it's still light outside" angle. As I expected, our mother was waiting for us when we walked up the basement stairs after leaving our bikes on the back porch, her face pulled tight, eyes piercing holes into our faces.

"Didn't I tell you to be home before dark?" she demanded.

We both copped our most pathetic and sorry expressions and said, "Yes."

Right on cue, I jumped in, "But it's not quite dark yet."

"It's not dark? Do you see any light in the sky?"

Without giving me a chance to answer she went on, "You know the rules. You are supposed to be home while the sun is still visible, not after it's gone down." She turned to my brother and said, "You're older. You are supposed to be the responsible one."

She adjusted her gaze to bring both of us back into her line of sight.

"Both of you, go to your rooms. Next time it will be the paddle."

Relief flooded over me. We had escaped both the paddle and losing our bike privileges. We turned, ready to scurry from the room and out of her sight, Kirk in the lead. He hadn't taken two steps toward the hallway when something fell out of his jacket pocket, hit the floor and rolled. It was a smoke bomb. The thud it made when it hit the floor was enough to get our mother's attention. Kirk was scrambling to pick it up when my mother beat him to it, scooping it up off the floor. She looked at it, looked at my brother, and her face went from dark to black. There was no mistaking it, she was furious.

"Where did you get this?" she asked.

By now Kirk's gaze was firmly fixed on his feet.

"I don't know," he said.

"You don't know?" she asked again.

"No," he said in a very quiet voice.

"Well, maybe the board on your butt will help you remember! You're lying. And this is why you are late."

She then turned to me.

"What were you doing? Were you both lighting these? Where did you get the matches? Do you understand how dangerous that is?"

She was firing questions like bullets from a gun.

"No, I wasn't, it was Kirk and Kip and Brad."

It was out of my mouth before I could think. I hated myself immediately, but saw no way around it. The only alternative would be to claim I was not with him and that would have brought an even bigger punishment for both of us. After all, I did try to get him on his bike sooner. If we had left when I wanted to, he wouldn't have been in such a hurry and would likely have secured the contraband more carefully, made it to his room and stashed it wherever he hid such things, avoiding this whole ugly mess.

"You are getting the paddle," she said to my brother and walked toward the garage where she kept it.

As much as I hated getting it myself, I think I hated it more when he got it. Even if I had committed no transgression and I knew I did not deserve it, I still felt a sort of guilty remorse in seeing my brother being punished. It was different if we were both in trouble. There was a sort of bond you felt when you were in on something together, got busted and had to suffer the consequences. Our mother was not cruel or extreme when she spanked us. A few firm whacks and it was over. It hurt of course, but not that much. I usually cried more out of humiliation than from the actual pain.

My mother's spankings were typically silent affairs. The admonishment came first and by the time she got around to the paddling part she had said all she wanted to say. This time was different. When my mother returned from the garage with the piece of left-over wood molding that served her purpose, and instructed my brother to bend over (thank goodness our routine did not involve pulling our pants down) she seemed even angrier.

"You are just like your father, lying, sneaking around, doing things that you know better than doing," she fumed as she laid the first whack across his bottom.

"Is that how you want to be when you grow up? Do you want to be like him? Do you?" she demanded.

Two, three, four, and finally a fifth crack of the paddle ended it.

"Go to your room, both of you," she said, delivering her final words to us for that night.

I was out of there before she completed the sentence, heading swiftly toward my room before she could change her mind and decide to dole me a few whacks, too. My heart was still racing as I began to comprehend that I had been spared not only one but two punishments.

Her words about our father echoed in my ears as I got ready for bed. My parents had separated and were in the process of their first divorce. My father had moved out earlier that spring and I was just now getting used to my parents living apart. Our daily routine had changed little if at all, but overall, I had to say things were actually better.

We now saw our father every Sunday. We had one whole day of his undivided time every week. At first it was awkward. Prior to these organized visits I could recall only a few times spent exclusively in his company. It was obvious he didn't know what to talk to us about, so I tried to help him by chattering about school, my favorite TV show, or the book I was reading. But now, several months into our new arrangement, we had settled into a pretty comfortable routine. I looked forward to our weekly visits.

I loved my mother deeply. She had been a constant source of security in my life, my mainstay. Now a second-grader, I could still remember those long, lazy days before I started kindergarten, days spent delighting in her company, playing *Go Fish* and *Old Maid*. While she worked in the yard I walked between the roses and lilies that lined the perimeter of our vegetable garden, giving each one a drink with my miniature watering can. Other times I would watch her at her sewing machine while she made dresses for both of us. And then there were our walks to the little grocery store in town.

Sometimes, while lying in bed waiting to fall asleep at night, I would imagine what I would do if she died. The thought of it made me cry so hard I would soak my pillowcase. I wanted her to be happy. But, I wanted to love my father, too. My mother's clear display of animosity toward my father posed a challenge to the achievement of that goal. Her words about my father conflicted me, calling into question how I could love someone who seemed to make her so miserable.

Chapter 19

In the Closet

"I remember thinking Dad was 'bad' in those days," I said, air quoting the word bad.

"But we didn't really know him. He worked so much. We only had Mom's observations to go on, and although she shared them infrequently, they usually weren't complimentary."

"That's why I didn't like hearing that I was just like him," Kirk said.

I nodded in understanding.

"I do have a few memories of him in my younger years," I said, thinking back to my recollection a few hours ago about sitting in his lap.

"Remember how we used to have such a ridiculously early bedtime? I swear it was like 8:00 p.m. or something, even in the summer. I just remember that sometimes I would be in bed and it would still be light outside," I said.

"My room was closer to the living room, so I could hear bits and pieces of *Laugh-in* or *Gunsmoke* or whatever Mom was watching on TV while I was trying to go to sleep. It was always so hot in my room. I remember lying there sweating and bored out of my mind until I finally fell asleep," Kirk said.

"Some nights I would lay there so long that, eventually, I would hear Dad come in. It had to have been well after 11:00 p.m., since he worked second shift. If I were feeling particularly brave, or just driven by extreme boredom, I would sneak down the hall and stand at the edge of the living room and see if he would notice me before Mom saw me and sent me back to my room. If he saw me, he would let me come and sit in his lap for a few minutes. Then, he would carry me back to bed and tuck me in," I said.

"I think he really wanted to make the whole family thing work with Mom, but he didn't have a clue how to do it," Kirk said.

"For one thing, his own father walked out on Gramma Millie when Dad was a boy. For another, they got married right out of high school, thanks to me," he continued, grinning. "Neither one of them had a chance to figure out what they wanted out of life."

"Yeah, getting married because you're pregnant isn't exactly a winning formula. It would have been different if they had dated for a long time and had tons in common. Plus, I don't remember ever seeing them kiss each other or hold hands. There didn't seem to be much affection between them," I said, pausing, "other than I suppose, pure lust in the beginning. And that always has a limited shelf life.

"I also don't remember seeing them just plain talking to each other very much. Or talking with us, for that matter. Our house was an eerily silent place. Oh, but they sure had some explosive fights," I said.

While my parents closely guarded whatever fondness they had for one another, they seemed to have no such compunction when it came to their feelings of anger and frustration toward each other. Or maybe, I thought, there were quite simply times when it could no longer be contained.

Kirk stared into space and simply nodded.

As a child I was prone to nightmares. Some were inspired by movies or stories, others were just random, frightening situations my young imagination created. After waking from a scary dream, I would immediately go into my parents' room and shake my mother awake. In the beginning she would patiently tell me there was nothing to be afraid of, then shuttle me back to my bed. But as the frequency of my nightmares increased, my mother's patience dwindled, her half-asleep response diminishing to a sleepy yet firm, "Go back to bed."

Being aware of the hardship my nightmares posed for my parents, I tried very hard to console myself when my dreams terrorized me. After coming fully awake, reassuring myself that the scene did not actually happen and that I was in my own bed, I would think back to what I was doing in my dream and rationalize that whatever it was could not ever actually occur in real life. I began to realize that just when the dream became really bad, when I started to scream, bringing forth nothing but throaty white noise, or when I tried to run, only to find I couldn't lift my feet, I would wake up. This awareness crept into my subconscious, enabling me at times to recognize that I was dreaming while I was still in the dream. Once I knew that I was dreaming I found that I could usually wake myself from it.

This newfound approach to managing my nightmares alleviated their former hold on me. One night in my dreams I heard loud noises. Was it the giant apes again? Were they slapping that poor woman onto the pavement again?

"Thwack! Thwack!" I concentrated hard, but I couldn't see the apes. I couldn't see anything. I waited, only to hear the noises repeating. Something about it felt ominous, even though no horrific visual accompanied it. I tried my new technique, telling myself I was dreaming, but I couldn't seem to bring myself out of it. The noise continued, becoming sharper and more distinct. I imagined two hard things hitting against one another, like a board slamming into a wall.

"Get out of my Life! Get out of my Life! Get out of my Life!" a voice screamed, in between the banging.

When the voice began chanting, "I hate you!" over and over, I recognized it as my mother's and began to think that maybe I wasn't dreaming. My mother was screaming from somewhere in our house. It didn't seem loud enough to be coming from her bedroom which was directly across the hall from mine. Where was she? What was happening?

"Leave me alone!" came her next plea, expelled from the top of her lungs. *Oh my God, someone was hurting her!*

I came immediately and fully awake, scrambled out of my bed and ran to my bedroom doorway where I paused to listen. My heart pounded, my stomach felt like some small animal was doing back flips in it as I made my way to into the hallway where I found Kirk. He was standing in his doorway looking in the direction of the ruckus, but the living room was dark. The noise was coming from farther away, probably the kitchen, which we could not see from where we stood.

"What is it?" I whispered to him.

We had never experienced an intruder in our house, but I could think of no other explanation. I had no idea what time it was. I knew my father was certainly not home by now. If he were here he would be fighting my mother's assailant. Unless, I thought, he, too, had been subdued. My mind began constructing all kinds of scenarios involving my father being captured, tied to a chair or knocked unconscious while the murderously violent intruder assaulted my mother.

"I don't know," Kirk said, carefully stepping into the hallway, speechlessly commanding me to follow him. I fell in quietly behind him and we tiptoed toward the kitchen where the noise seemed to be coming from. In the meantime, the banging continued but with less frequency. My mother's screams came to resemble more of a shouting beratement, sounding similar to the way she sounded when she was angry with us. She was still going on about hating the person and continued to insist that the intruder get out of her life.

"When we get to the kitchen you get to the phone and call the operator," Kirk instructed. "Ask for the police. I'll see what's going on."

As we made the turn from the living room into the kitchen we heard her scream the loudest yet.

"I'll take the kids. We'll leave, and you'll never see them again! This is the last time I'll let you do this to me!"

That's weird. Whoever had a hold of her knows us and based on her threat would seemingly be upset if he never saw us again. At that instant I realized she wasn't talking to an intruder and that our father had not been apprehended or knocked unconscious.

My mother's perpetrator was none other than my father. This premise was confirmed when we reached the kitchen. My mother stood in the utility closet in her nightgown, her head turned to the side facing us, back against the wall, hands balled into tight fists at her side. My father, wearing a t-shirt and jeans, had his hands on her shoulders, restraining her.

Seeing us, my mother sobbed, "Your father hit me!"

Hit her?

I struggled to shift gears from calling the police to comprehending the scene in front of me. As terrified as I was at the thought of our mother being accosted by an intruder, the reality I had just confronted was far more frightening. My mind began piecing together the scene that was taking place before we arrived in the kitchen, incorporating the banging noises that woke me up and the accusation she had just made.

Had those noises come from him hitting her? Had she hit him back?

The blurry lines in my mind filled in as I envisioned my parents slugging it out with one another, using a board bigger than the one my mother spanked us with to inflict pain on each other. She had screamed at him, telling him to get out of her life, and then threatened to take us and leave him.

I was practically glued to my brother, standing so close to him that our arms touched, both of us staring, wide-eyed, into the closet. At the time it didn't occur to me to question the location in which we found them, or even the cause of their brawl. Years later I surmised that Mom ambushed him in the kitchen right after he walked through the door, demanding to know where he had been. It was safe to assume that whatever answer he provided did not meet with her satisfaction and probably, she suspected, involved another woman. Somehow their argument led them to the closet that was just off the kitchen. At that moment I wasn't capable of analyzing cause and effect, nor did I care. I stood paralyzed in place, waiting fearfully for the next blow.

But it didn't come. Instead my father, out of breath, said, "I didn't hit your mother," releasing his hold on her and stepping back.

The look on his face conveyed defeat, fatigue, and embarrassment. I anxiously scanned my mother's face and her exposed arms and legs, looking for marks. I didn't see any, but the only light was coming from the closet in which they stood, and it was pretty faint. My father, however, looked much worse for the wear. His face was red and puffy, and I could see what looked like scratches on his neck.

"We were just having an argument," he said.

Tears ran down my cheeks. We were not an affectionate family, but I was so overcome with emotion -- fear, empathy, and shock -- that I felt my arm rising instinctively toward my brother's back, seeking something safe to hold onto. I caught myself, curbing my urge to embrace him, out of fear he would push me away. Instead, I grabbed a fistful of his bathrobe and squeezed tight.

I felt an involuntary sigh escape from me as the scene from my memory faded and returned my focus to the present. "It was bad enough seeing them like that with each other, but what made it worse was the fact that nothing was ever said about that incident. Or any of the ones that followed, for that matter. And no matter how many times it happened it never got any easier to see or hear. I honestly couldn't tell you if it happened only a few times or a hundred times. It was just so scary, it dominates my memory of their marriage," I said.

My thoughts drifted to the day after that first fight my brother and I witnessed. My father was absent as usual, either at work or temporarily banned from the house. My mother never uttered a word about the closet incident. If my brother had not been standing next to me the night before, I would have questioned whether the scene had actually taken place, believing that my initial perception had been accurate and that it had been nothing more than a bad dream. I remember watching her closely, looking for some clue as to the cause, and more importantly the corollary, of the previous night's clash. From her demeanor, to her words, to her facial expressions, she gave nothing away.

"I'm not saying that she should have tried to explain to a five and six-year-old the complexities of their marital conflict, but that night scared the shit out of me. I had no idea what was coming next. I braced for the worst. For example, was Dad ever coming home again? Could we expect Act Two to follow the next night? Was she really hurt? Hearing and seeing their anger toward one another was horrifying, but tip-toeing around the house the next day was worse. It was like this tension hung in the air. You couldn't see it or touch it, but you could feel it.

"I think it was the first time I noticed the silence, the first time the lack of communication in our house felt wrong to me. Before that, I just always took for granted that there wasn't a lot of talking in our house. I know she was just really introverted, I get that. But there are events in life that left unaddressed become bigger, badder, and uglier in your mind over time. I have finally reached the conclusion that she just isn't capable of talking about painful things," I said.

Kirk nodded again and reached for the bottle of Crown. He decided to skip the glasses this time and instead, raised it to his lips and tipped it back, taking a long sip. He then handed it to Matt.

Matt waved his hand, "I'm driving."

"Well I'm not," I said, relieving my brother of the bottle. I let the now familiar burn work its way down my throat and fill my still-empty stomach.

I set the bottle down. The three of us sat in silence. For the first time that day I felt tired. The effects of sleep deprivation, the Crown on my empty stomach, and the day's events had finally succeeded in dulling the adrenaline that had propelled me through the day.

"It's late," I said, turning to Matt, "we probably need to get going."

He was already getting up out of his chair.

As Kirk walked us out I told him about plans to meet Doris to discuss funeral preparations the next day. He shook his head. I fully expected that reaction, but still felt the need to inform him.

"Doris thinks the funeral will be Friday," I said, watching his face closely.

He looked away again in silence. This time I chose to fill the void.

"You have to be there. I need you there," I said, unable to imagine getting through the funeral without both of my brothers at my side.

After more silence he said, "I know Sis, it's just that I hate funerals."

"I know. I do too," I said, with the complete understanding that, like that night so long ago when we discovered our parents in heated combat, he felt most comfortable processing his feelings in solitude.

"We'll talk," he said, hugging me. As I got into the van I felt a chill go down my spine. Kirk's words mimicked those that my father had spoken to me just one night before, the last words I would ever hear him speak.

Chapter 20

Legacy

Matt and I got into the van. I focused on him as he fumbled for the keys in an effort to ward off the fiber optic threads of connectivity that my mind was attempting to forge between the story I had just resurrected with my brother, and a recent scene from my own marriage. Just moments ago I had acknowledged my extreme fatigue. I craved the release that some peaceful thoughts might bring to my rattled brain, and the relaxation that would accrue to my tension-sore muscles. But it was already too late. I gave in, knowing I did not have the will to redirect my tired mind at this point.

For years I was traumatized by both the perceived and real violence that my parents carried out on one another in the course of their physical confrontations. Like a hibernating bear, their anger would lie dormant for long periods of time. Just when you started to feel safe again, almost forgetting that the bear even existed, it would awaken again, snarling, clawing, and charging at you with full force.

Violent behavior, and so many other negatives I witnessed throughout my childhood, would never be part of my adult life, I had pledged to myself. But had I not, just three months earlier in a blind rage, accosted my own husband, blackening his eye with my fist, hitting him in a way I didn't even know I was capable of?

I shuddered inwardly at the memory of that night, still trying to rationalize my behavior, telling myself that nothing like that had ever happened between us before. We had had more than our share of screaming matches, but physicality had never entered the picture. It's not as if Matt and I had a routine of knocking each other around, I told myself. Maybe it wasn't so awful ….

But I couldn't deny that it really had been awful.

The only silver lining was that the incident took place far out of the sight of the kids. If they had been with us, or anywhere in the vicinity, it would have never happened. I told myself over and over. If we had taken a *family* vacation as I had advocated for the past three years, instead of our annual couples' get-away, he wouldn't have found himself in that situation and I wouldn't have been provoked to hit him.

Each time I revisited that night, I tried to see it his way. I *wanted* to see it his way. We had been drinking all day at the beach. His excuse was that he was intoxicated. Yes, I had to agree, he was drunk; so was I for that matter. But still ....

Could I ever be drunk enough to kiss a woman?

I once again returned an answer of no. It was the same answer I had returned every time I recounted the events of that night. No, I could not comprehend ever being so drunk that I would forget that I was both married and heterosexual.

And yet I had walked into the kitchen of our friends' villa to the sight of him fully lip-locked, his tongue visibly probing the mouth of another man. My shock, combined with the dullness of my alcohol-soaked senses, forced me to step back. I stood stunned in the hallway for a moment, processing the scene I had just witnessed. In mere seconds I felt instinctive rage rising from my gut, spreading like wildfire to my chest and down my arms. My fingers curled into a fist at my side and the idea came at me with the force of a speeding locomotive.

I'm going to punch him.

And once that thought got a hold on me it was too delicious to let go of. I turned and walked back to the kitchen only to find it empty. My focus was now so sharp that nothing could have deterred me from my mission. I retraced my steps, turned the corner toward one of the bedrooms and saw him there, weaving from side to side as he tried to make his way down the hallway ahead of me.

He nearly lost his balance when he turned toward me after I spoke his name. His face was void of a distinct expression, his eyes were open but seemed not to recognize me. I squeezed my already fisted right hand tighter. He opened his mouth to speak, but before he could utter a word I landed a blow, hard, fast, and solidly placed, to the sweet spot beneath his eye and above his cheekbone.

The force of impact, combined with his drunken, abject surprise, knocked him backward, slamming him into the wall behind him.

"I saw you!" I screeched, "I saw you!"

His face crumpled in hurt and disbelief. He reeled, trying to make sense of what had just happened, as his hand raised to touch the wound I had just inflicted. He wore the look of an unsuspecting child who was jolted from his peaceful play by a parent's angry words.

In spite of my fury and the hurt that precluded it, I instantly regretted my action. The look on his face cut me to the quick; guilt had already begun percolating in my core. Regardless of what I'd just witnessed, how could I have so decisively, without so much as a second thought, sought him out and assaulted him with such force?

The friends we were vacationing with quickly arrived on the scene and separated us, shuttling me to an extra bedroom in the villa and driving Matt back to our condo. Unable to sleep, I crept out to the pool after everyone went to bed and curled up in a chaise lounge until the sun came up, mulling over the scene I had just witnessed.

Was my husband gay? I had to admit the signs were present. It would explain a lot, his mysterious activities during my long days at work and while the kids were in school, our almost nonexistent sex life as of late. But if he were gay, why didn't he ask for a divorce? Our marriage had seen its share of conflicts, from managing money to redirecting our children, but one of my husband's strongest traits, I had always believed, was his loyalty. I knew with complete certainty when we married that I could count on his fidelity. I was positive that he wasn't capable of living a secret life. But then again, for the past four years I had failed to come up with a plausible explanation for what occupied his days. The subject was all but banned from our list of approved discussion topics. My mind batted the questions and my contrived answers back and forth like a tennis ball until I saw soft pink light appearing in the eastern sky.

As much as I wanted to catch the first flight home, I thought better of it. I needed to hear him out. The next day he apologized profusely, admitting that he had no right to disrespect me that way. He was truly sorry. He drank way too much. It was inexcusable. It wouldn't happen again. I appreciated his apology, something that I knew was not easy for him, but I was far more interested in getting to the heart of the matter and understanding the root cause.

I asked him point blank if he was gay. No, of course he wasn't gay, he was just drunk. But, I shot back, how could you be that drunk? Using my father as an example, I explained that no matter how much my dad had to drink there was no way, not a shred of a chance, he would tolerate being kissed by another man. And, I pointed out, I saw the two of them. He had seemed to be anything but an unwilling participant. The vision would remain forever etched in my mind. My husband's face tilted upward, his mouth engulfed by his partner, the two of them gently, longingly massaging the insides of each other's mouths with their tongues *in a way I could never remember him kissing me.*

My heart didn't believe his words, but my head was desperate for them to be true. I pushed away the recurring urge to take an early flight home. What would everyone think if I came home ahead of him? What would I tell the kids? No, we needed to stay and finish our vacation. When we got home we would work it out. I envisioned couples' counseling and lots more talk about that incident after we got home. But three months later that had yet to happen.

Whenever I raised the subject Matt would shut me up with a look and ask in an irritated voice, "Are we going to go there again? Can't you ever let anything go?" He had no interest in counseling and reminded me of the time we had gone years before. It had done us no good. Hadn't we found our own way through our problems? Plus, I was the one always harping about money; counseling was expensive. His words were effective in dredging up my own guilt, and by the time the conversation was over I was in full self-blame mode.

I would back down sheepishly, placing my fears firmly back into their box in the far reaches of my mind. We would resume our daily life, our conversations focused on what to have for dinner, work, and planning Cam's high school graduation party. Each time the topic bubbled up I allowed him to rationalize my concerns away. I would tell myself I needed to be forgiving and supportive. I would remind myself how much I loved our family, and that being married to him was a key part of that.

But I couldn't shake the nagging feeling that something between us was very wrong. Our years of conflict had worn on us, causing both of us to take our frustrations underground. He quit complaining that I worked too much, I stopped nagging him about getting a job. Skirting discussions regarding the issues that irritated us most did nothing to solve them, however; it just bred resentment and widened the void between us.

Was that how my mother felt that night in the closet? Had she reached some invisible yet palpable limit? Perhaps her trigger was the time of my father's arrival home? Had he been late? Or maybe she detected some remnant of an interaction with another woman, the scent of her perfume, a smear of lipstick, or maybe just a guilty look that she could no longer rationalize away? I recounted my own anger. As much as I regretted my behavior, I couldn't deny it was driven by my truest of feelings. I made the decision to hit Matt in a split second.

I wasn't certain I could characterize my reaction as being the result of a conscious decision. It felt more like pure instinct. The fact that my brain was clouded by alcohol at the time was pretty telling. Instead of mellowing my instinctive reaction, my foggy state of mind intensified it. But why was violence my go-to resolution? Was I wired this way?

The answer, I finally decided, was that it did not matter. No matter how completely wrong it was for Matt to make out with a man, punching him in the face in response was no more acceptable. I could not deny the parallel between my behavior and the scene I had witnessed between my parents in the closet of my childhood home so many years before. My smug and long-held belief that I had risen above my parents' style of conflict resolution was undeniably in question.

The act of dredging up the villa scene and the ushering in of all the unanswered questions that accompanied it had delivered me to a state of complete wakefulness. The fatigue I felt at Kirk's house was a distant memory. My urge to engage Matt in a conversation about the incident was strong, but I knew that I did not have the energy to entertain more conflict. Not now. Not this week. Not on that issue. But I also knew that my tenacious mind would not leave the topic be. Like the morning after witnessing my parents' conflict in the closet of my childhood home, I was left to contemplate the meaning and implications of my husband's behavior in the solitude of my own mind.

Chapter 21

The "D" Word

I struggled to fall asleep that night. The thoughts that surfaced during the ride back to Jill's house nipped at the corners of my consciousness like the dachshund who chased me on my bike as a kid, desperate to get its teeth into my skin.

Matt was already asleep, his snores growing increasingly loud. I turned onto my side, propped myself up on one elbow and looked at his face. The slivers of moonlight that seeped through the minuscule spaces between the blades of the window blinds illuminated sections of his face. We had been together for 22 years, married for 18 of those. I thought I knew everything there was to know about him, but that belief was called into question three months ago. The seeds of doubt that were planted that night in our friends' villa had blossomed into a thicket of concern that continued to plague me. Had our marriage run its course? More importantly, had I been living a lie that spanned more than two decades?

And yet, I could point to plenty of days since our vacation when our relationship felt the same as it always had, days when I let go of the nagging concerns and found myself forgetting all about the vacation incident. Today was a perfect example. He had been so supportive; his mere presence and the knowledge that he was there for me had made the day bearable. I knew he really loved me, and I loved him. Our family life was idyllic. Complete strangers often complimented the beauty of our family. We had been blessed with three beautiful, healthy children and the means to live a good life. It would be a shame, if not a sin, to disrupt the perfection we had created.

Throughout my adult years I had witnessed the unwinding of numerous marriages of friends and colleagues. I watched in sympathy, smug in my conviction that I would never find myself in that situation. Matt and I had an obligation to uphold, we were an example for others to follow. I knew firsthand that divorce left a mark on everyone in the family. My parents had cycled through four marriages each, and my father had engaged in a fifth before he cashed in his chips and exited this world. The thought of putting my children through the events I endured at the hands of my own parents' seemingly endless family reorganizations sent shivers down my spine.

I could not have imagined a more ideal family than the one I married into. Matt's parents had been together for nearly 50 years. The first time I attended Sunday dinner at his parents' house I was hooked. As I chatted with his parents and grandparents over cocktails I learned that this was a weekly thing. The idea of being part of a family who gathered every Sunday just to spend time together captivated me. But the closer I looked, the more contrasts I saw between our two families. Matt was in constant contact with his sisters, his parents and his grandparents. They shared every single holiday and special moment in each other's lives. It was the sort of family I had craved for as long as I could remember.

Matt could have been a three-headed monster and I would still have married him. But he wasn't a monster at all; he was intelligent, well-mannered, and respectful. Our relationship began as a friendship that gradually turned into romance. Initially he was an anomaly to me, demonstrating complete restraint when it came to sex. He had strong views about premarital sex, believing it was best to wait until we were married, or at least until such time that we were committed to doing so. I saw this as a sure sign he had been raised properly. I felt not only fortunate, but privileged to become a member of this wonderful family I had happened upon.

As I looked back, I had to admit the life we built had exceeded my every expectation on the family front. The families of Matt's two sisters and ours grew in lockstep, producing eight grandchildren in fewer than six years. My children came into this world amidst a shower of love, attention, and support in which they flourished. They regarded their five cousins as some of the most important people in their lives. I knew their bonds would be lasting, giving them yet another anchor of stability they could lean on throughout the course of their lives. Matt and I had given them the childhood I never had. I couldn't fathom taking it from them.

I thought again of my mother and father's union, reminding myself of the reasons for its failure, not just once, but twice. As an adult with almost 20 years of marriage under my belt, I believed I had pinpointed the issues. My parents were incompatible. That was the first strike. Second, they married under the duress of pregnancy. Finally, and perhaps most notably, my father had a regular practice of straying. There was no sugar coating it. Infidelity plagued his first four marriages to his first three wives.

Doris, wife number four, and I weren't close enough to discuss such things, but the fact that they were still married led me to believe he had finally gotten this habit in check. Either that or he was being very careful to cover his tracks. I remember with great clarity the first time I became aware of the concept of marital cheating. As I lay staring into the darkness, the vision of that day came back to me as clearly as if it had happened yesterday.

When our family acquired a second vehicle my mother began driving 20 miles into Maumee to shop at the larger and newer Foodmart store. The store was huge compared with the little market in downtown Grand Rapids and the choices seemingly endless. I loved those trips just as much as I had enjoyed my walks into town with her when I was younger. Kirk and I were each privileged with choosing our own breakfast cereals, a decision we didn't take lightly. Adding to the intrigue of our grocery excursions was the opportunity to choose the cookies we would eat for snacks and dessert for the upcoming week. The catch was that we were allowed just one choice between us. If we reached the cookie aisle and still hadn't reached a consensus, our mother would decide. We often began our debate in the car in order to assure that we reached agreement by the time we got inside the store.

We were standing in the cereal aisle, boxes in hand and engaging in a hot debate over which tasted better, Count Chocula or Franken Berry. My mother interrupted our banter to tell us we could each choose a toy from the limited but enticing selection comprising a few shelves adjacent to the cereal section. It was a rare treat to get a new toy outside of Christmas or our birthdays. Rather than question her motivation, we dumped our cereal boxes into the cart and raced over to the toy section. I pored over the choices, carefully considering every option. Squirt guns, balloons, jacks, jump ropes, and coloring books stared back at me from the shelves. I bypassed the cheap imitations of Barbie dolls, having learned that the arms and legs broke easily when you tried to put clothes on them. I zeroed in on a set of cardboard dolls that came with five sets of plastic cling-on clothes. The pieces of the outfits could be mixed and matched in seemingly endless combinations. The versatility of the play options this choice offered was too appealing to resist. Kirk studied his alternatives long and hard: cap guns, play money, super balls, and marbles. Finally, he settled on a bag full of green army figures.

Kirk and I wasted no time tearing the wrappers off of our new treasures as my mother pulled out of the Foodmart parking lot, our focus firmly fixed on the task of playing. Kirk set about posing his plastic army all around the back seat and arm rests while I tried the first outfit on my one-dimensional doll. We were engrossed in our new amusements, paying no mind to our surroundings or the stopping and going of the car.

I felt the brakes, and something about the abruptness of our stop caused both my brother and me to look up. Through the windshield I could see nothing but a forest of thick trees behind a small parking area. The same scenes were visible through the side windows in the backseat. To the left, in front of the trees, was a large grassy area dotted here and there with people. A mixture of adults and children were playing baseball on the far end of the grassy area. Two kids on bicycles whizzed by my window. I didn't recognize the place, but it looked a lot like the park in Grand Rapids where we often played, only bigger.

"Where are we, Mommy?" I asked, my anticipation growing in hopes that we were here to play.

She seemed not to hear me. My eyes were fixed on the back of her head as I awaited her reply. When it didn't come I opened my mouth to repeat the question, just as she turned the wheel hard to the right and accelerated again. I followed her gaze and saw a man walking toward us. As the car got closer I could see it was my father. That's funny, I thought, Mommy didn't mention that we were coming to see Daddy. And what was he doing in a park? Wasn't he working?

My father had not quite reached the side window my mother had rolled down when she went off on him. My mother's brown eyes were typically expressionless, making it difficult to read her moods much of the time. From my vantage point I could see clearly her reflection in the side, rear-view mirror as she addressed my father. Her face was pulled tight, her eyes squinting upward, creating lines across her forehead. Her eyes sparked as if a fire burned behind them.

"So, this is what you do at lunch time?" she demanded.

"She's just someone from the plant. We were just talking and enjoying the day," he replied quietly, as if trying to shush her with the tone of his voice. "Can we not do this in front of the kids?" he asked softly, almost pleading.

"Why? Don't you think they should know?" she more stated than asked. Her voice was now high-pitched and shaking with emotion. She turned her head toward the picnic area beyond where my father stood. Following her gaze, I saw a woman gathering up what appeared to be the remains of a lunch spread. I noticed her blonde hair and red dress, but she was too far away for me to see her face. She stole a glance our way every so often as she busied herself with clearing the spot. Before my father could reply my mother turned to us, our faces nearly in the front seat from leaning so far forward in our attempt not to miss anything that was transpiring, and said, "Your father has a girlfriend!"

At this point my brother and I turned our attention back to the woman in the red dress who was now scurrying away from the spot, blanket draped loosely across her forearm, trash and other remains in the other. The pace at which she moved, and her tense posture, suggested nervousness, discomfort, and a desire to get out of there quickly. While our mother couldn't seem to tear her gaze away from the woman, my father never once looked back, as if refusing to acknowledge that he had been with her -- or anyone, for that matter.

My father was leaning into the car through the side window, hand on the steering wheel and trying to calm my mother down. The scene was beginning to attract the attention of numerous passers-by. I noticed one woman staring at the front window with a big grin on her face. I couldn't imagine what she found amusing about the situation.

"Come on," he said, "why don't you let the kids play for a minute and we can talk about this."

"I don't want to talk to you about this. I'm sick of it. I've listened to all your excuses for being late coming home. I've heard you talk about all the overtime you are working and your second job. I'm beginning to understand all of the *work* you're doing." After pausing to catch her breath she charged onward.

"I want a divorce," she said, jerking her head forward, fixing her gaze firmly out the front window again.

"Come on," he pleaded, his face wearing a look that conveyed impatience, frustration, and mild disgust, "we were just having lunch."

"Dressed like that?" my mother shot back. "You're a liar. You'll hear from my lawyer," she said, ending the conversation as she rolled up the window.

She stared straight ahead, put the car in gear and pulled forward. Kirk and I simultaneously whipped our bodies around to look through the back window at our dad. He was shaking his bent head and walking slowly in the opposite direction from where he came. He probably figured it would be best to get in his car and head back to work, leaving his lunch date, who was long gone by now, or maybe hiding in the woods, to find her own way. Or maybe he waited for us to pull away and then went to rescue her.

The scene left me feeling sick to my stomach. The fear and doubt it instilled stayed with me for days. And like the closet scene, it was never discussed. For days afterward, I walked on eggshells, wondering if my father was going to leave. But in the end, it turned out to be just another one of the many times my mother would threaten divorce. That word, divorce, became more feared by me more than the sum total of giant apes, faceless bad guys, and vampires who appeared in my nightmares. Its mention was always preceded by some dramatic and fear-inducing scene involving both of my parents.

Chapter 22

Faithful

I would come to regard the spectacle I witnessed that day in the park as the first time I associated my father with the term "unfaithful husband." Over the years I would watch his dalliances with other women undo successive marriages. My childhood orientation to marital infidelity and the continued reinforcement of its consequences instilled a sense of caution within me. The thought of having to worry constantly about whether my future husband was romancing other women seemed both exhausting and heart breaking. Matt's strict moral code reinforced the notion that he was the perfect man for me. I knew I would never have to worry about him straying; he had proven that to me with the platonic resolve he demonstrated during the first two years of our courtship.

My preoccupation with my future partner's ability to be true kept me from leveling this same focus on myself. I had always regarded my values as staunch in this regard. I couldn't imagine inflicting upon my own family the kind of pain I watched my mother endure. It never once occurred to me that I could even be tempted to stray, let alone follow through. And yet I had done just that. In the aftermath of my affair I repeatedly tried to rationalize my behavior, telling myself it wasn't really an affair. Affairs, I had always believed, were premeditated and involved people who possessed some dysfunction that prevented them from upholding their end of the bargain in a relationship. I had always theorized that my father was affected by his own father's abandonment, the example that it established in his young mind rendering him forever unwilling or unable to commit to one partner.

While I had seen plenty of bad examples throughout my childhood, I took for granted that my awareness of the corresponding negative consequences would keep me firmly in line. I later realized it was this line of thinking that got me in trouble. Affairs, I now knew, didn't always advertise their potential in advance. Rather, they presented themselves in the most unlikely of forms.

Even now, years later, I struggled to come to terms with the how and why of my fall from grace. If I were to have been asked at the time, I would have reported that I was indeed a happily married woman. Our youngest child, Austin, was just under a year old, Rachel and Cameron were thriving. I was living my dream. My subconscious assumption that I had no reason to be wary of a diversion could not have been further from reality.

My relationship with Josh began innocently enough. We met through work. The first thing I noticed about him was his sarcasm, a brand of humor I happened to share. We hit it off immediately and quickly established a habit of giving one another a hard time in what we mutually understood to be a joking manner. The ease that existed between us unwittingly took our professionally-based banter to a more personal level. Before I knew it, the focus of his compliments had shifted from my competence in my job to how beautiful he thought I was.

One after another silent warnings went off in my head, telling me to retreat to the confines of the professional boundaries I had long ago established for myself. I needed to remind him that I was happily married, and it was not appropriate to talk to me that way. Somehow, no matter how many strict talking-tos I had with myself, I could not find a way to resist the mysterious and delicious feelings he created in me. Not only did the will to deter him elude me, I found myself wanting more, more of him, more of his admiration, more of the look he gave me that always made the blood rush to my cheeks. The mirror he held up to me provided a whole new reflection of myself. I felt accomplished, intelligent, and physically desirable in a way I had never felt before.

He sensed my unspoken willingness to continue our dance and pushed closer and closer. Our mutual respect for one another, combined with the sparks flying between us, became an irresistible combination. I became a hormonal time bomb. It was only a matter of time before I detonated. By the time we finally crossed the line I had become practically manic, my feelings wildly swinging back and forth between euphoria and guilt. I was an addict and he was my drug. My brain knew how bad he was for me, but I had no idea how to make myself stop wanting more.

The ceaseless wrestling match that ensued between my conscience and my behavior killed my appetite. I lost weight. The physical change, coupled with my inability to focus and my general inward withdrawal, did not go unnoticed by Matt. He questioned me. What was going on? Was I interested in someone else? No, of course not, I insisted. I hedged, buying time that I prayed would allow me to figure out just exactly what was going on with me. *What was my problem?*

This sort of thing had never happened before. Not to me. I had never so much as looked at another man since I began dating Matt, and certainly not since I married him. But I couldn't control my feelings for Josh. Our relationship had awakened something within me. Exactly what, I could not put my finger on, but I was desperate not to lose it.

I had actually talked about Josh quite openly in the beginning. My blindness to the infatuation between us kept me from guarding the details of our burgeoning relationship. In my mind it was strictly professional. I had no reason to hide anything from my husband. Josh turned me on to Ayn Rand and I became an immediate fan, somehow finding time to read *Atlas Shrugged* and *The Fountainhead* in the same month. Over dinner or before bed I chattered on to Matt about the characters and the themes of her stories. As things progressed between Josh and me I continued to talk about him but shifted the focus to work related topics, while trying to convince myself we were nothing more than acquaintances who operated in the same professional sphere.

Meanwhile, Matt put the pieces together and finally challenged me about Josh. It seemed, Matt asserted, like we were more than friends. He didn't accuse me of having an affair but asked if I had feelings for Josh. Cornered, and having exhausted all tolerance for the inner turmoil that was eating me alive, I spilled my guts.

In hindsight, I realized my confession was one of desperation. Knowing I didn't have the will to save myself, I hoped that my husband would. Thoughts of divorce had begun to rise to the surface of my consciousness as fast as I could slam them back down. Divorce ranked number one on the list of my parents' transgressions that I would not repeat -- under any circumstances. Matt and I were aligned in our conviction that marital vows were not to be broken. Regardless of the sin I had just confessed to committing, he had no interest in enacting the first divorce in his family. No interest in sharing custody of our children. No stomach for explaining to his colleagues and friends that he was getting a divorce, thereby making him damaged goods. Just as my father's girlfriend had done in the park so many years ago, we tidied up, brushed ourselves off and moved on.

I let go of my extracurricular love interest, but continued to be troubled not only by its genesis but also the extreme

to which I had allowed myself to be taken by it. I actually
contemplated divorcing my husband. For what? I barely
knew Josh.

Once again, I felt shame as I absorbed the full extent of
my weakness and continued to be frustrated by my lack of
understanding of my own motivation. I reasoned that the
attraction began on the heels of having our third child. We had
let our roles as parents trump our roles of being partners. We
had stopped paying attention to one another as individuals.
The unforeseen implications of Matt's recent career change
had me off balance, I told myself. The combination of those
factors provided a plausible yet still unsatisfactory explanation.
I couldn't stop thinking about the passion that existed between
Josh and me, and what a stark contrast it presented to the
friendship that had served as the foundation of Matt's and my
relationship so many years ago.

Our reconciliation was blissful at first, our near-miss
incident reminding us both of our deep appreciation for
one another. We made a point to schedule date nights and
reintroduced romance into our relationship. I was hopeful we
could create the passion we had missed out on by starting out
as friends, but within a few months our second honeymoon was
over. Matt became distant and distracted. When I remarked on
the change, he denied that anything was wrong and insinuated
that just because we reconciled did not mean he had forgotten
my misstep, that I shouldn't expect him to kiss my ass forever.

Matt's social interactions with the friends he met at the
coffee shop continued. He became increasingly close with
Stephen, a guy he met at the gym. Small gifts began to appear
around the house; a coffee grinder, homemade cookies, nut
bread, all from Stephen. Something about their friendship
troubled me. I couldn't shake the feeling that Matt was hiding
something from me. I asked to meet Stephen, suggesting we
all get together for drinks, but Matt put me off, saying that

Stephen's job required him to work almost every evening. I told myself I was overreacting, but at the same time, he had never before engaged in a friendship that excluded me. It was just different, I told myself, and that's why it seemed odd. I should be happy for him.

I began to feel he was deliberately paying me back for my transgression. My guilt drove me to suck it up and bear it. By now, all that remained of my brief love interest was shame and remorse, laced with a good dose of self-loathing. When I did occasionally weaken and complain to Matt about the time he spent with Stephen, he would roll his eyes and dismiss me with a rhetorical question like, "Oh, so I'm not allowed to have friends?" He would then bolster the question that didn't invite a response with something along the lines of, "You have friends. You had a really *good* friend as I recall. And because *you* have a guilty conscience you don't trust me. Stephen is a guy, for God's sake. It's not like I'm hanging out with some woman I met at a bar."

I lay awake for hours trying to make sense of the vacation incident, overlaying upon it the relationship he had cultivated with Stephen four years earlier. No, I finally concluded, he hadn't been hanging out with a woman he met at a bar. But maybe another woman wasn't the real threat.

Chapter 23

All That Was Good

Following the closet scene and the park incident, the contentiousness between my parents ebbed and flowed. At times the seas upon which their relationship floated were calm and peaceful, other times they were dark and stormy. I felt like a boat without a rudder, sailing aimlessly at sea, my course at the mercy of the wind. I was incapable of predicting when the blue skies above me would turn black and unleash bolts of thunder and torrents of rain. The increasingly frequent conflict between my parents put me on edge. Even when things appeared to be fine, when my mother's face wore her natural, albeit serious look, but absent the furrowed brow, I still found myself anticipating the next storm. And it always seemed to come.

We already had a well-established pattern of spending weekends with our grandparents, and as the turmoil between our parents escalated, Gramma and Grampa's house became our sanctuary, the place we could go and forget the unsettling goings-on in our own house. One particular weekend we were with them on the heels of yet another showdown between our parents. The day before, our mother had stood in the doorway of our living room, suitcases in hand, and told our father she was leaving, and she may or may not return. That evening we spent a rare and tense night alone with our father.

The next day he dropped us off at Gramma's on his way to work. He was pulling 12-hour shifts all weekend, he said, and would pick us up Sunday.

Grampa opened the door and bent down so we were at eye level. Saying not a word, he let his dancing blue eyes do all the talking and grinned from ear to ear. He patted our behinds as we ran past him and plopped ourselves into chairs at the kitchen table. I breathed in the rich and smoky scents of coffee laced with bacon, a hallmark of Gramma's kitchen. Our visits always began with a snack.

At home we were required to remove our shoes in the garage before entering the house, but Gramma had no such rule. I was thankful for this. Traversing her green Astroturf kitchen floor felt like walking barefoot across a giant hairbrush. The spaces in between the stiff filaments attracted crumbs and stray food particles the way Velcro attracts fuzz. The tiny bits of debris had a way of sticking to the bottom of bare feet, something I didn't much care for. In Gramma's defense, she was a career woman and didn't have time to keep her house spotless.

Grampa rummaged in the cupboard and extracted our plastic cowboy-boot cups, filled them with milk and set the red one in front of me and the blue one in front of Kirk. He then placed a plate of oatmeal cookies in the middle of the table, caught my eye and winked but still said nothing. He settled into the chair between us, left arm resting on his stomach and holding his upward bent right elbow in support of his right cheek.

His index finger was extended along his jawbone, thumb tucked under his chin, and the remaining three fingers tucked in. He watched us as we chewed away, the smile never leaving his face. The pose, the silence, the smile, all epitomized our Grampa -- who rarely spoke, and when he did his delivery was brusque, making you think he was cross. You had only to look into his eyes to see the offsetting tenderness, rendering his tone and manner of speaking completely harmless. Eventually he said, "Once you finish up it'll be about time to go pick up your Gramma."

We knew the routine without being told. Kirk and I would climb into the backseat of his red VW Bug and Grampa would make the 20-minute drive to the Waterville branch of the First National Bank. He would pull into the parking lot and back into a space so that we could look straight ahead and see the door from which my Gramma would eventually emerge. We always arrived promptly at the 5:00 p.m. closing time. Her actual departure time would depend on how long it took her and the other tellers to count out and balance the funds in their drawers. From the parking lot we could see into the bank through several enormous windows on the side of the building, often catching a glimpse of Gramma, who was stationed in the teller stand next to the window. Eventually we would see the lights extinguish, and within a few moments she and her coworkers would appear on the sidewalk, where they would all wait until her boss, Hal, locked the door.

Once in the car, Gramma would greet us warmly, then immediately launch into a tirade about Hal, Betty, or Evelyn, her co-workers, and the latest, most irritating or entertaining acts they had committed. Kirk and I would often imitate these scenarios in our pretend-play at home. But in the moment, we listened from the backseat, spellbound. Tonight we were going to McDonalds, something we only did with our grandparents. Afterward they were taking us to see the Disney animated movie, *The Aristocats*.

Eating out was both a novelty and a treat. We knew that going to McDonalds might also involve getting a milkshake or an apple pie, creating even greater anticipation. Sometimes there would be McDonald's-themed toys or games for purchase. We knew we needed merely to show some interest, say something like, "Grampa, look! They have stuffed Ronald McDonald dolls this week," and we would walk out the door with one in our hands.

Our grandparents worked from a seemingly endless list of activities deemed to be fun by a kid's standards. In addition to our dinner and movie nights, our weekends with them often involved day trips. Grampa maintained a family membership to the Toledo Zoo and we went with them at least once a month, weather permitting. Sometimes our parents would accompany us, but we never went without Gramma and Grampa. Even today I cannot walk through those gates without thinking of my grandparents. After church on Sunday, Grampa might drive us in his navy-blue Lincoln to Port Clinton, Mansfield, or Columbus to check out some new sight or attraction that my Gramma was interested in. We petted and fed deer, rode in a rattle-trap train through a makeshift jungle that housed giant, roaring plastic dinosaurs, and drove through an African Safari park where we looked at lions, zebras, and tigers through the closed windows of the car.

Our days always ended back at Gramma's house. Gramma and Grampa sat in their respective recliners. Kirk and I shared the couch, reclining at opposite ends, our feet in the middle, within perfect viewing proximity of the console TV on the opposite wall. The prospect of watching *Lawrence Welk* at home would have had both of us playing in our rooms in favor of enduring a geriatric display of pink and blue chiffon floating against a backdrop of antiquated music. But everything was fun and entertaining at Gramma's. Watching TV always necessitated snacking, and even though we knew that any request within reason would be indulged, it was always up to me to ask. If Kirk got hungry before I made the pitch, he would nudge me with his foot or give me a look, jerking his head toward the kitchen.

I always waited for a commercial break, knowing that the timing was precarious. There needed to be adequate silence for Gramma to hear me, but if I waited too long she might launch into a critique of Bobby and Cissy's last number or the arrangement of the Beer Barrel Polka performance. I had seen her commentary last through entire commercial breaks, spilling into the program when it resumed. My Gramma loved to sing and played the piano and organ. She had strong views about all things musical, and as with all her other views, she wasn't prone to holding them back. At what I perceived to be just the right moment, I asked.

"Gramma?"

"Yes, honey?" she was looking directly at me over her glasses, rocking slowly back and forth in her recliner, a relaxed smile on her face. Our Gramma had many words of endearment for us. When she called us "honey" it came out sounding like "hun-ye."

"Can we have something to eat?" I asked.

"Sure! What sounds good?" Looking over at my Grampa, she then said, "Bernard, don't we have some ice cream?"

My Grampa, who kept his hearing aid turned down, rarely heard anything Gramma said the first time and tonight was no exception. She continued to look at him with anticipation. He was fixated on the TV, cheek resting on his index finger, thumb tucked under his chin, and completely oblivious to her question. She waited a mere few more seconds before saying loudly in an exasperated tone, "BERnard!"

My Gramma had a deep, baritone voice. An enthusiastic member of the Zoar Lutheran Church choir, she sang with the men in the back row. In sharp contrast to my Grampa's infrequent verbalizations, Gramma was rarely quiet. She spoke almost constantly. If the volume of a household's verbalization could be rated on a scale of ten, with one being the least and ten being the most, our house would be a one and hers would be a ten. The fact that my Grampa was hard of hearing was no deterrent. She could satisfy herself with long periods of one-sided conversation, going for many minutes before requiring any input from others. She could also be quite demanding.

For all of the foregoing reasons, my Grampa had found it beneficial to his peace of mind to keep his hearing aid on low, which of course, aggravated Gramma tremendously.

"What, Thelm?" he asked, turning his head slightly to look at her, chin still in hand, flashing his shiny blue eyes her way.

"I said, do we have some ice cream? Why can't you ever hear me the first time?"

My Gramma's whole face was squinted up in irritation. For as many times as this exact exchange had occurred between them, I would have thought by now she would anticipate my Grampa's response, or rather lack of response, and that the pained expression she now wore would have diminished to one of mild displeasure.

Communication between the two of them was as predictable as the performance of *Adios, Au Revoir, Auf Wiedersehen* that closed the *Lawrence Welk Show* every Saturday night. Each time I witnessed their hallmark bantering I couldn't help but wonder why she ever expected something different to happen. Whatever the reason, it never failed to entertain us, and tonight was no different. Kirk and I shared sideways glances, doing our best to contain our giggles.

"I don't know," he said in an agitated voice, getting up out of his recliner and turning toward the kitchen. As soon as his back was to her, he looked our way and winked. This was the signal to follow him into the kitchen. I picked my way through the minefield of crumbs and food particles on the prickly floor. Kirk and I stood behind him, his silhouette dark against the light projecting from the freezer side of their avocado green Frigidaire.

In the light, wisps of his hair stood out on each side of his head as if infused with static. The ceiling light above made the bald spot on the top of his head appear smooth and shiny. He extracted the carton of ice cream and we sat at the table waiting patiently for our bowls. Setting two bowls of chocolate chip ice cream in front of us, he handed us each a spoon and we made our way back to the couch. Gramma allowed us to eat in the living room in front of the TV, an indulgence we were not permitted at home. We did not take the privilege lightly and were very careful not to spill or make a mess.

After *Lawrence Welk* it was bedtime. We went over to Gramma's chair to kiss her goodnight. Her face was stern and sullen at rest, especially when she looked at you over her glasses. As we approached her she smiled, changing her countenance completely. Her eyes softened, the lines on her face smoothed and the corners around her mouth turned upward, transforming her face in a dramatic way. Grampa's hair was graying, but Gramma's shoulder length hair was still dark brown in color. Lacking any distinct style, she combed the loose curls away from her face and secured them with bobby pins.

She grabbed me around the waist and pulled me onto her lap. She was tall for a woman, and while she was not fat she had a rather large, hard belly that protruded forward. Getting onto her lap was a bit of a feat but she always managed to get me in position to give me a big, hearty hug and lots of kisses. Sometimes she would pull both Kirk and me in at the same time, and somehow, we all three fit.

Once we were settled in her lap she would sing us a song. Our favorite was the one about the three little fishes swimming over the dam. She play-acted while singing the words, making deep swishing and bullfrog noises of the chorus, "a-boom-boom, diddem, baddum, waddum, SHOO, a-boom-boom, diddumm, baddum, waddum, SHOO, and they swam and they swam right over the dam," with her baritone voice, her facial expressions mimicking the emotions of the little fishes all the while. When that was over we would go over to Grampa and kiss his stubbly cheek. He would look at us with his playful blue eyes, say goodnight and swat us both softly on the behind as we walked toward our room upstairs.

The next morning, we went to church, a firmly established component of our weekend routine. When we returned I changed out of my dress, back into my play clothes and wandered into Gramma's room. I went immediately to the bench that stood in front of her dressing table and perched myself atop the gold velvet cushion. As I waited for her to finish changing out of her church clothes in the adjoining bathroom, I made faces in the trifold mirror mounted on top of the table and tried to decide if I was pretty. I determined that I liked my appearance much better before Mommy cut all my hair off, and before I lost both of my front teeth. I was further disappointed by the fact that as my hair grew out its color was stubbornly dark. Mommy said the long sandy-brown braid she cut off was lighter because it was made of baby hair. Most all children's hair, she explained, turned darker as they grew older.

Gramma interrupted my self-assessment.

"Whatcha doing honey?" she asked, walking toward me.

A glimpse into her bathroom revealed a number of undergarments strewn over the shower door. My Gramma was a staunch believer in girdles. The whole notion of wearing something so tight and confining seemed nothing short of awful to me. Being much younger and still slight in build, I was hopeful I would never need such binding foundations. But then I remembered seeing pictures of Gramma when she was younger, and she was very skinny then, too. Maybe things changed. Someday I may get a larger mid-section and also find that the only way to contain it was by wearing a girdle.

She allowed me free reign over her dressing table where she kept her perfume, makeup, and jewelry, and let me try on anything I wanted. She wore only costume pieces, chunky necklaces, bracelets, brooches, and earrings. Delicate jewelry would have made no sense for a woman with my grandmother's tall, big-boned stature. Her earrings were all the clip-on variety, making them easy for me to model since my ears were not pierced. Knowing she would say yes, but always feeling as though I should ask, I said, "Can I try on your jewelry?"

"Yes, honey," she said, sitting on the end of the bed behind me.

I eagerly unlatched the section of the tabletop that opened upward to reveal a deep well that was appointed with compartments housing her stash of accessories. I began carefully sorting through her collection, admiring old favorites and looking for new things she may have added since the last time I looked. A large brooch shaped like a daisy, its petals white enamel, the center a cluster of raised metal dots painted a shiny yellow, called to me. It was beautiful but much too big for me. I selected a white on black cameo necklace, matching earrings and a large gold bangle bracelet to complete my look. I stood up and turned toward her and asked, "What do you think?"

"Oh, that's so nice," she crooned, "you look so pretty! Let's see what I can give you to take home," she mused, sitting down on the vanity bench beside me and sifting through her piles of baubles.

This was my favorite part. She would find pieces and tell me the story of how she wore them or where she got them, setting her keepsakes aside and looking for others she could give to me to put into my own jewelry box at home. We settled on a round brooch with two-tone pink stones and a matching cuff bracelet. It would be years before I could wear the pieces without looking like I was playing dress-up, but I was thrilled to have them.

"It's a shame," she said, "your mother never liked jewelry." She became quiet as she sorted through some more pieces and then said, almost absent-mindedly, "You know, honey, your Daddy can't help it that the girls like him."

She continued returning each of her pieces to her vanity cache, her attention never leaving her task, never turning to me, and not inviting a question or a reply. I looked at her blankly. What did she mean? I had a vision of my father minding his own business when the woman from the park accosted him, throwing her arms around him and declaring her love for him. Was that how it went? Even so, why did he not just tell her he was already married ... and had two kids, for God's sake? My mind was aflutter with this conundrum when I heard Grampa yell from downstairs that Daddy was here to pick up my brother and me.

We returned home, and to our delight our mother was already there waiting for us.

One more crisis averted.

Chapter 24

Merry Christmas

My little brother, Jay, proved to be the final breath of life that was drawn into my parents' marriage. We stayed with our grandparents when my mother went into labor. When Grampa took us home after my mother returned home from the hospital I raced inside, full of anticipation. He was so tiny and wrinkled. I was not allowed to hold him at first, but in time my mother gave me training. I had to be sitting down on the couch, arms fully extended, and once the bundle was laid in my arms I gently curled my elbows in to encase him.

I watched his pink face and listened to his involuntary grunts and squeaks, his tiny fists closed, and occasionally he jerked this way or that as if he were temporarily overcome by a spasm. In spite of his curious appearance, I loved the way he smelled, fresh mixed with a sweet saltiness. My wish for a sister had not come true, but I was very content with my new little brother.

My mother allowed me to help more in the coming months, holding a bottle in his mouth, burping him and changing his diaper. More of the gardening responsibilities fell to Kirk and me since our mother was busy with Jay. I didn't mind. The combined need for quiet in the house during Jay's nap time and our mounting boredom with playing alone in our back yard prompted her to grant us some additional freedoms. We were allowed to play with Jimmy and Sara Walters, who lived at the other end of the alley and whom we walked to school with every day. Our play area was expanded to include their house, as well as the empty lot on the other side of our neighbor, Mrs. Calvin's house. There were rules of course, which mostly entailed the two of us staying together at all times. Each time we went to play at the Walters' house she watched us from the kitchen window as we crossed the street, and until we disappeared from her view down the alley.

In the fall I started the second grade, somewhat apprehensively. During my first-grade year I found myself far too many times in the spotlight. Our music teacher, Mrs. Whitman, tortured our entire class by making each of us sing a song she taught us about fall leaves, a cappella and completely solo. Mr. Coffie, our gym teacher, introduced us to the requirements of the Presidential Physical Fitness Test. The numerous requirements of the test were carried out individually and in front of the rest of the first-grade class. Showcasing my slow running pace and weak arms that were unable to sustain a flexed arm hang for the meager six seconds required, and my subpar performance in every other area of the test, was humiliating and demotivating.

I credit our president's award for firmly establishing the belief in my young mind that I possessed zero athletic ability. Isolating my performance, even in areas where I excelled, like flash card drills, distressed me. Standing alone at the head of the class, I sensed every eye in the room boring into me. It made me feel vulnerable, as if my audience could see through my skull and into my brain and all of its carefully guarded contents: my thoughts, my fears, my secrets, all exposed.

But second grade was different. There was no embarrassing solo singing requirement and now that we were all reading, we performed our assignments independently. I still couldn't do the flexed arm hang to save my life, but I no longer cared. What I lacked in physical talent, I learned, based on my near-perfect Iowa Basic Skills test scores, I made up for in intellectual ability. I quickly tired of the second-grade section of the school library and began checking out books at the fifth- and sixth-grade levels.

My mother owned a set of 10 classic novels and although the number of pages and advanced vocabulary were intimidating, I decided to give *Alice in Wonderland* a try. My world was forever changed. My self-consciousness eased as I embraced my newly discovered talent, reveling in the appreciation of my classmates when I was named to their spelling-bee team, or soaking in the praise of my teacher when I made the best score on this test or that assignment. I had found two new loves, school and reading.

Fall turned blissfully into the Christmas season. Our annual tradition involved attending the late Christmas Eve church service. I easily picked out Gramma's voice in the choir's rendition of the Little Drummer Boy; her hearty "rumpf, rumpf, rumpf" sounds mimicking a drum were distinct, reminding me of the sounds she made when she sang us the fish song. After church we opened presents from Gramma and Grampa at their house. I was thrilled with the box of *10* new Nancy Drew books Gramma wrapped for me, and if that weren't enough she also gave me a jewelry box shaped like a piano; inside of it was a small blue enamel pin shaped like a dog. Jay played with the boxes and paper, practically ignoring his new tricycle. Kirk carefully took a few practice swings with his new baseball bat and then tried on his new glove, repeatedly punching his fist into it.

The next morning we jumped out of bed as early as our tired bodies permitted, running first into our parents' room and shaking them awake. After stopping and collecting Jay from his crib, Mommy and Daddy followed us into the living room and the five of us gathered by our Christmas tree. Kirk and I eagerly tore into the gifts Santa had left us, and Jay once again crawled around in the mounds of discarded paper and empty boxes, completely ignoring his new blocks and the See'n'Say Farmer Says toy. After Kirk and I had opened everything, we busied ourselves with constructing plans of how to integrate our new toys. Kirk's G.I. Joes would plan a rescue mission for my Barbie and Francie dolls. We would play radio. Kirk would be the DJ and I would be a famous singer lip-syncing to songs playing on my new record player. I may even get him to sing with me, playing David Partridge, while I played his sister Laurie. I decided to keep that idea to myself and see how things went.

I walked over to the tree to retrieve my new set of play dishes. The number of play scenarios involving plastic dinnerware and food was virtually endless, especially when you combine this with the cardboard kitchen appliances I already owned. Turning away with the box of dishes in my hand, I noticed my parents standing off to the side.

My mother was facing my father, whose back was to the tree and me. I had a full and unobstructed view of her face, which bore a huge smile. She was holding a half-sheet of paper in her hand.

"Merry Christmas! I'm divorcing you!" she exclaimed, pushing the paper in front of his face.

I froze.

The inevitable, bad thing I had dreaded for what seemed like forever was finally happening. All the defenses that were brought to bear -- my new little brother, the discovery of my advanced reading skills, not even the arrival of the most important holiday of the year -- could keep the enemy of my family's happiness at bay. My mother had finally made good on her ultimate threat. She had obviously planned ahead so she could make her dramatic presentation at this moment, right here on Christmas Day in front of the tree Kirk and I had decorated with such great enthusiasm.

I saw Kirk out of the corner of my eye, his gaze fixed on the two of them. As if snapping out of trances simultaneously, we busied ourselves with our toys as if nothing unusual had occurred, as if we hadn't heard our mother's gleeful announcement.

Eventually my father came into the living room with some sort of suitcase. He knelt in front of Kirk and me to say goodbye. I tried very hard not to cry, but when he hugged me and whispered, "Don't worry, we will see each other soon," the wall I tried so desperately to construct caved in, giving way to tears. My brother, stone-faced as ever, hugged my father back and said goodbye. Maybe he felt like he needed to be strong for both of us.

We watched as my father stood up, walked into the kitchen, and disappeared around the corner. We stood very still, watching the spot where we last glimpsed him, hearing the car door open then close, then the sound of the engine starting.

As his car pulled away, the roar of the engine faded to nothing more than a low hum and gradually disappeared into the crisp, quiet air of Christmas morning.

Chapter 25

The Wolf in Wolf's Clothing

I ended the call and settled back onto the pillows, not yet ready to face the day. Matt's side of the bed was empty. I vaguely remembered hearing him moving around earlier, the rustling of cloth and zipper as he dressed and the quiet click of the latch as he closed the door behind him.

Talking to Jennie had bolstered my spirits. It was unbelievable that he chose to end his life, she said, after everything Dad had been through, his marriages, the houses, all his hard work, after everything he had accomplished. You kids meant so much to him, she reminded me, as she had done so many times in my life. She encouraged me to remember all the good times and focus on the positive. So sad, it was just so sad, she crooned. Her voice, gentle and upbeat, conveyed hope and an undaunted sense of optimism.

She had always had that effect on me. When she entered my life I was a gawky, acne-ravaged teenager who reeked of insecurity. She drew me like a fly to sticky paper. From the moment she met my father's three children she loved us, completely and unconditionally. From the very beginning she gave me something to look forward to. Later, she represented something to aspire to.

I lived with her and my father while I attended the University of Toledo. Reminiscing on those days never failed to bring forth memories of her fragrant pot roast, the homey yet stylish manner in which she decorated, the flattering way she dressed, her ever-present smile, and lighthearted laugh. A licensed cosmetologist, she had been doing hair for more than 10 years. I eagerly turned over to her the complete responsibility for my own hair. I found myself wanting to be like her. The way she dressed, the easy way she could carry on a conversation with anyone, and the kind and loving way she treated everyone served as benchmarks that would remain with me throughout my life. I couldn't imagine how my father could have ever strayed, how he could ever find another woman superior to her. She was pretty, youthful, positive, and energetic. She was financially self-sufficient. And she loved us.

Years later, during one of my many conversations with my father in which we pondered the deeper elements of our respective lives, he lamented the end of their marriage. He admitted he had made a big mistake. If he had it to do over, he had said, he would have found a way to make it right, to get her back. Despite the fact I knew it would never happen, his admission made me happy. As I lay in bed reflecting on Jennie, having just spoken to her, I couldn't help but think that he would never have made his last, awful decision to end his life if they had remained together.

Jennie and my father got together after my parents' second divorce, at a time when our relationship with our father was strained. He had not yet reestablished a presence in our lives, making our early interactions with her as infrequent as they were with him. She gave our father the boost he needed to coax us back into his life after our mother moved us to Wyoming. It was during our twice-annual visits home that Jennie ingratiated herself to us, becoming the centerpiece of our newly formed family. Her bright, unencumbered personality and the ease with which she imparted affection stood in stark contrast to our stepfather. Spending time with Dad and Jennie fortified us and taught us what a happy family life was like.

It was impossible to think about that time in my life without also thinking about the *other* step-parent at that time. Glen entered our lives in the midst of my parents' second divorce, after my father moved out. It was spring of my fifth-grade school year.

We were experiencing a rare reprieve from the usual cold and gloomy northwestern Ohio spring weather. The sun shone brightly through the bare branches of the trees, illuminating the first signs of fuzzy buds on their tips. Daffodils poked through the crusted and cold soil, exposing their bright yellow mantles. The fresh spring weather energized our walk home from school that day. Kirk and I raced the Walters kids to their house. I came in last, as always. Sara Walters, while a year younger, was a tomboy and beat me handily. The three birthdays that had come and gone rendered me taller, but no more able bodied than I was in the second grade. Kirk and I were arguing about my loss as we walked in the door. I was well aware of my athletic shortcomings, but that didn't stop me from finding excuses for them.

"Sara runs like a boy," I said.

"No, she doesn't, you run like a girl," he said.

"She got a head-start," I said.

"Nuh-uh, and even if she did, you should have been ready," he said.

"Just shut up," I said, as I walked into the kitchen.

"That's no way to talk to your brother," my mother said.

I looked up to see my mother and a man I had never seen before standing next to her. Something about their proximity to one another suggested a closeness that was beyond friendly. She smiled broadly.

"This is Glen," she said to us, "and these are my kids, Kirk and Amber," she said to Glen.

"Say hi to Glen," she said, smiling even bigger, exposing both rows of her teeth in the process.

I looked at him and said, "Hi."

I was immediately struck by his height. He was almost a head shorter than my mother. His reddish-brown hair was parted on the side and combed meticulously into place. His broad face, flanked with matching sideburns, wore a big smile. His white undershirt was visible through the V-neck collar of his fitted burgundy and white pullover. His jeans just grazed the tops of his shiny black boots.

"How was school?" he asked me. His voice was forcibly deep, as if he were trying to add a few inches to his height through the volume of his voice.

"Fine," I said.

Kirk, without giving him eye contact, said, "Hi," and kept on going, walking into the living room.

"Wait a minute," our mother said to him.

He stopped, turned partway toward her and said, "What?"

"Where are you going in such a hurry?" she asked, irritation in her voice.

"I need to do my homework," he replied.

"Go ahead, I'll catch up with you next time," Glen chimed in.

Next time? The comment registered as I puzzled over the nature of their relationship. The answer to my question came as

I heard Glen say to my mother, "Well, I need to get going." He turned toward her, and I noticed they were holding hands. With his free right hand, he touched my mother's face, bringing it toward him, then began kissing her on the mouth.

I wanted to look away, but it was as if my feet were glued to the floor. I had never seen anyone kiss this way, not even on television. My face felt hot. I finally found the will to move my body and walked over to the sink to get a drink of water while they finished. When it was finally over, I heard him behind me asking, "What's the matter, did that embarrass you?"

As if it wasn't bad enough to see my mother and a man I'd just met tonguing one another in the kitchen of the home in which I had spent my entire life, the one my *parents* had lived in together, to make matters worse he wanted to talk about it? Are you kidding me?

"No," I stammered, "I just wanted a drink of water."

"You better get used to it," he said, "I really care about your mother and you're going to be seeing more of me around here."

He squeezed her hand once more, the two of them gazing into each other's eyes for a lingering moment, then he walked out the kitchen door. I watched him through the kitchen window as he got into a truck that oddly, I hadn't noticed in front of our house earlier. As he drove away I focused on calming the butterflies in my stomach.

So she was moving on to another man? Why him? How did they meet? The questions rolled around in my head. Dare I ask her? I tried to gather up the courage, but as I turned away from the window I realized it was pointless. The room was empty except for me. She'd disappeared before I could ask.

Things started out amicably enough between Glen and us. On one of his next visits Glen brought a puppy -- a brownish-black, wiggling, pink-tongued shepherd mix -- which he presented to Kirk, who was instantly smitten. He decided to name his new best friend Brutus. Our mother conditioned keeping him on Kirk's commitment to take complete responsibility for him. The presentation of Brutus gave rise to one of those rare moments when my brother's face fully displayed the distinct pleasure he felt. I was happy for him, seeing his delight in getting his very own pet. Glen told us Brutus would grow into a much bigger adult dog.

I was apprehensive about how Brutus would get along with my cat. A gift from my Gramma, Missy had enjoyed free reign in our house since she was a kitten. She sprinted straight for the shelter of my bedroom when Brutus came bounding out of the cardboard box he was transported in. I hoped he would be nice to her and that they would be friends.

The early days of Mom and Glen's courtship focused on acquainting our two families. Glen had two sons who were close to Kirk and me in age. When they visited, we played in our back yard, and sometimes went to the park or out for ice cream. Other times we would go visit Glen's parents who lived in a suburb of Detroit. Having spent my entire life in a small town, I found their house to be a novelty. Set on a quiet street with a dozen or so similar houses, the modest one-story sat on a small lot and had a driveway that led to a single-car detached garage in the back. The tidy little neighborhood felt safe and secluded, yet it was surrounded by the city. The end of their street intersected with a busy, four-lane highway and we could see smokestacks from nearby factories.

The inside of the house was as neat as the exterior, but completely joyless. After exchanging greetings with Glen's parents, we would go out to the tiny back yard and play baseball or tag until we got bored. But there was nothing inside the house to interest us, either. The living room was appointed with a sofa and chairs that looked as if no one ever sat in them. There were no board games to be found and the television was never turned on. My mother and Glen would sit with his mother at the kitchen table and talk.

Glen's mother wore her short blonde hair teased and sprayed. Although her hair was not nearly as profuse as my mother's, you got the sense that if the wind blew, the weight of her hair might tip her frail body over. She dressed in ankle pants and a matching shell, the fabric having nothing to cling to other than her bony shoulders and hips. It was hard to believe that Glen, with his squatty, husky physique, came from her. She alternated between lighting, inhaling and exhaling a continuous chain of cigarettes as she reported the current events of the family in her flat, Kentucky-accented voice.

Glen's father was equally small and frail. He sported a full head of gray hair, parted on the side, a mustache, and wore wire-rimmed glasses. After greeting us he would disappear down the hallway that led to the bedrooms or go outside and sit in a lawn chair and smoke. He rarely spoke to us and we, having no idea what to say to him, didn't speak to him either. Eventually we learned that he was an alcoholic. I could never recall seeing him drink during our visits, but I often wondered if that is what he did back in his bedroom. Glen neither drank nor smoked and self-righteously lectured us on the evils of both. This quality seemed to endear him to our mother. She revered him for overcoming what he described as a harsh childhood spent with an alcoholic parent. And while we had never seen our father drunk, I was pretty sure drinking was involved in some of the many unexplained absences that permeated his two marriages to our mother.

Glen was also going through a divorce, from a woman he characterized as fat and disagreeable. She and her boyfriend, John, Glen claimed, were always trying to undermine his ability to see his two sons. Frequently Glen would arrive at his designated time to pick them up, only to find no one at home. His soon-to-be-ex-wife, Peggy, we learned, was fighting for full custody of the boys. Glen responded to this threat by showing up at the home he had shared with Peggy -- my mother, my brothers and me in tow -- on a night when he somehow knew there would be no one home. He then directed the removal of his pick of the household furniture. We all helped to load the booty, which included among other things his beloved black vinyl recliner, into the back of his truck, and later, into our house.

That would teach Peggy to fuck with him, he had said. His rants about "Fat Ass Peggy" and all that had been wrong in his marriage to her eventually bled into lectures that decreed the many shortfalls of our own family. Kirk and I were spoiled, he said, sparing Jay any criticism since he was barely four years old. Kirk should be mowing the yard by now and I should be setting the table and doing the dishes by myself every night. We had too many toys, and worse yet, we didn't show adequate appreciation for all that we had, he opined.

Glen wasted no time in trying to shape us up. Dandelions, a sure sign of spring, were flaunting their bristly, yellow mantles in every corner of our yard. As we stood before him in our garage one late spring morning, Glen informed us that dandelions were weeds. Did we know that? Um, no, we didn't. To us they were a promise of the coming summer, a splash of cheery color, and a distraction. Fresh blossoms, we had discovered, when rubbed on the inside of your forearm, left their bright mustard color behind. Flicking the blooms off stems in the schoolyard while chanting, "Mama had a baby and her head popped off," entertained us during countless springtime recesses. What child could resist the urge to pluck the carcass of a spent bloom and hurtle the dainty seeds into the breeze with a single hard blow?

Glen marched Kirk and me out to the front yard and demonstrated the proper removal of a dandelion, using a forked weed digger to extract not just the flowering part and leaves above ground, but also the root. He handed each of us a tool and told us not to come inside until all the dandelions had been removed from the front yard.

"Don't think about trying to take a shortcut and pick them instead of digging them out," he warned us. He would be checking our work. We were to put our extracted weeds into a bucket and he would inspect them to assure that each plant's roots were intact. Our instructions were to come get him when we finished, and after he approved the front, we were to start on the back yard. I viewed the sea of yellow before me and groaned inwardly as I thought about the back yard that was easily six times the size of the front.

In an instant he had managed to transform something I regarded pleasantly into something I despised. It was one thing to assign a legitimate chore. We were no strangers to helping around the house. The dandelion exercise was just one more example of how Glen's standards often bordered on fanaticism. His military background had taught him the merits of a clutterless, spotless, and perfectly angled world.

But it was more than that. The specifications he required in a task as simple as placing a glass in the cabinet was a means of imposing control. He enjoyed watching our faces as he made one after another ridiculous demand of us, daring us to smirk or roll our eyes. If he sensed that we were inwardly mocking him he would up the requirements of the task at hand or add more to our list. And when we did slip up and give him a valid opportunity to reprimand us, it was all he could do to wipe the satisfied smile from his face.

Chapter 26

Lucky

Within a matter of months Glen had garrisoned complete control of our household, making no attempt to preserve any aspect of our former lives. Regulating everything from the breakfast cereal we ate to the way towels were folded, and the television programs we watched, he firmly believed he was making our lives better. We were the lucky beneficiaries of his countless wisdoms. My mother's disgust with our father and everything associated with their past life together had her embracing Glen, his changes, and his control with open arms. She seemed indifferent to maintaining even a shred of her former lifestyle.

It didn't take long for his zest for sucking the joy out of anything that provided us satisfaction to spread its focus to our relationship with our father. The time we spent with him was an annoyance to Glen. He looked for things to criticize each time we returned from a visit with our father, accusing me of acting snooty, Kirk of acting cocky and both of us of acting spoiled. He couldn't control how we behaved with our father, he lectured us, but he could control how we behaved in this house.

My mother sat silently at first, but it wasn't long before she began throwing in her two-cents-worth during Glen's dissertations about our father. This gave Glen all the encouragement he needed to wage a full-on campaign against our father, lending justification to his interrogations and eventually leading to my meeting with Judge Swartz. In spite of the ease with which my mother handed him control of our family, I would soon learn it wasn't enough for the four of us to follow his orders, he also needed us to fear him.

From the moment he first met Missy, Glen made it clear that he disliked cats. In fact, he told me, he hated them and thought them to be completely worthless creatures. You couldn't trust them, they were sneaky, he knowingly asserted. As the comfort level in his new role as ruler of our roost increased he felt less compelled to curb his natural urges. He would eye Missy across the room, watching her out of the corner of his eye until she found a spot to curl up. He would wait until she settled herself and closed her eyes. At that moment he would slap a rolled newspaper onto the end of the table next to him or release the lever on his recliner to create a loud and sudden noise, sending her tearing from the room. Once he quelled his laughter he would follow it with commentary about her stupidity.

I didn't trust him around her and did my best to keep her hidden in my room. In spite of my efforts to sequester her, she would eventually become bored with the confines of my bedroom or need to use her litter box and I would have to let her out. One night I was in the living room watching TV with my mother and brothers when I heard a racket coming from Kirk's room. Brutus was growling. I heard him jumping and scratching a hard surface, creating intermittent scraping and banging noises in the process.

"Hey, Amber! Come see what your cat's doing," Glen called, laughing loudly.

I jumped up and as soon as I reached the hallway I saw Glen standing in the doorway of Kirk's room. He was laughing and pointing upward. I looked up at the half-open door and saw Missy balancing precariously on the top of it. The banging and scratching noises were generated by Brutus -- who was jumping up on the door as Glen taunted him.

"Get the kitty" he directed Brutus, a look of sheer delight on his face.

Missy was hissing, every hair on her back raised, her tail standing straight up. I was terrified for her safety, having quickly determined that she would not be able to balance herself for long on the few inches of surface that the top of the door provided.

"Stop it! Take her down!" I ordered, my eyes fixed on her rigid form perched above my head, not thinking for a moment about whom I was commanding.

He feigned a look of innocence.

"She must have jumped up there."

"She couldn't get up there by herself, she's going to fall," I said, the volume in my voice escalating.

"Oh, stop being a baby," he replied, the humor quickly draining from his face, steel hardening in his eyes.

"Cats know how to balance themselves. It's what they do. I was just having a little fun and I knew she wouldn't get hurt."

He stepped closer to me, his eyes boring into mine.

"You don't tell me what to do. You're a little fucking baby," he said, pointing his index finger in my face. He turned back to Brutus, instructing him one last time.

"Get the kitty!"

Brutus jumped on the door as Missy, who had had enough, leaped from her perch toward my brother's bed. I knew that there was no way she would reach the top of the bed safely. I lunged forward in an effort to retrieve her, but Glen got her first, catching her in one hand rather awkwardly.

"Here," he said, "get the little bitch out of here," throwing her at me. Her claws were extended defensively and she scratched me as I caught her.

I held her tight and ran past him to my room. My legs were weak from the adrenaline that the fear for her safety had pumped into my system. I shut the door behind me, desperately wanting to slam it, but knowing better.

It didn't matter. He was right behind me.

He kicked the door open, causing it to slam into the wall behind it. I jumped at the noise, sitting up straight on my bed where I had plopped myself. Missy, whose heart was beating a fast rhythm onto the crook of my arm, jumped, clawing me in her haste to find a safe haven. She leaped out of my arms, off the bed, then scurried beneath it and out of sight. I desperately wanted to follow her, knowing I was about to pay for talking back to Glen.

Before Glen could start on me, my mother appeared behind him.

"What's wrong?" she asked.

"This one has a real attitude," he said, pointing at me and looking at her.

"I was just playing with her stupid-ass cat and she got all pissed off and screamed in my face. It's that disrespect again. I keep telling you these kids are spoiled."

Knowing I was already in deep and feeling I had little to lose, I interjected, "He put her on top of Kirk's door! I didn't scream at him. I just wanted him to get her down."

My mother turned to Glen, "She was probably just afraid that Missy was going to get hurt. She's not used to Brutus yet, and she's never had anyone playing rough with her."

"I wasn't playing rough with her, you dumb-ass! You don't know what the fuck you're talking about. All you've ever done is mother these three bratty-ass kids," he said.

He was facing her now. Even though I was viewing his profile it was impossible not to see the anger seething from his eyes and the tight line his mouth was drawn in.

"Why don't we just let her calm down?" my mother suggested. Her facial expression was composed but her eyes revealed a glimmer of fear. She delivered the words evenly, but they lacked conviction. He now stood just inches from her. She leaned backward in an effort to create some space between the two of them.

Her non-verbal submissiveness failed to satisfy him. He went on.

"I'll do whatever the fuck I want. You don't tell me what to do in my own house," he said, wagging his index finger in her face.

"Are we understood?" he demanded.

"Yes," she said, her mouth quivering.

He turned, chest puffed outward, and walked out of the room. I heard the sound of the footrest extending on his recliner, indicating he was in his chair and that one more conflict was over.

My mother stood there a few minutes longer, before speaking.

"I know it's hard sometimes, but it will get easier. We just need to do things his way. You'll see."

Funny, I thought we were already doing that.

Chapter 27

Gunning for Glen

I eventually learned that Glen and my father worked together at the Ford plant. They had been friends before Glen took up with my mother. As soon as my father got wind of their relationship he and Glen became arch enemies. This, Glen told us, suited him just fine. The end of their friendship was my father's loss, not his. Glen was too good for him anyway.

Meanwhile, my mother remained firmly within the bounds that Glen established for her, keeping the peace between the two of them. This allowed his focus to be directed exclusively on her children. My distaste for conflict had me looking for the positive, something I could grab hold of that would help me to get on board the ship that was already sailing at full speed. When he wasn't wagging his finger at me, calling me stupid or swearing at me, I looked hard for something to like. I continued to come up empty handed.

Glen considered himself an expert on a host of topics -- ranging from college football to health and fitness and music. His preferences in each category were deemed to be the best, the ideal. Anyone who held an alternative view was just plain unenlightened. Having completed several tours in the Navy, he often spoke of places he had visited. Despite the beautiful scenery and impressive architecture the photos contained, he claimed that Naples, Italy was nothing but a shit hole. The women there were whores, he said. He was an avid reader of *Playboy* and *Hustler* and considered himself an authority on the female anatomy. He seemed to feel it was his duty to comment on virtually every woman he encountered. As we walked through the grocery store or into the Post Office he shared his assessment with any of us who happened to be within earshot.

"Did you see her tits?"

"Now, *that* is one fat ass."

"She looks easy."

I questioned the benefit my mother derived from their relationship. I tried not to think about that night I asked him to carry me to bed and what transpired afterwards, but his comment about her not being used to affection stuck in my head. I shuddered at his definition of affection, but had to concede that the two of them were physically attentive to one another in a way she and my father never were. She also had someone in her corner, an ally against our father, the enemy she fought through two marriages spanning nine years.

Glen never left the house to do anything but attend his single job, unlike my father who was rarely home between the two or three jobs he juggled most times. She reveled in his constant presence in our lives. With few exceptions, the five of us did everything together, from eating meals to grocery shopping to watching television.

He never left us alone.

Several months after I spoke with Judge Swartz, I awoke in the middle of the night. After conducting a quick mental inventory, I confirmed that it wasn't a dream that had interrupted my slumber. I listened for the dull, unintelligible murmur from the television or shreds of an exchange between my mother and Glen. When the silence persisted, I relaxed and attempted to drift off again. Although I couldn't hear anything, I had a feeling something was amiss, like something had occurred just before I awoke.

Realizing that going back to sleep was out of the question, I crept out of my bed and padded quietly to my bedroom door. I pressed my ear against the wood panel and listened as hard as I could. At last I identified the faint voices of my mother and Glen, probably in the kitchen. I slowly turned the knob and cracked my door open slightly. I could hear my mother's voice and another male voice that didn't belong to Glen. I strained harder to hear.

"We searched the whole area and didn't find anyone," said the male voice.

"I know he was back there. I've been waiting for this. He threatened me at work, said he had a sawed-off shotgun and it was only a matter of time until he got to me," Glen said.

"We have a big back yard. How do we know he's not hiding somewhere else?" asked my mother.

"We searched your back yard, too," said the male voice. "Look, he may very well have been out there, but he's gone now. Probably figured you called the police and by the time we got here he got away."

As I listened, questions formed in my mind, each one tightening the knot that had become resident in my stomach.

My mother and Glen were talking to the police? Who threatened Glen with a sawed-off shotgun? Who was hiding in our back yard?

The threat of an armed intruder added a new and darker twist to my former brand of midnight drama. I could feel the pulse in my neck and in my chest, the sound of my heartbeat reverberating in my ear. I wanted to sneak into Kirk's room, but I had no way of gauging how much longer the meeting with the policeman would last and I didn't want to risk being caught listening. Whatever was going on, I instinctively felt it was not meant for my ears. I stood as still as I could and eased the door open a bit wider, praying it wouldn't creak, and pushed my head out into the hallway.

"What do we do if he comes back?" my mother asked.

"We will assign an officer to watch your house from dusk to dawn. If he comes back, we'll be close by. We'll get him," said the policeman. "I'll make sure the officer keeps an eye on the area around the pond and the back yard. In the mean time I suggest you file a restraining order against your ex-husband."

Her ex-husband? They were talking about my father?

I gasped involuntarily, immediately clapping my hand over my mouth to contain the small noise I made. I was stunned. My father threatened Glen with a gun? I couldn't suppress the visual that began forming in my mind's eye. I pictured my father crouched in the thick brush that surrounded our pond and buffered us from the depths of its deadly waters, gun in hand. A man on a mission, he darted between the cover of one tree after the other as he made his way past the garden and toward our house.

Then what?

Was he going to shoot Glen in our house? While he was sitting in his black recliner? Was he after our mother too? I shivered.

Sensing that their conversation was winding down, I carefully closed my door and returned to bed. I lay awake for a long time that night trying to digest what I had overheard. We already knew that Glen and my father didn't like each other. I didn't like Glen, either. Not one bit. But imagining my father shooting him chilled me to the core. And what about our mother? Did Daddy have it in for her too? No, I decided. Probably just Glen. I lay awake long after I heard my mother and Glen retire to their room across the hall from mine.

The next morning Glen dispelled any notion I may have had that the matter I overheard them discussing the night before would be kept secret. He wasted no time informing Kirk and me of our father's attempt to kill him, explaining that our father was jealous because our mother now loved Glen. He said that our father was also angry because of the judge's ruling that declared him unfit. He deserved every bit of it, Glen said. He wasted his chances by chasing women and drinking instead of being a good husband. If Glen had his way our father would never see us again. Charges would be filed, but it would take time. In the meantime, we needed to think seriously about whether we wanted to see our father at all.

The situation between our father and us was already awkward. I found it difficult to look him in the eye when he picked us up for our bi-weekly Sunday visits. I wondered if he knew I was complicit in my mother and Glen's scheme to pollute the judge's opinion of him. Unlike them, my father never mentioned the divorce or asked about my mother and Glen at all. Once we were in the car with him, he would attempt to engage us in a discussion about where we wanted to go. None of us dared mention the bowling alley. Instead we went to movies and visited our Gramma Millie or our cousins. After the initial ice was broken our interactions loosened up, but my visits with him were plagued by the constant worry that he would mention Glen, my mother or the divorce, and what I would say if he did.

I became even more nervous after the gun allegation. I wanted to ask him if it was true. Did he really hide out on the banks of our pond with a gun that he intended to use to shoot Glen? I often found myself studying my father from the backseat as he drove, seeing just part of his face in the rear-view mirror. He looked the same to me, wavy brown hair parted on the side and trimmed neat, blue eyes filled with intensity as he watched the road, their sparkle returning when he arched his head to look at us in the mirror and ask, "How's everybody doing back there?"

His countenance tended toward neutrality of expression most of the time, but when he did flash a smile, the corners of my mouth turned up automatically, mirroring his without thinking or trying. He seemed tender to me. His arm naturally found itself around my shoulders when I stood near him. When he looked at me it felt like he really saw me, like I had his complete attention. I recalled only a few times when he yelled at my brothers and me, and he never once laid a hand on any of us.

The need for communication burned inside of me, but I had no model for initiating it. I somehow sensed that this man with whom I had never had a real conversation would tell me the truth. Maybe it was the possibility of hearing that truth that kept me from finding the words to form the question. I couldn't bring myself to broach with him any of the topics that weighed on my mind. So, we continued, each of us holding on tightly to our sins, denying ourselves the chance for redemption.

Every night before I went to sleep I peeked through the space between the roller blind and my bedroom window. As much as I disliked the idea that my father was the reason for our house being watched, I felt a sense of relief each night when I saw the patrol car in its now regular spot. I could go to sleep free of the concern that I would awaken to my mother screaming amidst bullets flying through one of our windows.

In the weeks that followed I felt myself swaying toward my mother and Glen's side until the scale finally tipped. Had I not overheard the policeman that night I would have questioned the validity of the allegation. Still, I thought, Glen could have made the whole thing up. I heard the policeman say he had not actually seen my father. I turned over in my mind the question of Glen's honesty. Would he make something like that up to get back at my father? By now my mother was completely beholden to Glen, and her desire to avenge my father's numerous and unforgivable transgressions had her ready to believe him capable of anything. Glen could have easily convinced her at this point.

In spite of my skepticism, I allowed myself to be persuaded. Although I didn't fear my father, I told myself he was dangerous. Eventually, my heart believed the words my mind spoke to it.

It was I who reported to my father that we didn't want to go with him one late summer Sunday when he came to pick us up for our bi-weekly visit.

"What do you mean, you don't want to come?" he asked.

"We just don't," I said.

Kirk remained silent, but I knew he would follow my lead.

"Why don't we just get in the car and we can talk about it on the way? It's OK," he said.

"No, we don't want to go," I said.

He looked at Kirk, whose face was expressionless, his eyes fixed firmly forward, not looking at anything in particular. Our father stood on the front porch for a few moments longer, looking sideways off into the distance as if deciding what to do.

Finally, he said, "OK, well I'll see you in two weeks, then."

He turned and walked down the single step of our porch onto the sidewalk and got into his car. I closed the door without waiting to see if he looked back at me or waved as he drove away.

Two weeks later he returned and the same scene played out again. After his third rejected attempt to see us he stopped coming. I had butterflies in my stomach on that fourth Sunday. A part of me desperately wanted him to come again. If he did, I told myself, I would go this time. It would just be too mean not to. When noon came and went with no knock at the front door I felt the butterflies dissipate, the space in my stomach now filling with what felt like heavy stones.

What had I done?

My guilty mind flashed forward to the future. Images of my father with a new wife and new children formed in my head. What if that happened? Would he forget about us? Would he stop loving us?

Would we ever see him again?

Chapter 28

A Real Family

My mother and Glen were married just a few days before Christmas, less than a year after we had first met him. I tried to be happy about it for her sake.

"You are finally part of a real family," Glen told us repeatedly.

While the advertising campaign might have worked with those unfamiliar with the inner workings of our new family, I could find little in my new life to be happy about. New rules were instituted regarding Kirk's and my privileges. Gone were the days of jumping on our bikes and riding up the alley, drifting between the houses of the handful of kids who lived within a three-block radius.

My mother had no jurisdiction over us anymore. If we sought a privilege, it had to be through Glen. Most often he would find a reason to deny it, because a chore wasn't completed, or its quality did not meet with his satisfaction, or he just felt like saying no. We had stopped inviting kids to come over to our house. Glen's interrogations of them, or belittling of us in front of them, became too much of an embarrassment.

Worst of all, the former oasis provided by our grandparents had all but dried up. From the first of their meetings Gramma eyed Glen suspiciously, watching him over her glasses while one after another cussword slipped from his mouth, a customary embellishment to one of his Navy stories. Her eyes moved occasionally to my mother, who sat in silence, her hand never leaving Glen's. The look of distaste Gramma wore on her face left no question about her feelings regarding her daughter's new beau, but she held her tongue. Grampa, not equipped for confrontation, sat in his chair, his chin resting on his hand, hard blue eyes trained on Glen, saying nothing.

Gramma drew the line when Glen began interfering with us at her house. During one of our visits he shooed us into the living room before Grampa could serve us our cookies and milk. We were rude, he said, sitting at the table like it was ours and expecting to be served, we needed to be more respectful.

Gramma told him that this was her house and she had been giving her grandkids cookies since they were old enough to eat them. We weren't rude. We were fine, polite children. He responded by telling her we were spoiled, and that she was a big part of the problem. He was in charge of us, not she. The visit ended with the five of us heading out the door only a few minutes after we arrived. Shortly after that incident our weekend visits tapered off entirely. What little time we spent with our grandparents always included Glen, and since he had no use for church, our former Sunday tradition vanished, too.

Tension had long existed between my mother and Gramma. My Gramma spoke her mind and on more than one occasion something she said to my mother would infuriate her, sending her out of the house in silent anger. Despite their differences, my mother always encouraged the bond between my grandmother and me. She never disparaged Gramma in front of me.

Now that our father had receded into the background of our lives, Glen focused his negative commentary on Gramma, often referring to her as "Fat Thelma." He belittled all the things I loved about her -- her deep voice, her tirades about her co-workers, the way she spoke to Grampa. His insults were like little knives cutting away at me, exacerbating the animosity I already felt toward him. Anxiety replaced the former joy of visiting Gramma. The fear of being reprimanded and the possibility of witnessing an ugly argument between the two of them made me jumpy. It was hard to be at ease while at her house. I no longer sought her lap and stopped asking for snacks. Time at her house soon became just like time at our own house.

Adjusting to the contrast of life with Glen would have been difficult under any circumstances. The fact that it happened so quickly compounded the challenge. As hard as it was for me, it was 10 times so for my brother. Glen's drive to establish himself as head of our household created natural tension between he and Kirk. It didn't matter that he was only 11 years old, Kirk's natural athleticism begged for Glen to prove his superiority.

Kirk revealed himself to a select few, and from his earliest interactions with Glen he seemed resolved that this man, this spoiler of all that had been good in our lives, would never see inside of him. Kirk applied his lack of vocalization universally, and was equally detached in both happy and unhappy circumstances. He didn't complain or talk back to Glen when he was given an undesirable chore, and at the same time demonstrated no desire to draw Glen into his life.

If you didn't know Kirk and you saw him in his most natural and relaxed form, you would think that something had irritated him. He held his lips in a straight line and his eyes intently focused, although not looking at anything in particular, and he could go for hours without uttering a word. Answers to questions were brief and utilitarian, and Kirk never initiated conversation. The contradiction his smile presented was completely disarming. Like our father, that simple expressive act prompted an involuntary and identical response. Kirk's face personified his thoughtful nature, and at the same time, closely guarded the bounty of treasure that existed within him, his love of fun and sense of humor, his creative talent and imagination. Kirk could impersonate Gramma talking to "BERnard" perfectly and his contrived substitute lyrics for commercial jingles elicited giggles from me every time. He directed the construction of our Matchbox car village made from cardboard, plastic margarine dishes, and old cereal boxes, and incorporated the clubhouse in our back yard, presiding over it from the branches of our apple tree. The contrast between his interior and exterior created the effect of two people living in the same body.

By now Brutus was house-trained, but he was prone to occasional accidents. Glen didn't believe in accidents. Kirk had agreed to take on the responsibility of a dog. There were no acceptable excuses. One afternoon, shortly after Glen officially became our stepfather, Brutus did his business on the dining room floor. Glen, Kirk, and I were watching TV in the living room. Kirk and I were seated on the floor, and seemed to be the only ones to notice the sharply offensive scent as it cascaded through the dining room doorway and filled our nostrils. Knowing better than to wait until he was told, Kirk jumped up and commenced clean up.

I went on immediate alert, glancing as inconspicuously as possible to my side where Glen was seated in his recliner, trying to judge whether he noticed what was going on. To my surprise he was engrossed in a magazine. Maybe he didn't notice? Perhaps my brother would escape reprimand this time? I returned my focus to the television and relaxed a bit.

My brother returned, the job complete, and took his spot next to me on the floor. He had no sooner sat down when I heard Glen snap the lever on the black recliner. The sound of the footrest releasing could be heard from any room in the house. No matter where we were or what we were doing, that loud, punctuated clap garnered our complete attention, issuing a warning that Glen was on the move and might soon be headed our way. Having already learned the lesson that ignoring him only exacerbated his anger, Kirk and I both turned to look at him.

He laid the magazine down on the table next to him, leaned forward in his chair and looking squarely at my brother said, "I want to talk to you."

My earlier assessment couldn't have been more wrong. Not only did he notice Brutus' accident, he had spent the entire time it had taken Kirk to complete the cleaning regimen getting worked up about it.

I couldn't see my brother's face, but I imagined it looked as it always did. He continued to look at Glen from his position on the floor, a few feet away.

Glen waited a few seconds and said, "When I say I want to talk to you, that means you need to come and stand in front of me."

His emotion escalated with each word. He spoke evenly and quietly, but the anger hovered dangerously, a hair's breadth beneath the surface.

Kirk hesitated just long enough to send Glen flying out of his chair. He took the three steps to my brother at a speed he rarely exhibited. He was already red-faced, his arms stiff at his sides, flexing, ready for a rumble. Kirk was standing by now and from my vantage point on the floor I could see the dark cloud that had settled over his face. Glen stood mere inches from Kirk, his chest pushed into him, his body laboring to contain itself. Kirk's body faced him, his eyes grazing the tops of Glen's shoulder, refusing to look at him directly.

Glen was seething now, his breath coming hard, his whole body flexed to the point of a barely perceptible quiver.

"How many times do I have to tell you to look at me when I'm talking to you?" Glen demanded, even more quietly.

The scene in front of me was fast becoming ugly. I could no longer resist the urge to distance myself from the blow-up that was coming. As nonchalantly as possible I scooted myself backwards, got up off the floor and walked to the couch. I would have gone to my room but the two of them were blocking the path to the hallway. Kirk turned his face slowly to Glen and shot daggers of death from his eyes. Unable to contain his fury any longer, Glen's right arm that had been tensed for combat rose violently and slapped my brother hard across the face, sending his head reeling to the right.

The combination of the assault to both his body and his pride dropped a curtain of tormented outrage onto my brother's face. His head remained stubbornly facing a hard right, fixed in the position in which the slap had placed it. He stood there, inches from Glen, lip quivering, color rising in his face as the tears finally escaped from the vault that housed his emotions, and slid down his cheeks.

Satisfied with his first victory, Glen stepped back, breathing deeply.

"Get your ass in your room! And you better make damn well sure that dog doesn't shit on the floor again or you and I are going to have some real problems," he said, turning back toward his recliner.

I watched my brother, red-faced, arms stiff and hands squeezed tightly at his side, turn and take three steps before he disappeared into the hallway. I felt the corners of my mouth twitching; my heart was racing. I wanted to scream at the injustice of the scene I had just watched. I wanted my mother to storm into the room, stand in front of Glen's recliner and berate him for once. Even better, she should slap him. But I already understood the improbability of either of those things happening. I forced myself up from the couch and went to my room.

As I passed Glen's chair I fought the urge to kick him, to tear at him with my fists and knock his stupid glasses off his fat, ugly face. I half expected him to find some fault with the way in which I walked past him, or to banish me from the back of the house thinking that I may try to go to Kirk and offer him some comfort. But Glen did nothing, his attention now focused on the current issue of *Playboy*. As I walked past my brother's closed door I felt an ache deep within me. I wanted to go in there and sit on the edge of his bed and commiserate about our situation, about this man who so clearly delighted in making our lives miserable, and whose control over our lives seemed to have no limit. But I knew my brother. If I had even attempted such a thing he would have told me to get out and leave him alone. That was how he handled things.

Chapter 29

Control

Glen's first triumph in reducing my brother to tears had
the effect of a shark tasting blood. At last he had found the
formula to break through Kirk's protective armor. He seemed
determined to break my brother, ever seeking new and creative
ways to demean him, and unable to hide his satisfaction when
he succeeded After several incidents involving a plugged toilet,
Glen banished Kirk from our one-and-only bathroom. If he
couldn't figure out how to use a toilet without plugging it up,
Glen told him, he didn't deserve the privilege. From now on he
would use the bathroom in our basement.

To call the commode that stood behind a rickety wooden
door in our basement a bathroom was a gross exaggeration.
The tiny room was lit by a single, bare light bulb, activated
by a chain. At any given time, there may be a dozen or more
spider webs lining the walls and ceiling. Dirt and dust lurked
in the corners. The act of getting to the basement toilet was
daunting enough. Situated at the opposite end from the
stairway, the full length of the basement had to be crossed. If
you were brave enough to make the trip by the dim glow that
came through the basement windows, you could save time
fumbling for the light string that dangled in the middle of the
room. But at nighttime there was no choice. It was pitch black
down there.

My contact with that room was kept to a deliberate minimum. I could count on one hand the times I had used that toilet, and all of them were based entirely on necessity. Not wanting to interrupt whatever play I was involved in, I occasionally didn't allow myself adequate time to make it from the back yard to the upstairs bathroom. Avoiding the embarrassment of wetting my pants was the only motivation I had found to make me want to use that toilet. My haste to get there on time absorbed my focus completely until I had situated myself at last on the seat. The whole time I was peeing, I scanned the walls and floor in front of me to make sure nothing was poised to jump on me. As soon as I finished I got out of there as fast as I could, pulling my pants up on my way out, not wanting to spend even one more second than necessary in there.

Using that bathroom was unpleasant, but thankfully my experiences had been quick, none of them involving going number two. While peeing can usually be done quickly, pooping can take a lot of time and requires some level of relaxation in order to properly execute. It was hard to concentrate when you were on the constant look out for some creepy crawly thing to jump on you. Kirk's ban from the upstairs bathroom was focused specifically on number two, which meant he had little hope of a quick in-and-out experience. In addition to the darkness and spiders, our basement was not heated, so it could be freezing down there in the winter.

Even though boys have more tolerance for spiders and the cold, I knew my brother hated having to use that room as much as I did. But complaining would be useless, and only satisfy his tormentor, so he endured his punishment in silence. Regardless of the time of day or night that nature called, he hoisted the heavy basement door up and latched it, felt his way down the dark, cold stairway and made his way across the room to take care of his business.

The time Kirk made the mistake of leaving discarded clothes at the end of his bed, instead of placing them in the laundry basket, found Glen in a particularly foul mood and at the end of his patience with our collective forgetfulness. He had no choice but to up the ante on the consequences. Glen discovered the clothes during an inspection of Kirk's room after Kirk had left for school that morning. He promptly got into his truck, drove to the school, retrieved my brother from his classroom and took him home to put his clothes away. His motivation this time was to humiliate Kirk in front of his classmates.

He would learn, Glen told him that night at the dinner table, or his life would just keep getting harder.

Chapter 30

Unanswered Questions

I jumped at the sound of my ring tone. Inhaling deeply, I tried to shake off the accumulated tension in my shoulders. Seeing it was my brother calling, I touched the green button and brought the phone to my ear.

"Hi, Jay."

"Hey, Amber. Did I wake you up?" he asked, in response to the strange way my voice came across.

"No, I was just laying here. I've been awake a while, just haven't ejected myself from the mattress yet," I replied. By now my breathing had returned to normal, the memories of those days receding to the depths of my mind where they had long ago been banished.

"We didn't get a chance to talk yesterday after the meeting with the minister," he said, "and I just wanted to fill you in."

Today was Thursday. My father's funeral was scheduled for tomorrow. The meeting Jay referred to had taken place the day before. In spite of the unexpected tragedy my father's death posed, Matt and I attempted to carry out some of the happier objectives of our trip, shuttling the kids between houses so they could spend as much quality-cousin time as possible.

Matt's cousin volunteered to drive Cameron to East Lansing for his two-day orientation that started yesterday and would be complete this afternoon. I hated to miss it, but activities had to be reprioritized. I spent the better part of Monday afternoon at the funeral home with Doris, and yesterday we found ourselves at the mall buying clothes for our family to wear to my father's final farewell. He would be angry with me if he knew I spent money on clothes for his funeral, telling me to wear what we brought with us -- even if that meant shorts and t-shirts. But I knew if the situation were reversed he would have worn nothing less than his best suit to my final send off.

The purpose of yesterday's meeting was for the minister, who had been designated to deliver the eulogy, to gather stories about our father to assist him in creating a fitting and accurate tribute. My father had a long and troubled history with religion. In our younger days he attended church with our family when his work schedule permitted, which was very seldom. Later, his second wife, Jennie, persuaded him to give church another go. To his surprise, he found satisfaction and fulfillment in attending Sunday services.

All too soon, the minister with whom my father had bonded resigned his position in the midst of allegations of an affair with a parishioner. My father never overcame his disappointment with the behavior of this man whom he had come to regard as a beacon of righteousness, someone he could look to in times of weakness and temptation, someone better than himself. Other than weddings and funerals, he never again stepped inside of a church. Doris, on the other hand, attended a new-age church fairly regularly. Given my father's lack of religious ties, she engaged the minister of her church, Pastor Lewis, to preside over his memorial service. Since he had never actually met my father, he needed to collect input from those of us who knew him well.

I participated in the meeting by phone while sitting in the van outside the mall. Jay and Glynis were on site at Dad's with Doris and a handful of other close relatives. Kirk was maintaining his seclusion and did not attend. No surprise there. We resurrected some of our fondest memories, talked about his love of cars, his devotion to his children and grandchildren, and the success he achieved in spite of his humble beginnings. Success achieved through hard work and determination. I gave my input to Pastor Lewis and dropped off after 30 minutes to refocus on my to-do list for the day. I had already found that keeping myself occupied was key to getting through the days, one at a time. Jay's comment piqued my curiosity. What transpired after I hung up that Jay wanted to fill me in on?

"OK," I said, "what is it? Did something happen after I dropped off?"

"Not after. Before. Glynis and I arrived at Dad's early, and Pastor Lewis was asking me about Dad. I gave him a brief history and when I got to the part about how Dad and I spent so much time together on car projects in his barn, he asked me to give him a tour. He wanted to get a feel for the place and said it would be nice if I showed it to him. I got ready to walk out there with Pastor Lewis when Doris tells me I'm going to need a key. I reminded her that Dad gave me a key a long time ago. She then looks directly into my eyes, you know, with that menacing stare she likes to give people when she wants them to know she means business."

"Then she says, 'You *did* have a key. I changed the locks yesterday.'"

"She then looked at Pastor Lewis and said, 'I'll take you out there.'"

Jay continued, "So all of a sudden she has to change the locks? It felt like, between the way she looked at me and the fact that she didn't offer to give me a new key, that she was insinuating I couldn't be trusted. Like she was afraid I'd go out there and steal something."

"Wow," I said, reflecting on yet another curious attribute of her behavior since my father's death a mere four days earlier. In that moment I resigned myself to the reality that I wasn't going to be given access to my father's final words, allegedly left on his computer, any time soon, or maybe ever.

Why? What is she hiding or protecting?

I then added to my list of Doris' strange behavior, the fact that she had locked my brother out of his father's barn – the place that both had come to know as a sanctuary. A place to which Jay had enjoyed free and unlimited access just a few days ago.

Finally, I said, "Well, I guess it's her right. It's her house. But the way she's been acting sure is odd. It seems like she's either expecting some confrontation from us or she wants to create one."

Tension churned in the pit of my stomach. Other than the robotic execution of the numerous tasks I had assigned myself this past week, my entire focus was aimed at managing my grief and comprehending my future without my father. I tried to push away the anxiety I felt at her reluctance to share his last words with me, telling myself she was just stressed. But this latest bit of information made it more difficult to deny that she was posturing.

For what? And why? Why did she have to make the situation worse by adding tension and drama?

"That sucks," I sighed. "What a slap in the face! It was a place the two of you shared. I mean sure, she went out there on occasion, but I can't recall her being involved in his cars, certainly not the way you were."

"Yeah, well, I just wanted you to know," Jay said, disappointment and frustration coming through in his voice.

"Other than that, how are you doing?" I asked.

"Oh, you know, the same. Dreading tomorrow," he said.

"Me too. I'm pretty sure Kirk's going to be there. I know it will take every ounce of his will, but he knows we need him there," I said.

"OK, well, I love you Amber. I'll see you tomorrow," Jay said.

"Love you too brother, and yes, I'll see you tomorrow," I said, pausing for a moment before I took the phone from my ear. I looked at the screen and noted it was only 10:15 in the morning. I already felt tired and I had only been awake for an hour.

Willing myself to throw my legs over the side of the mattress, I heard the click of the door opening and saw Matt's face peering through the crack. Seeing me sitting up, he opened the door and stepped through.

"You're awake," he said.

"Yes, I am," I said, forcing a smile. He walked over and sat down next to me as I reiterated Jay's conversation with him.

"Well, we always knew Doris was a bit of a hard-ass," he said. "I guess technically you aren't related anymore. You aren't family. It seems like she's trying to protect what's hers."

"You mean like Dad's estate?" I asked, knowing full well that is what he meant, the thought of which had been teasing the corners of my consciousness.

"Yes, it sure seems that way," he said.

"Well that's fine, but he's not even in the ground yet. Plus, does she really think Jay's going to steal from her? Dad told all three of us that his will leaves her everything. Add to that the fact that other than the house and barn there are probably not a lot of assets to talk about. Does she really think we'll challenge that? All I care about is getting some keepsakes and anything he may have wanted the kids and me to have. Shit, I can't believe we're even talking about this. I couldn't care less about his stuff," I said.

"I know you don't, and neither do your brothers, but she does," he said.

"You're probably right. It's just sickening to think that four days into his departure she is so laser-focused on protecting his material remains. It's difficult for me to comprehend that mindset," I said.

As much as I didn't like the message Matt's words conveyed, I appreciated his candor, a trait I knew I could always expect from him. I had to admit there were times I could have done without it, most notably when he was using it to point out one of my shortcomings. *That was how relationships went, right? The qualities about your partner that attracted you in the beginning had a way of becoming annoying later on down the road.* Entertaining that thought more fully, I reminded myself that he had to feel the same way. He had found my drive and determination to better myself attractive at the onset, but I knew these attributes had become frustrations to him at some point.

Here I go again, I thought, as my mind shifted gears and went straight down the rabbit hole I had found myself frequenting as of late. Continuing my struggle to put all the pieces together and see the larger picture, I thought back to our early days in Houston. For the first year we were dizzy with the excitement of all that was new; our home -- complete with a pool and hot tub that could be used year-round -- new restaurants, and the endless entertainment options offered by a city so much larger than the one we had left. It felt like vacation.

Matt busied himself with all the settling-in activities; undertaking maintenance and decor projects to personalize our new home to our family, learning how to service the pool, exploring local grocery stores and eventually venturing into the city where he found his gym of choice. Before we knew it, a year had passed. Ever the dog with a bone, shortly after the first anniversary of our move I broached the employment topic with him.

"Are you still planning on it?" I asked.

"Oh yes, definitely," he said. Houston was booming compared to Toledo, the closest "big" city to our former home in Whitehouse. He was confident he would be able to find something.

In the meantime, he spent his days exploring the city, reporting to me each evening on this antique shop he had found or that lighting store. Matt always had a dozen or so projects on his list and sourcing home improvement supplies was a priority. He forged friendships at the gym and described to me the group of four he met in the course of his daily workouts. I was thrilled at how easily he took to our adopted city, relieved that this move I had pushed so hard for seemed to suit all of us beautifully. Meanwhile I threw myself into my new job, intent on demonstrating my value to this company that was responsible for bringing our family to this new and wonderful city.

The change was subtle and gradual. Matt's dinnertime accounts of his day became generic, and eventually our conversation focused almost exclusively on my workday and the kids. I tried to draw him out, probing for details, but he became increasingly vague. Matt handled the shuttling of the kids during the day, delivering each of them to and from their practices and activities. At some point I began receiving calls from the kids in the afternoon. Practice ended over 20 minutes ago -- did I know if Dad was on his way? Yes, they had tried calling him, but he hadn't answered. He didn't answer when I tried calling him, either. The increasing frequency of this occurrence ramped up the anxiety that his reticence regarding his daily activities had created in me.

I trod carefully. I had no desire to aggravate our situation with more conflict. It was clear he didn't want to talk about his daily activities.

But why?

The strain of containing my growing concerns, and the suspicion that accompanied his lack of disclosure, eventually got the best of me. On the heels of an incident that had him picking up Austin three hours late from football practice, I unloaded on him. He became immediately defensive. He was stuck in traffic. It was no big deal. Austin was safe, and yes, he had to wait, but why was I making such an issue of it? He didn't tell me how to do my job. I didn't have any appreciation for the challenges he faced each day, he said, I was too absorbed in my own world.

I understood all of that, but why didn't he ever answer his phone? Completely ignoring the question, he continued his attack on my absence, the excessive hours I worked, and my complete lack of appreciation for all that he did for our family.

And so it went. I knew better than to expect to get anywhere with him if I acted out in an angry or accusatory way. I tried talking, broaching the delicate subjects when we were both in good spirits. His responses regarding his daily activities were stubbornly vague, entailing the gym, the grocery store, and the generic category of "errands." His practice of not picking up the phone expanded from disregarding my purposeful attempts to locate him to virtually every call I placed to him during the day.

And then there was the issue of work. I continued to press him in as casual a manner as I could muster. Did he need help with his resume? Did he want me to introduce him to one of the recruiters I worked with? He never outright told me that he had no intention of getting a job, but he never made any effort to find one, either. I updated his resume and helped him post it on a handful of job websites. By now I was engaged in a full-on battle with myself in an effort to remain positive and supportive, to resist the urge to unleash the anger and resentment that grew within me each passing day.

Meanwhile my work schedule provided both justification and ammunition to counter the challenges I directed at Matt's secret life. My job had me in the office no less than 10 hours a day and working another 10 that I parsed out of our evenings and over the weekends. We rarely ate dinner before 8:00 p.m. in response to my long days. Year-end and annual proxy season placed additional demands on me, sometimes requiring seven-day work weeks for months on end. The newly public company's feverish tempo infected me with the belief that there was no work that could wait until tomorrow. I couldn't recall a single week that I took completely off, declining to look at emails or take calls. Matt knew work was something I loved. And because I loved it, he could appeal to my sense of guilt by insinuating that my job was a selfish indulgence.

In the beginning I felt a lot of pressure to prove myself, to justify what I knew to be a costly relocation package, and to assure that I was earning my keep. Later, I had to admit, my time at the office became an escape, a means of shielding myself from the growing void in our relationship. As I looked back I saw his point. My obsession with performing well and ingratiating myself with my new employer did seem a bit excessive. It was this line of thinking that gave rise to the job change I recently made. Having not succeeded in motivating a change in Matt's behavior I focused on my own. The aftermath of seeing my husband in the arms of another man reinforced this perspective. My initial feelings of anger and resentment were quickly replaced by guilt.

It's my fault. I pushed him away by working so many hours and hassling him about getting a job. I've been selfish. After all, he gave me his 100% support for the move to Houston. I need to be more supportive of him.

Chapter 31

No Matter What

I was so deeply engaged in my marital analysis that I jumped when Matt said, "Jill made breakfast if you're hungry." Seeing my reaction, he asked, "Are you OK?"

I nodded and smiled.

"Yes. I was just in deep thought about this whole situation with Doris. Breakfast. Yes, that would probably be a good thing. I'll come down and give it a try." I had to acknowledge the fact that my stomach had continued to show little interest in food these past few days.

"OK, I'll see you downstairs," he said, heading toward the door.

"All right, thanks honey," I said, watching him until the door closed behind him.

I felt my phone buzzing next to me. I picked it up and scanned my email. Nothing too pressing. What did I expect, I had only been on my new job at Michaelson Industries for two weeks? I pushed away the discomfort I felt at not being more engaged. This is the way normal jobs work, I told myself. Most people would be falling all over themselves with excitement at having gotten a bigger job with more pay, that miraculously was at the same time less demanding. What kind of idiot feels uncomfortable because their work email account isn't blowing up?

Me, that's who.

There I go again, obsessing over work.

I was both proud and grateful to have inherited my father's work ethic. I reflected on my first job, thinking how ironic it was that Glen was responsible for it. I held no delusion that his motivation in any way contemplated my interests, but nonetheless I had to credit him with helping me discover the satisfaction that accompanied a job well done. And the money that went along with it wasn't too bad, either. It was 1975 and the news was filled with headlines about job cuts and the sagging economy.

Glen had recently been fired from his job after losing his temper and punching his boss in the face. We were living off of the child support my father paid and the unemployment money that Glen earned. My mother had never worked outside the home. In recent years she had taken on some ad hoc babysitting jobs for a few of the rare working mothers in Grand Rapids. This work had dried up, probably because the parents had gotten a good look at our newest family member and wanted their children to have no part of it.

While grocery shopping with my mother, I noticed that she used pieces of paper that looked like a cross between play money and coupons to pay the cashier. These, she explained, were food stamps. The government gives them to people who don't make enough money to afford groceries. For the first time in my life I was confronted with the reality of money. Our father, the worker of two or three jobs at any one time, had always provided us with not only the necessities, but also countless other "nice-to-haves". Pretty dresses hung in my closet, and I slept in a canopy bed dressed in a purple floral coverlet that hosted a sea of stuffed animals. Our house, while not extravagant, was nice and spacious. My mother was proud of her furniture, all of which she had purchased brand new. I never thought twice about opening the door of our refrigerator and finding food inside of it.

My new reality was reinforced when my mother signed us up for the free lunch program at school. In response to the look of utter mortification on my face, she assured me that the school would keep it secret. But, I responded, the teacher takes a count every day for lunch. I feared I would be singled out. She explained that the office managed the process behind the scenes. To my great relief, I found that my teacher never made a distinction between those who were paying for their lunches and those who were on the free program.

This all changed the day our teacher, Mrs. Beckman, was sick, and a substitute teacher took her place. In an act of complete senselessness, the sub asked for a show of hands for the free lunch program. I picked up a pencil and looked down at my desk, quickly extracting a paper from within so that I could pretend I was completing my homework assignment. I felt the heat rising from my chest and spreading all the way to my cheeks. I knew they must be pink or worse yet, bright red. I focused on getting my nervousness in check, willing my pounding heart to slow its pace, and relax so as not to draw undue attention to myself. I reminded myself to breathe.

My eyes never left my desk, so they could not see if any of my classmates raised their hands. Just when I began to think that the hour-long moment had passed, I heard Tommy Newton, the cutest boy in the fifth-grade and my on-and-off boyfriend, say, "Amber does, but she didn't raise her hand." As my mind comprehended his words, my head jerked up and I could see that he was pointing at me.

"No, I don't," I shot back without any thought or planning. My response was instinctively protective. My pride would not allow me to be looked upon by my entire class as someone who could not afford to pay for her lunch. I would gladly do without lunch before I let that happen. Thankfully, the brainless substitute didn't belabor the point, noted the count, and moved on to announcing our first subject of the day. I relaxed, feeling the temperature of my face returning to normal. So much for keeping a secret.

Shortly afterward, Glen and my mother announced that they had taken on a newspaper route, our mother would manage it and Kirk and I would deliver the papers. Our new job paid $20 per week to both my brother and me. At the onset we were less than excited about the notion of delivering papers on each of the year's 365 days. But the enticement of earning $20 each week danced in our minds and very quickly won us over. My mother split the route by location, giving each of us about 30 customers. Every day after school we changed clothes and counted out our papers, adding a few extras in case of a mishap, or in the event that someone stopped us and wanted to buy a single copy. After loading my newspapers into the wire basket of my hot pink bike and securing them with a bungee cord, I jumped on my flowered banana seat and set out to deliver the daily news to my half of the town of Grand Rapids.

Despite the early weekend mornings, the hardships that rain, wind, and snow posed, customers who repeatedly didn't answer their doors on collection day, and flat bicycle tires, we loved our jobs. The money was a great motivator, but even more so was the freedom those few hours a day afforded us. Out from under Glen's critical eye we performed our work without having to contend with his belittling comments or controlling directives. If a disgruntled customer called to complain about a wet or windblown paper my mother handed the phone to me.

I learned to take extra care, placing each customer's newspaper in a protected area so that it stayed dry and couldn't be carried away by the wind. This assured that I wouldn't be called to deliver a replacement after supper, and more importantly it gained the respect and admiration of my customers. To my great delight, many of my appreciative subscribers responded by tipping me each week. I sometimes earned an extra $5 each week, and at Christmas time, up to $50.

Customer compliments flushed me with pride and drove me to work even harder. I had found something in addition to my schoolwork that I was good at, something Glen could not demean. The ultimate judges of my success were my customers, and all 30 of them couldn't be wrong. The entrepreneurial bug infected Kirk and me as we grasped the cause-effect relationship between effort and profit. We began a campaign to obtain additional customers and were rewarded with prizes and recognition from *The Toledo Blade's* subscription department.

Believing that the sky was the limit, we donned our parkas and snow pants that winter and took our snow-shoveling business door-to-door. We charged $5 for every sidewalk, and always ran out of daylight and energy before we ran out of customers who were willing to hire us. That newspaper route not only taught me the value of a job well done and the pride in earning my own money, it provided a distraction from the negativity that had settled over our lives, fueling a belief in me that anything was possible. So began my love affair with work . . . .

I sighed deeply, my musings having brought me no closer to dispelling the worries that nagged me about my marriage. We had both made mistakes. But we both wanted our marriage to work. I was confident of that. Our relationship had had its share of peaks and valleys, but even in my moments of greatest doubt I always came back to the one thing that bound us, our family. What would I do without the security and safety of the family we had created together? After my affair we discussed divorce and quickly dismissed the idea, reconfirming our shared conviction to keep our family together.

I had to admit that the vacation incident had invited the notion of divorce, but I had stubbornly tried to hold it at bay, desperate to keep it from joining forces with the doubts that Matt's secret life had instilled in me. But there had been days when the urge was too difficult to resist. I found myself imagining the details of my life without Matt, the lightness I would feel at ridding myself of the obsessive worry over what he did all day.

I would have complete control over our family finances, and would get a smaller, more affordable house. I would no longer be beholden to his willful refusal to contribute income. At times I could feel the peace that would occupy the space currently consumed by our many conflicts. The fantasy lingered sometimes for an entire day.

But all I had to do was think about holidays absent the kids, shared custody, and the disappointment that breaking my contract would inflict, not only on our children, but also on the rest of the family. This thought was all that was required to bring me back from the brink and fortify my determination to make things work. *I could do it*, I told myself, *no matter what it took.*

Chapter 32

A New Frontier

In contrast to the entrepreneurial success my brother and I were experiencing, our family's household financial situation did not improve. The months stretched on and still Glen didn't find work. In the spring of 1976 our mother announced that we were moving to Wyoming. As soon as we could sell our house, ideally by mid-summer, we would be on our way with the goal of arriving before school started in the fall. Glen, my mother explained, had family in Wyoming who told him that oilfield jobs were plentiful and high-paying. The oil industry seemed to be weathering the recession much better than the auto industry.

"Wyoming?" I repeated, trying to register what I had just heard.

"Why?" I asked, refusing to believe this was the only place in the world where Glen could find employment. What about California or Florida, or any other state that was desirable?

"I just told you, Glen thinks he can get a job there," she said, and sensing my resistance went on to add, "we just can't make ends meet on what we get from your father and Glen's unemployment is about to run out."

By now I had become accustomed to every negative aspect of our lives being somehow attributed to my father.

"What about Dad? What about Gramma and Grampa? What about our paper route?" My mind began compiling a list of everything that existed here, in Grand Rapids, Ohio, and that would be left behind.

"You know your grandparents are retiring in Michigan, so you aren't going to be seeing them as much," she explained. "We will see them sometimes during holidays, and when we come to visit in the summer."

"How often?" I asked, ticking through the list of important holidays, the best of which had all been celebrated with my grandparents.

"I don't know right now. That will depend. They're buying a motor home so maybe they will come see us," she said.

In spite of the wall Glen had erected between my Gramma and us, knowing that she lived on the other side of town gave me comfort. At times when I felt I couldn't take one more minute of him, after one of his demeaning lectures, calling me stupid, or making me repeat a job over and over just to goad me, I would throw myself onto my bed and think about running away to her house. The consequences would be severe if I ever dared, but the option presented an imaginary lifeline I could grab onto if I ever succeeded in finding the courage.

When my grandparents announced their plans to retire in Michigan, four hours away, I tried to counter my extreme disappointment by telling myself we would still see them on major holidays. I re-spun my runaway fantasy, envisioning a future where I spent occasional weekends at their new place. Without Glen. I had only recently accepted the reality of their departure, and now this? I couldn't remember how many states lay between Ohio and Wyoming, but I knew there were more than three. The distance between our new homes would make spending weekends at her house a virtual impossibility.

As I was trying to picture the U.S. map in my mind it occurred to me that she had not responded to the question about my father. As I opened my mouth to re-ask the question she cut me off.

"Your father doesn't know we are moving and you can't tell him."

I stared hard at her and thought for a minute.

"You mean, not tell him at all?"

"Yes, that is what I mean," she said, adding, "if he finds out he may try to take me to court to stop us from moving. You remember how difficult he was during the divorce. Plus, you haven't even wanted to see him lately."

I let the sting of her words set in. *True, I had rejected him. But, it was because of the harassment and bad-mouthing that followed every Sunday visit, first from Glen and eventually from my mother, too.*

Oh, and there was that whole gun incident.

In the year that had since passed I found myself less and less concerned about the thought of my father threatening Glen with a gun. Having gotten to know Glen much better, I found myself fantasizing on a pretty regular basis about hurting him myself. My go-to scenario had Kirk holding him down while I kicked him in the stomach until he cried.

I was certain he would cry, because he was a bully, and I had learned firsthand from Sara Walters that bullies cower when their victims fight back. She had taken to kicking me during our walks home from school. After the second time when I came home crying, my mother coached me to fight back if she did it again. The very next day after she landed her foot firmly in my behind I hauled off and whacked her with my very full and heavy satchel, taking her completely by surprise.

Her face clouded up and she burst into tears. I walked on, leaving her standing there and crying like a baby. She never kicked me again.

I thought back to my conversation with the judge, and then to that Sunday when I bluntly told my father that we didn't want to see him, and a wave of guilt swept over me. I was getting what I deserved. Now we were going to be taken so far away that my father would never be able to see us.

I felt like I was being systematically stripped of everything that was important in my life, things I never even considered I could lose. My grandparents. My father. The security of knowing that your family can afford to pay for things like your school lunch.

And our paper route -- the only positive thing I could claim since Glen had entered our lives.

I would be completely cut off from everyone except for Mom and Glen. Glen would have no one watching over him, no one who seemed to know, as my Grandmother did, that he was a really bad man.

"Once we get there we will let your Dad know where we are. He will be able to bring you guys back to visit at Christmas and in the summer," my mother said.

She paused for a moment and continued, "But he hasn't been much of a father to you lately, so I wouldn't hold my breath."

I felt the final slap of her words as a feeling of utter helplessness settled over me. How much more could he do to us? It was clear to me that we were moving because of Glen. He was the one who punched his boss in the face and got fired. Fired from a job at the same company that still employed my father, a job that paid my father enough to easily support our family. Glen had squandered a good-paying job at a time when work was scarce.

All because he couldn't control his nasty temper and violent tendencies.

My growing hatred for him surprised even me. Before he appeared in my life I couldn't think of a single person I felt that way about. He gleefully took away everything we loved, making sure we knew how much he enjoyed it. My mother was so completely under his control that I had long since relinquished any hope for defense or protection from her. He had proven that even she was not exempt from his controlling abuse and hair-trigger temper, treating her on occasion as badly as he treated us. *How could she love him?*

On the last day of school, my sixth-grade class threw me a going-away party complete with presents, cake, and decorations. My walk home that afternoon was somber. I couldn't stop thinking about how nice it would be to enter junior high school with the safety net of my friends, most of whom had been my classmates since kindergarten. For years I had taken for granted the benefit of inheriting teachers who had taught Kirk the year before. Something about being recognized by my family name on the first day of class made the venture into a new academic year feel safe and comfortable.

I tried to imagine what it would be like to be a complete unknown. The thought of it made me uneasy. I tried to cheer myself up by recalling my experiences with new kids who had come to my school over the years. The teacher introduced them in front of the class, describing their families, where they had moved from, and what sports or activities they enjoyed. Sometimes the new student would bring cupcakes or cookies. By lunchtime the new kid was being fawned over by the whole class, invited to play tag and dodge ball at recess, and having his or her choice of lunch tables to grace. I decided I could go for that. While being the center of attention was not something

I usually sought, I could handle a day or two in the spotlight if it made the job of making friends easier.

I questioned my mother about Wyoming in hopes of gleaning some information that would make me feel like living there would at least be an even trade-off, that the benefits would outweigh some of the negatives of living in Grand Rapids. But as I thought about it, there really weren't any negatives of living in Grand Rapids. It had been my home for the duration of my young life. All our relatives lived nearby. The fact that it was such a small town did not, at this point in my life, concern me.

And then there was my father. I found myself again in a crisis of conscience. We were forbidden to tell our father about the move. The one good thing about our current estrangement was that I didn't have to feel awkward, or like I was lying by not telling him something of this magnitude. Later, after he found out, I could avoid feeling guilty by reminding myself that I never had the opportunity to tell him. Last Christmas, when he stopped by to drop off gifts for us, we engaged in some brief, strained conversation with him at the front door. I felt bad after he left, wishing I had said more, but his unannounced visit had found me unprepared and tongue-tied.

Our new home would be near Yellowstone Park in a town called Cody. My mother explained that Cody's proximity to one of the most famous national parks in the U.S., and the fact that Buffalo Bill Cody was born there back in the 1800s, made it a popular stopping point for tourists traveling to and from Yellowstone. I knew of Buffalo Bill, but I was less than impressed. Our mother also told us that the town of Cody was bigger than Grand Rapids. She seemed excited about the move to a new town and a new house. My emotions swung from apprehensive sadness to excitement at the unknown that lay ahead.

Our house in Grand Rapids sold quickly and we began preparing for the move. The first order of business was to find a house in Cody and for Glen to secure a job. Our excitement ramped up tremendously when we learned that we were going to visit Cody before our actual move. We were going to buy a camper and drive more than 1,500 miles to preview the town that would soon become our new home. We had never taken a vacation and I had never traveled more than a few hundred miles from our home in Grand Rapids. At last I found something to get excited about.

The route my mother and Glen mapped out for us would take us north through Michigan and then west through Wisconsin, Minnesota, and South Dakota. On our return trip we would follow a more southern path. This plan maximized the sites we would be able to see on our roundtrip drive. Mackinac Bridge, Mount Rushmore, and The Black Hills of South Dakota were just a few of the stops earmarked to visit. It went without saying that we would spend some time in Yellowstone Park once we reached Wyoming. We also had the opportunity to add some stops that we discovered along the way. Billboards boasting the amenities of a place called Wall Drug peppered the interstate. By the time we reached Wall, South Dakota, we could barely contain our excitement at being able to experience an attraction so world renowned.

Glen drove, towing our new pop-up camper behind us. The bed of our pick-up truck was now appointed with a camper top. My brothers and I rode in the back while Mom and Glen sat up front in the cab. From the two side windows in the camper top we watched the landscape transition from lush green, forested vistas to vast stretches of prairie. Being both out of earshot and eyesight of Glen, our days passed blissfully. We played cards and a variety of other games we concocted that involved spotting attributes of passing cars, billboards, and license plates.

Just when I began to wonder if the mountains we had heard so much about really existed, I looked up to see my mother banging on the window that separated our two travel compartments. Once she got our attention she pointed excitedly out the front window. My brothers and I crowded our three little faces around the opening and took in our first view of the mountains far ahead in the distance. With each passing mile the mountains loomed larger on the horizon, bringing into sharper focus their majesty and beauty.

Despite the fact that we were on a vacation and a new life with better opportunities hovered on the horizon, Glen's temperament was as foul as ever. Just a few days into our journey, we were settling in for the night at a campground that was anchored by a small lake and boasted hundreds of campsites sprinkled among thick clusters of pine trees. After supper my brothers and I went to use the shower facilities while our mother and Glen readied our camper for bed. By the time I finished, it was dark outside. The glow of lanterns and campfires illuminated my path back to our campsite. Aside from a few summer nights when I had been invited to sleep in Kirk's tent in our back yard, I had never camped before. I breathed in the cool and smoky night air on my walk back. The stars were already dancing above me, lighting my path.

Approaching our campsite, I could see the light radiating from the Coleman lantern inside our camper, projecting the silhouettes of my mother and Glen onto the canvas sides. Satisfied that I had navigated back from the lavatory facilities correctly, I turned my attention back to the light show above me. Being naturally clumsy and prone to tripping and falling, I had learned to take extra care when doing even the most mundane physical activities. After a few seconds of upward gazing I returned my focus to the path in front of me to assure I was still on track.

Once again our camper came into focus, but this time
I noticed the silhouettes inside had changed position. The
shadows of Glen and my mother now stood so close to one
another that no light showed between their two forms.

I felt immediately alert to danger, but could not articulate
the reason.

I watched as his figure separated from hers just far enough
to gather the leverage and space required to put his hands on
her shoulders and shove her backward onto the bed behind her.
She fell backward onto the bed behind her.

He was on her instantly, his right hand raised high like
a pistol that was cocked and ready to fire. Blades of his hair
hung between them like slender daggers, the shadow of his
head seemed ready to burst from the strain of containing his
anger. And then, unable to contain his fury any longer, he fired,
bringing his hand down and slapping her hard in the face.

By now I had stopped and was standing very still in the
middle of the pathway, staring at the canvas sides of our
camper, fearing that something even more awful would happen
if I averted my gaze for even a second. The churning in my
stomach spread to my bowels and I clenched reflexively. I tried
to pull myself together as I ticked through a list of options.

Intervening was out of the question. I had no wish to
redirect his violent anger toward me. I had never before seen
him hit my mother. His mood at the onset of our trip had been
uncharacteristically upbeat, but in a matter of just a few days
it turned to nasty and confrontational. The close proximity of
the five of us for days on end seemed to rattle him. I guessed
that the privacy of the moment he thought he shared with my
mother enticed him to let loose the control he would have
otherwise exercised. A surprise entry by me would cause him
to question just how much I had seen and would likely further
incite his temper.

I stared at the canvas before me, silently willing him to stop. Next, I willed my mother to bite him or head butt him long enough to get him off of her. I decided that if she succeeded in making her way out the camper door, I would make my presence known in an effort to thwart any further violence.

Mere seconds had passed, yet I felt like I had stood in that spot for hours, hair dripping, shampoo and soap clutched in my hand. As I struggled to come up with a more viable solution, I watched his arm cock once more and fire three more successive rounds at the same side of her face. All the while she lay there defenseless. The only movement I could discern was the jerking of her head in response to the impact of his hand.

When at last he got up off the bed, I snapped out of my trance. I felt an urgent need to distance myself from the ugly scene I had just witnessed. My clouded brain could conceive of only one option. I turned, scurried back to the lavatory and commenced taking yet another shower. I stayed there as long as I thought I could without raising concerns for my whereabouts, letting the hot water pour down my back, wishing it could wash away the scene I had just witnessed.

Finally, I turned off the faucet, stepped out onto the cold cement floor and dried myself off with my wet towel. I walked slowly back to our campsite. When the canvas sides of our camper once again came into view I half expected to see their shadows brawling on the bed. To my great relief I saw only my mother's silhouette this time. Glen was nowhere to be seen. Good. I knew if I saw him at that moment my face would be unable to disguise the intense disgust I felt. Facial expressions that veered on either side of neutral tended to provoke him, and I had no desire to further incite his anger. I hoped he had gone somewhere to cool off and would come back in a better mood.

I tried not to stare at my mother as I entered the camper, but my sideways glances confirmed a welt on her right cheek, the one I had seen that bastard slap at least four times. I asked if she was going to take a shower, to which she replied she didn't think so. I was struggling to find some other topic to engage her in, when she suggested I go outside with my brothers. They were getting ready to toast marshmallows. I knew I was being dismissed, so I did as I was told.

Glen eventually returned, and the few hours that remained before bedtime were spent in tense silence. The two of them barely looked at one another. The next morning I was grateful to climb into the sanctuary of the camper top with my two brothers, buffered from Glen once again.

Chapter 33

Cody

We rolled into Cody on July third, just in time to witness the town's famous Stampede Days, a three-day celebration of Independence Day that takes place each year, complete with parades, rodeos and mock shoot-outs. Cowboys and Indians in full regalia seemed to be on every street corner. As we pushed our way through the throngs of observers lining the streets along the parade route I began to understand what was meant by the term "tourist town." Traffic was backed up on each of the four major highways that led to and from town, the vehicles bearing license plates from virtually every state in the union. The hotels all boasted signs that read "No Vacancy." The air was filled with excitement, music, and a constant barrage of gunfire from the cowboys and Indians who pretended to shoot at one another.

The single highway that led to the east entrance of Yellowstone Park passed through Cody. This encouraged vigorous development of all things pertaining to hospitality, and little else. Main Street was lined with western-wear and boot shops, souvenir stores, and the historic Irma Hotel, named for Buffalo Bill Cody's daughter. Scattered in between these tourist attractions were a few restaurants, a JC Penney, movie theatre, and a few restaurants. Old Trail Town, a collection of authentic, local buildings dating back to the late 1800s,

was located west of town not far from the Cody Stampede, a
stadium that hosted a rodeo every night in the summer months.
The third gem in the town's triple crown of attractions was the
Buffalo Bill Historical Center, a museum boasting collections
of western-themed art as well as an impressive collection of
firearms, and the actual home in which Bill Cody was born.

As tourists, we were charmed by everything the town
offered, and there was still enough kid in us to revel in
the mock gun fights on the street corners. The mountains
were beautiful and every campground we stayed in boasted
incredible forested vistas, complete with rolling rivers and
water so clear you could see the rocks in the riverbed. After we
extinguished our lanterns at night, the dark became so thick
and black that you couldn't see your hand in front of your face,
but if you walked to a clearing the starlight was breathtaking. I
marveled at how the sky here could be so much bigger than the
sky back home.

My brothers and I camped under the stars for the first time.
We fell asleep to the scent of pine, the feel of the crisp air on
our faces and the sound of water tumbling over the rocks in
a nearby stream. We returned home more positive about our
move than ever. I decided to make the best of it and allowed
myself to feel excitement for the first time at the prospects of
new friends, a new house and a new life.

My mother collected newspapers during our visit and
proceeded to call about available houses after we returned.
Within a few weeks she reported to us that she had secured
a rental home. It was a one-story brick house on the west
side of town. Our house in Grand Rapids was white with
black shutters. The prospect of a brick house, something
altogether different, was appealing. One of my best friends
lived in a brick house in the country and I had always thought
it beautiful. I pictured ours looking just like it and placed a
mental checkmark in the plus column.

My mind quickly returned to the part about it being a "rental" house. Why were we renting, I asked my mother? Didn't we get money when we sold our house? She explained that houses cost a lot more in Cody, and right now we couldn't afford to buy one. After Glen got established in his new job we could save up and buy a house within a few years.

When our Ryder truck pulled up in front of our new house my visions of grandeur were quickly dashed. The house, as advertised, was indeed made of brick, but otherwise boasted no distinctive characteristics. It was located a little over a mile from downtown, just off the highway on a street named Gulch that ran alongside a cemetery. The front of our new house faced the service entrance where the caretaker accessed the graveyard with his backhoe and other pieces of equipment essential to burying the dead and maintaining their gravesites. Row after row of headstones was visible through the chain-link fence.

The grass in our tiny yard was sparse, and even if there had been room for a garden I could not envision plants surviving in the rock-hard soil that seemed to host nothing more than sagebrush and pine trees, plants so self-sufficient you would have to work hard to kill them. A white plank fence stood between the tiny front yard and the street. A short sidewalk led from the driveway to the cement stoop outside the front door. Other than two scrubby evergreens that flanked each end of the fence in front, the yard was void of shrubbery.

I had to admit it was a nice house. It was just so different from the one we left. I remained positive, telling myself that the inside probably made up for the lackluster yard. But that was not the case. The living room was a fourth the size of the one we had left, and accordingly held a fourth of my mother's furniture. Without a dining room and basement, the only solution was to pile the extra pieces into the garage, leaving little room for anything but a path to walk in and out. Our kitchen was painted a cheerful yellow, but it wasn't big enough to hold our table. The picnic table that had sat on the lower patio of our home in Ohio for as long as I could remember became our kitchen table. It fit so long as it was pushed up next to the window when it was not in use.

I now had the answer to the question of what more Glen could take from us. Not only did we not own our new home, it paled in comparison to the one we left behind. My mother's plans to buy a home of our own never materialized. In spite of Glen's job and the job my mother took working at the Mini Mart, money would continue to be tight for the duration of their marriage.

Fortunately for Kirk and me, tourist towns needed lots of cheap labor and businesses offered jobs to kids as young as 12 and 13. We landed our first jobs at the Cody Cafeteria, Kirk as a dishwasher and me as a busgirl. From that point on, I always had a job. Despite all of Glen's shortcomings, his one saving grace was that he never asked us to turn our earnings over to him. The money I earned from cleaning hotel rooms, doing laundry, working at the local drive-in burger restaurant, sacking groceries, and eventually waitressing was mine to keep. I used it to buy the things our family couldn't afford, like clothes, a bicycle, lunches and Cokes, and eventually a car.

Years later I would realize that all of those jobs contributed to my self-esteem, despite the insecurities that riddled me during that period of my life. Our family's lack of prosperity under Glen's stewardship helped me to discover my love of earning and the feeling of satisfaction that accompanied the ability to provide for myself. I developed an early drive to get a good-paying job as an adult. No one in my family had earned a college degree. Maybe I would be the first.

Through whatever means necessary, I was determined to achieve the standard of living I had enjoyed before Glen entered my life, to live in a nice home, drive a reliable car, and afford decent clothes.

Aside from the financial benefits of being self-sufficient, there was also the knowledge that if I ever found myself beholden to a husband as monstrous as Glen, I could simply pack my bags and move on, leaving the son-of-a-bitch far behind me.

Chapter 34

That Girl

I walked through the double glass doors of Cody Junior High School expecting it to be like Grand Rapids Elementary where the environment had been kind, friendly, and inviting, and whose teachers had rehearsed the entire class roster so that they would be able to correctly pronounce each student's name on the first day of school.

Within seconds I knew I had completely miscalculated the situation. The lobby was swarming with kids. I winced involuntarily at the rising clamor created by hundreds of grunting, laughing, boisterous teenagers. I had the sensation that I was shrinking into the crowd as I pushed my way to my locker, bouncing off of countless bodies in the process.

As self-conscious as I felt, I finally realized that no one seemed to even notice me, and I relaxed a bit. Kids were clustered in small groups, girls whispering and giggling behind raised hands into each other's ears, boys puffing up their chests, eying the squads of girls out of the corners of their eyes, slapping each other on the back and referring to one another by nicknames like "Beast" and "The Hammer." I dared not make eye contact, but my curiosity had me straining to discern what all the chatter was about. It seemed as if I had entered a different world, like I was a foreigner struggling to understand the native language.

I felt woefully out of my league. My heart fell further as I distilled the scene in front of me, realizing I had no tools with which to compete, no special skills I could pull out of my book bag and transform myself with. I milled about the throng of students, looking anxiously for my assigned classrooms. By lunchtime I hadn't exchanged a single hello. Not one teacher introduced me as a new student. By the fourth period I found myself feeling grateful for my invisibility. What did I have to talk about, anyway? My excellent report card from sixth-grade? The stellar reviews from my paper route customers? The bits and pieces of repartee that caught my ears were focused on lip gloss, Friday night's game, the upcoming fall dance, and which boys had asked which girls.

The scene of my seventh-grade entrance fantasy played in my mind and I almost laughed at what I now understood to be a completely ridiculous expectation. I realized that if I was going to find a friend I was going to have to take the first step in initiating contact. The thought terrified me. What if I was rejected? What if I was laughed at? I hadn't made a new friend since kindergarten and couldn't even remember how I did it then. My guess was that the teacher facilitated the process.

When the lunch bell rang I anxiously scanned the crowd of students heading toward the cafeteria. In the few weeks following our arrival to Cody I had met two girls who lived on my street. I couldn't call us friends yet, but they both seemed nice. If I could find either one of them I was certain they would invite me to join them. At least I hoped they would. I soon realized that finding anyone in the crowd of what seemed like hundreds of seventh-graders was next to impossible. I walked slowly out the doors, giving myself a final few minutes to catch someone's eye and possibly receive an invitation.

At last I resigned myself to going it alone. I wandered around the grassy area outside of the junior high school building until I found an obscure bench and sat down to eat my lunch in solitude. I fought the feeling of humiliation that was slowly seeping over me at being the only kid who didn't belong. I finished quickly, the stress of the morning having diminished my appetite.

When small groups of students began trickling out of the cafeteria I studied them closely. The girls all seemed to be wearing the same kind of jeans and the same kind of tennis shoes. I would later learn that the brand of jeans was Levi and the style was the 501 Button Fly. The tennis shoes were made by Nike, discernible by a marking on the sides that looked like a large, sideways apostrophe. I was mystified by the similarity of dress. How had they all known what to wear? Who had decided and how had she informed the rest of the seventh-grade girls?

The more I observed, the more self-conscious I became about my own attire. I looked down at the jeans I was wearing. I had purchased them at J.C. Penney the year before with my paper-route money. When putting them on that morning for the first time in several months, I realized to my great disappointment, that my legs had gotten longer over the summer. My pant legs hovered a good two inches above the tops of my shoes. When I tried on a second pair, the only other pair I owned, I found them to be every bit as short. Ransacking my closet for other options, I found little to choose from other than dresses, which had been a staple of my sixth-grade wardrobe. I decided the jeans were the lesser of the two evils.

As I sat watching the crowds of students, I knew I needed to buy some new clothes if I was going to fit in. Unfortunately, the savings from my paper route had dried up. I chastised myself for wasting it on silly trinkets during our vacation earlier that summer. The truth of the matter was I wasn't really a great saver to begin with. The knowledge that another payday was always just a week away had me spending freely on books, records, and candy. I also bought gifts for my brothers on their birthdays, for everyone at Christmas and my mom for Mother's Day. I bought my own clothes, but that had never been my first priority. I should have saved more. I started thinking about another paper route. The residents of Cody had to enjoy reading the news too, didn't they?

I had completely lost myself in thoughts of how I could earn some money when a group of girls walked directly in front of me. They were talking quietly, their focus consumed by whatever they were discussing. My mood sank further as I noticed the hairstyle that was consistent among the four of them. Although the overall length varied, each of them wore it parted down the middle and feathered on the sides. I felt a split second of satisfaction. I had known about that trend, I had even gotten my hair cut that way. *But he wouldn't have it.* I felt my frustration beginning to build.

I still longed sometimes for the waist-length mane I had worn until the middle of my kindergarten year. My mother sometimes showed me the braid that had been cut from my hair and that she had retained as a keepsake. Its qualities, sandy blonde in color and silky in texture, were far superior in my view to what grew in its place. On the heels of a two-week bout of chicken pox and impetigo, and the twice-daily shampoos necessary to rid me of infection, my mother had decided a shorter cut would be much easier. To my disappointment my hair grew out much darker and wavier than the braid she cut off before my sixth birthday. Coercing my cowlick-ridden locks into any type of smooth and trained style was a near impossibility.

My mother had attended cosmetology school before she and my father divorced the second time, and possessed adequate skills to trim both my brothers' and my hair. Salon visits were expensive, and our current family budget didn't allow for such luxuries. My mother recognized that I was now at an age where my appearance was becoming more important to me, and knowing that her expertise couldn't compare with someone who practiced his or her craft every day, she offered to take me to a salon before I started seventh-grade.

I was thrilled, spending the week before my appointment thumbing through magazines and focusing intently on TV shows and commercials, seeking the perfect new look for myself. The stylist, Vivienne, was herself quite trendy-looking. She wore heavy but flattering make-up, including bright red lipstick and fake eyelashes that fluttered up and down like butterfly wings. Her reddish-brown hair was so thick and tightly curled it appeared to be suspended in mid-air. She wore denim jeans and a matching jacket with her high heels. She smiled, her red lips revealing a full set of perfectly straight white teeth.

At the onset of my appointment she immediately engaged me in a discussion about what I wanted in a hairstyle. I unfolded the magazine photos I had brought along with me, one of which was of Farrah Fawcett, and showed them to her. She nodded appreciatively as she gently raked her fingers through my shoulder length hair, assessing its fit for the style, telling me that all the girls my age were asking for the "Farrah Fawcett."

I beamed from ear to ear as I looked in the mirror at the finished product. I absolutely loved it! She had masterfully blended my bangs into each side of the middle part of my hair, the sides feathering beautifully, if not perfectly. She explained that the fullness of my hair and its natural wave were perfect for this style. I would just need to use a blow dryer and brush to counteract the cowlicks and to train my hair to part in the middle. She went on to say that my hair would look even more like the picture after my bangs grew out more.

I was so thrilled with my transformation I couldn't imagine it looking any better. My mother smiled when I met her in the waiting area and echoed my reaction. She told me that the new cut looked really good and flattered my features. I practically floated to the car, smiling all the way home and stealing glances of my reflection in the outside rear-view mirror. This was just the boost I needed. I could walk into seventh-grade with complete confidence!

Chapter 35

Defeated

My happiness was sapped the moment I walked through the door and Glen summoned me to his recliner. I didn't care what he thought, I told myself as he diverted his focus from his magazine and began to study me closely. *Nothing could make me feel bad right now, not even him.* I reveled in a rare moment of unrelenting optimism, the smile still illuminating my face. I watched as the corners of his mouth curled up and that smug expression settled across his face, and then he burst into one of his artificially loud belly laughs.

"You look ridiculous," he said. "Did you look in the mirror before you left?"

Turning to my mother he said, "You let her leave that way? The middle part in her hair makes her nose look huge. And you *paid* for this?"

I swallowed hard in an effort to maintain my composure.

Don't let him ruin this.

Don't give in.

Don't let him make you cry.

He stood up and began circling me, taking in the view from all angles. He was so intent on his inspection he hadn't thought to put down the magazine. I felt the pages brushing my arm as he stepped around me.

"Take her back," he said, looking at my mother.

"Take her back there and tell them to fix it," he said, The all-too-familiar expression of contempt had now replaced his former look of smug amusement.

No.

Please no!

I whipped around to look at my mother. I desperately needed her to stand up for me this time. I couldn't bear the thought of giving up the boost of self-esteem that my new hairstyle had bestowed upon me.

Why did he care? What difference did my hair make to him, dammit! But I knew why he cared. He saw my happiness and the air of self-confidence I had been unable to contain when I walked through the door. I needed to be kept in my place, to continue to believe that I wasn't worthy of acceptance, otherwise he would lose all control over me. And he wasn't about to let that happen.

It was no surprise when my mother conceded. The tears streamed down my cheeks as she drove me back to the salon in silence. I detested him, despised him, loathed him. On and on I went, sifting through every verb my mind could conjure up to describe the intense hatred I felt for him. I resurrected my fantasy that quickly began to evolve from kicking him, to bashing his face with my fists. Even these thoughts gave me no comfort.

The strong chemical scent of permanent wave solution assaulted my nostrils as we walked through the door. In the euphoria of my earlier visit I hadn't even noticed the stench that was now nearly gagging me. I willed myself to get a grip on my emotions, but the freshness of the wound rendered me incapable of sustaining my composure. I embarrassed myself by crying as I watched strand upon strand fall to the floor, claiming the bits of trimmed hair were irritating my eyes.

It's just hair. You're being dramatic. Calm down.

And yet I couldn't shake the feelings of sadness and defeat that accompanied each snip. Vivienne stole glances at me through the cage of lashes that rimmed her eyes, her silent pity tearing a hole in my heart.

It was so unfair that a complete stranger could feel my pain and yet my own mother was powerless to alleviate it. I wanted to go live with Vivienne, with anyone who would have me, for God's sake. I bid a final, silent goodbye to the bits of myself that littered the floor before I weakly thanked Vivienne and left with my mother.

My first day of seventh-grade ended in similar defeat. My subjects and teachers were fine, but the learning element of school was low on my list of priorities. On that first day of school I discovered one more thing I had taken for granted -- friends and a sense of belonging. Never in my life had I lacked for someone to sit with at lunchtime. I had even enjoyed occasional satisfaction that accompanied being picked first for softball or relay teams in PE -- despite the fact that I lacked even a shred athletic talent. I had never once questioned whether I was liked by my classmates.

Later that night before getting into bed, I stared at myself in the mirror, probing its reflection, and trying to see it as if it were unfamiliar to me, as it I were seeing myself for the first time. I then added one more problem to my list of woes. I wasn't pretty. Not at all. When had that changed, I wondered?

The image staring back at me had developed a big nose at some point. My hair, thanks to Glen, had been returned to a shorter version of its former wavy, shapeless, and unflattering state. The clusters of pimples and angry red marks littering my complexion provided ample evidence of the fully formed case of acne I had already been battling for a year. My teeth were crooked, the two in the front crossing on top of each other. My eyes and lashes served as the source of the compliments I had garnered over the years. I agreed that they were OK, even nice, but not enough to offset my long list of negatives.

No, I decided, the girl staring at me from my mirror was nothing like the girls I had seen that day. Girls with long, lustrous hair, white toothy smiles, cute little noses and smooth complexions. Some even boasted breasts -- real ones -- not just "bee stings", the term my Gramma had often used to refer to the barely noticeable bumps on my chest, but fully formed boobs that required a real bra.

The weeks stretched into months with little change. If anything, my predicament worsened. I reeked of insecurity and the circling seventh-grade sharks could smell blood and wasted no time going for the kill. That first week I was called out on my 'high-water pants" by a group of snickering and pointing girls, outfitted in their 501s. My big nose became the focus and major source of entertainment for a group of boys who rode my bus. Every morning as I made my way down the aisle to my seat, the Kempton brothers would yell at me as I passed, "Hey, is that a spider skiing down your nose?" I wasn't sure what bothered me more, the knock on my appearance or the stupidity of the insult. *Spiders don't ski.* I marveled at how everyone within earshot got such a bang out of this stupid joke.

I began to realize that these kids, the snickering bystanders as I came to know them, had identified an important survival technique, one that kept them far from the fire that seemed to be constantly lit beneath my rear end. The fear that they themselves might next be singled out prompted the snickering bystanders to join the gibing in an effort to keep the focus on the current victim and firmly off of themselves.

Just when I felt that things couldn't get any worse, tiny filaments of a lifeline began to appear. After a few months, the cumulative acts of correcting a partner's paper in math, shyly joining in the conversation at my art table, and commiserating with the other non-athletes in PE, began to affect a shift in my woeful universe. A nod here, a wave there, and being included in an occasional spontaneous gossip session in the hallway between classes – all seemingly inconsequential gestures– did wonders to ease my suffering, even if only for brief moments.

I was still far from being able to boast true friendships and the existence of a flourishing social life, but flashes of hope glimmered on the horizon. I longed to cultivate these budding relationships, but the restrictions Glen imposed made that a near impossibility. His belief that allowing Kirk and me to interact with other teenagers would only lead us into temptation in the forms of drinking, sex, and drugs, resulted in an obsessive motivation within him to account for our every move.

I might have succeeded in convincing him to allow me to invite a friend over, but I had no desire to expose a would-be friend to my stepfather. There was no doubt in my mind that exposing someone I hoped to impress to Glen's humorless jokes, unfiltered criticisms, and relentless probing questions would be a deal-breaker. I knew that my best bet -- my only bet-- was to do all that I could during school hours to transform my few acquaintances into something more enduring. Mondays were torturous. The kids who had gone to Friday night's game would huddle together before the start of each class and commence reliving the highlights of the evening. Reports were shared and validated as to who was going with whom as a result of the romantic interactions that transpired.

Other newsworthy reports focused on the movie that everyone seemed to have seen on Saturday night. I busied myself at my desk, pretending not to hear, but hanging on every word, crafting scenes in my mind that included me in the antics and stories that they shared.

My brothers made the school adjustment far more successfully than I did. Jay, having just entered the first-grade, was experiencing the delights of being the new kid that I had envisioned for myself before we moved. He was welcomed by his class, loved his teacher, and was not yet old enough to feel the social sting of Glen's obsessive control.

Kirk, although held to the same restrictions as I, seemed to acclimate easily. Despite his introverted personality, my brother exuded confidence. The expression on his face conveyed the combined messages that one, he wasn't one to back down, and two, he didn't give a crap what anyone else thought about him. His participation in sports, and the fact that he outsized every kid in his grade and most in the grade above him, gave him an edge that I didn't have. The hours spent at football and wrestling practices provided him with a forum for free interaction that couldn't be carried out in the classroom. It provided a means of excelling beyond academics, one that was universally appreciated. Kirk didn't have to talk. People talked to him. He had something they coveted: athletic success.

As I contemplated my own predicament and the lack of opportunities that existed for building friendships, I considered taking up a sport. Granted, I not only lacked athletic talent, I didn't even like sports. My physical prowess was limited to activities like riding my bike and playing badminton and croquet. I had always come in last in my grade-school field day competitions and I had never once passed the Presidential Physical Fitness Test. My talent was firmly rooted in the academic arena. At least I could differentiate myself in a positive way on this basis.

Unfortunately, being smart was not something that garnered friendships or status in the cutthroat world of junior high school. My mother's height, at just under 6-feet, represented an anomaly for a female of her era. She had told me that she played basketball as a girl and at some point in my younger life I had made the connection between being tall and playing basketball. I was already 5-feet-6 and towered over most of the boys in my grade (another notch in my belt of disgrace). As I began to consider the merits of playing a sport, basketball became the obvious choice. Joining the team would grant me an extra hour of access each day to a subset of seventh-grade girls. The additional opportunity that the handful of away-games requiring lengthy bus rides provided, completed my recipe for building a social network.

I talked to my mother first, and as I expected she did not encourage me, saying that Glen would probably not go for it. I wasn't surprised at her reaction. Unlike my brother, I had hardly established myself as a sports enthusiast. Glen would easily suspect that my motivation had more to do with socializing than learning the game of basketball. I persisted, arguing that Kirk was allowed, why not me? Eventually I wore her down and she somehow persuaded Glen to let me go out for basketball.

He conditioned his approval on the requirement that I take full responsibility for every aspect of my commitment to the sport. I could not expect either he or my mother to pick me up after practice. This meant that I would be walking home in some of the coldest weather of the year and that on some nights it would be dark by the time I reached the house, but I didn't care. The gift of even this tiny morsel of freedom, and the opportunities it presented, was worth the nearly mile-long walk in any weather.

It began gloriously. My coach, Miss Samuel, was sweet and encouraging. She never yelled or became angry, even if we missed a shot or fouled during scrimmages. I was far from passionate about my new sport, but I was determined to be successful. My lack of speed and overall poor coordination made a challenge of grasping a lay-up and pretty much every other aspect of the sport. But the girls were nice to me, making me at last feel like I was beginning to fit in.

Chapter 36

Dignity

One afternoon at practice we were performing free-throw drills. This involved dribbling to the line from center court, and then taking five successive shots. As each of us took our turn the rest of the team observed from the bleachers. This should have been an unnerving exercise for me, given my lack of talent, but the supportive environment at practices had shifted my focus away from my athletic shortcomings. I found myself putting my all into every practice. I was able to concentrate fully on the drill without any self-consciousness. Unfortunately, this added focus had done little so far to improve my ability to sink the ball. I took my first shot and missed. The ball bounced off the rim on my second attempt. As I dribbled and aimed, preparing to make my third shot, Misty Marvin, a very popular and outgoing girl, yelled to me from the bench, affecting a drum roll on the bench in front of her "You're gonnaaaaaaaaa MISS!"

Laughter erupted from the sidelines. I felt the heat rising in my face as I said a silent prayer that my involuntary reaction would cease before I turned beet red and alerted everyone in the room to my embarrassment. I tried to ignore Misty as I took yet another shot which to my great dismay didn't even come close to the basket. Meanwhile, the snickering bystander phenomenon afflicted the entire crowd on the sidelines and the volume of laughter ratcheted to a new high, scattering my already rattled concentration.

The whole scene lasted less than two minutes but it felt like an hour. I had the sensation of every bleacher seat in the gym being filled with laughing, pointing spectators, all yelling for me to miss, when in fact there were only about 20 seats occupied, all of them by my teammates. This was one of those moments when a witty or flippant response would have been a Godsend. Had I possessed even an ounce of confidence I could have laughed it off and caught Misty off guard by throwing the ball at her face, telling her to "think fast," secretly hoping she wouldn't be able to dodge it in time to avoid having the ball wipe the stupid smirk off her face. Standing up to Misty represented the equivalent of swimming in the Olympics. My level of conditioning barely permitted me to tread water. I dismissed my brief urge to stand up to her, knowing that such an act stretched beyond the boundaries of my capabilities.

At that moment I was driven by an almost primal need to remove myself from the stage upon which I stood. It was the only solution I could come up with to get everyone's attention off me. I stared at the net before me, trying to refocus, but I couldn't push the vision of the humiliating sideline circus I envisioned from my mind. If I could just make this last shot I would vindicate myself. I felt the tears welling, clotting in my throat as if someone had stuffed a gag in there. I had to make a split-second decision. I could either take the final shot and risk bursting into tears in front of the whole team -- or pack it in. Accepting the reality that I could no longer hold my composure, I chose the latter.

I bounced the basketball as hard as I could onto the court in front of me and made a run for the locker room, desperately hoping to get there before the dam in my throat burst and gave way to full-on sobbing. Was it not enough that she was popular, that she could do and say anything she wanted and the whole school would follow her? Was it not enough that I lived a life of virtual invisibility, that she had never said two words to me in the three months I had shared her grade? Did she also have to humiliate me in front of the whole team that had become my last hope for salvaging my seventh-grade year?

Of course she did. I had come to understand the unwritten rules that governed teenage abuse and how it always found a path to those who believed they were most deserving of it. People like me. She had pegged me to be exactly what I was. A loser. I was crying uncontrollably by the time Coach Samuel entered the locker room.

"Hey, hey, hey now," she said, sitting next to me on the bench in front of my locker, "don't let that get to you. I talked to Misty. She didn't mean to hurt your feelings. She was joking. She and her friends have a way of ribbing each other, but they all know it's just in fun. I explained to her that those sorts of comments are OK with her close friends who understand that it's in fun, but that others can be really hurt by it."

She paused, patting my knee, then went on, "Those girls, your teammates, really support you."

I tried to quiet the gasping sobs that escaped from my throat, shielding my face from her to hide my convulsing, snotty, tear-soaked face. I hated myself for allowing Misty to hurt my feelings. My hierarchy placed being pitied several rungs below being made fun of.

I endured the ribbing on the bus each morning by ignoring it, averting my gaze and pretending not to hear the taunts while I immersed myself in a book. I refused to give my tormentors the satisfaction of knowing how much they hurt me. Dignity was all I had left. But today, I had lost that too. I allowed Misty to highlight in front of my entire team just how deserving of sympathy I was.

"You are at a tough age. Kids can be so mean to one another. I know it's hard but try to shake it off."

After another few minutes of uninterrupted crying on my part she stood next to me, putting her arm around my shoulder and asked quietly, "Is everything else OK? Is there something else bothering you?" She paused briefly and then asked, "Is everything OK at home?"

"Oh yes," I wanted to say, "oh HELL yes there's something else bothering me, and yes, it has everything to do with my home! In fact, I can't think of a single fucking thing that *isn't* wrong at home right now. My stepfather is a sadistic, perverted son-of-a-bitch who makes my six-year-old brother and I rub his smelly feet at night. My mother is nice and loves me and all, but he has control of her, too. She can't help me. I can't take a bath without worrying that he will pick the lock, so he can watch me and masturbate in front of me. He's insanely jealous of my 14-year-old brother who is now taller than him and who he is constantly trying to provoke into a fist fight. Just a few weeks ago my six-year-old brother had to be rushed to the ER because Glen "accidentally" split his head open with a plastic rowboat oar. Oh God, yes," I wanted to scream, *"there is most definitely something wrong at home!"*

But instead, getting my tears somewhat in check, I turned to her and said, "No, nothing is going on at home. It has just been hard adjusting to this new school and moving so far away from my old home and my old friends."

I mustered a half smile and she hugged me a little tighter.

"You can come talk to me any time about anything. Don't worry about what Misty or anyone else thinks. You are a sweet girl," Coach Samuel eyed me closely.

I gathered up my things, wanting to be long gone before the team finished practice and made its way into the locker room. I couldn't bear the thought of Misty apologizing, and even more,

I couldn't bear the thought of her not. As I made my way out the door I thought about how cruel life could be.

In spite of the misery I felt, I had to admit that Coach Samuel's concern for me felt nice. I was immediately reminded of Vivienne. For the second time in a three-month span, two outsiders -- virtual strangers to my life -- had seemed to sense the sadness that pervaded my existence. How had they known? I had no idea. As much as I was comforted by the thought of someone, anyone, taking up for me, I was bitterly disappointed by the reality that rendered both of my Good Samaritans powerless to help me, even if I were brave enough to tell them the truth. It wasn't fair.

On my walk home that night I thought about Glen and how much I hated him. Why couldn't my mother see it? She always talked about how we didn't have money. Glen had a job, but somehow, we were still struggling. Funny how we were "struggling" but there was a brand-new Norton motorcycle in the garage. And how during one of our shopping recent trips to Billings, my mother, brothers and myself had sat in the car for hours while he played poker in some seedy hotel room. Strange indeed, how we had no money. I missed our house in Ohio and thought about all of the happy memories that I associated with it. The big yard, the endless, quiet streets where we rode our bikes. And now we lived in a house so tiny it couldn't hold our furniture. There was no yard to speak of. We lived across the street from a cemetery, for God's sake.

"Make sure that you can support yourself," my mother would advise me, "don't ever put yourself in a situation where you have to rely on a man."

It was at times like these, moments when I felt I had reached a new and unimaginable low point, that I would promise myself that no matter what it took, I would beat that son-of-a-bitch. I routinely fantasized about physically hurting him, but the satisfaction that these thoughts offered was fleeting. I began to find much greater fulfillment in devising mental images of my own future. I was determined to succeed. I would go to college, and afterward, I would land a high-paying job in a big city far, far away from him. I would live in a beautifully furnished high-rise apartment with a great view. I would wear nice clothes, cut my hair however I liked, and lead a busy and fulfilling social life. I would go where I wanted, when I wanted.

I grudgingly returned my thoughts to the present as I crossed the front yard and made my way to the front door. Back to reality.

Chapter 37

Jennie

My father played the hand he was dealt. He undoubtedly knew
that any appeal he made to the court regarding the fact that his
children had been taken 1,500 miles away without so much
as a heads-up would fall on deaf ears. He made the best of the
situation. He established a pattern of calling us every Sunday
night. He vowed to arrange visits home for us every Christmas
and in the summer. At this point my brothers and I were more
than happy to readmit him into our lives.

I welcomed both the easing of the guilt I had felt for
so long, and the hope that hearing my father's voice every
Sunday night offered. Those short conversations provided a
connection, remote as it was, to the world from which I had
come. A world that now felt so far away I often wondered if
it had really existed. Glen's rants about our father tapered off.
The satisfaction that Glen accrued from stealing my father's
children combined with the physical distance that now existed
between them served to neutralize Glen's thirst for the conflict.

Our first trip to visit our father had us busting at the
seams with excitement. We were going to fly on an airplane,
something we had never done before, and we were going to
meet his girlfriend, Jennie, whom we had only talked with
on the phone. We knew from our Sunday conversations that

he and Jennie were now living together. They had met before we moved to Wyoming. Her voice came across sunny and happy through the long-distance line. She said she was looking forward to meeting us. I had high hopes.

The baggage-claim area came into view as the escalator descended. At first I could only see the feet of the people comprising the crowd that had gathered to greet our flight. As legs and then torsos, and eventually faces, came into view, I scanned the throng anxiously looking for my father.

At last he came into view. Several years had passed, but he looked exactly as I remembered him. He was smiling, his arms crossed in front of him. The petite woman standing next to him wore glasses and a huge smile. Her brown hair fell below her shoulders. Seemingly unable to contain her enthusiasm, her arm bent upward at the elbow and waved to us. I ran toward them, reaching my father first. I fell into him, realizing in that instant how happy I was to see him. Next, I turned to Jennie. She bent down and wrapped her arms around me, telling me all the while how glad she was that we came to visit. I pulled away and waited patiently while she repeated the exercise with each of my brothers.

The smile never left her face. She asked how our flight was. I relayed all the details of what I had to drink (a Coke), where we sat, how empty the plane was and how exciting it was to fly on an airplane for the very first time. She listened intently, interjecting several reinforcing, "ohs," and, "uh-huhs," before I finished. She conveyed an air of sincerity and approachability that made me feel like I had known her my entire life.

As we walked to the car with our luggage, I blabbered away about school, my favorite subjects and whatever other mundane details of my life happened to surface. She listened intently, and when I finally came up for air she told me that my father had told her so much about me, how I did so well in school and my love of reading. She said she was so happy to meet me at last and looked forward to getting to know my brothers and me over the next week. She was perfect. There was not a single thing more she could have done or said to endear herself to me in that moment.

Jennie outlined our itinerary while my father drove us from the airport. We were going to open our Christmas gifts when we got to Dad's house. Tomorrow we would relax, the day after we would see our Gramma Millie and our cousins, and one day would be dedicated to a movie and dinner out. We could each choose something we wanted to do during the week and it would be added to our schedule. The remainder of our time would be spent hanging out at home.

My father lived in a trailer house on the edge of his best friend, Dave's, property. It was smaller than our house in Cody. My brothers and I slept between two bunk beds in the second bedroom and the living room couch. It was far from glamorous. Over the course of the next few decades, my father went on to build three beautiful and spacious homes that aesthically put the trailer to shame. But my memories of that time with Dad and Jennie are some of the very best of my childhood. It wasn't just what we did, it was how it felt to be with them. The atmosphere of their home was cheerful and lighthearted. Their happiness trickled over us like a gentle spring rain. Our pastimes of watching TV, playing cards and visiting my Gramma were somehow elevated to a higher level of enjoyment.

Jennie took me to the salon where she worked and preformed what I came to regard as her own brand of magic on me. She trimmed my hair, styled it and taught me how to harness my natural waves. I was careful to steer her away from a middle part lest I be subjected to another correction when I returned home. She gave me a brush and styling mousse to take with me so that I could duplicate the effect when I got back home.

As I sat waiting for her to finish up with another client I watched her closely. From her appearance to her bubbly and warm personality, she embodied everything I wanted to be. She chatted away effortlessly with her clients, who nearly always hugged her when they left. Everyone loved her for the same reasons I did. She was kind and selfless, you only had to spend five minutes with her to feel that she cared about you. And the best part was that she genuinely did care.

Jennie picked up on my admiration of her wardrobe and responded by ensuring that my Christmas and birthday gifts comprised clothes and shoes. She sent me big bottles of my favorite shampoo and conditioner, her packages always containing a hand-written card with some cheerful message. She baked the most wonderful chocolate-chip cookies and knew how to cook a pot roast that actually tasted good. She put her special touch on everything she did, from filling our Christmas stockings with oranges and candy, to baking a double batch of her sugary cutouts, frosted and beautifully decorated, for us every Christmas. At last, a bright spot had appeared in our lives. When they married two years after our move, the only thing that could have made me happier was to have been there to celebrate with them.

The one and only downside of our visits was the immense letdown that came after returning to Cody. A feeling somewhere between sadness and loss settled over me as I walked through the door of our cemetery house. Each time I came home I vowed to imprint all the happy times in the forefront of my mind. But the passage of time always seemed to confound my plans. School, my part-time job, and warding off the angry gloom that pervaded our house left little space for the frivolous memories that occupied a mere two weeks each year.

In spite of the comfort I felt with Jennie and my father, I couldn't fathom telling them about my life in Cody. The conflict between my father and Glen was bigger than life to me. I envisioned nothing less than a shootout between the two of them if I ever let slip even a sliver of the real story that was playing in the theatre of our Cody home. My father had been punished enough. I didn't want to provoke him, and I certainly didn't want to jeopardize my two weeks of heaven each year.

Chapter 38

The Bribe

The loneliness of my first year in Cody and the unexpected challenges that accompanied the establishment of friendships humbled me. Thankfully, the bonds I forged in grade school remained strong. I kept in touch with a handful of my friends from Grand Rapids, corresponding with them regularly. The act of reading and returning the letters I received served to remind me of another time and place when I was accepted. I regarded these connections as the only remaining outlet for my true feelings. These people had known me since the birth of my social self -- and they still loved me. I had no reason to guard myself or the topics that I shared with them. Or so I thought.

My innocent presumption changed drastically one day when Glen, having intercepted one of my letters before my mother mailed it, proceeded to read it out loud in front of my entire family. In it I had described in great detail the physical attributes of several boys upon whom I had crushes. I went on to fabricate a story about how one of them really liked me too, and that I expected we would be to the stage of kissing soon.

Glen laughed his head off at my embellishment. He, like my entire seventh-grade class, knew that I possessed no self-confidence and lacked all of the necessary attributes to attract a boyfriend, let alone kiss one. He delighted in my humiliation. That would teach me, he said, to exaggerate to such a degree and to pretend that I was something that I clearly wasn't. And, he added with a smug look, I was far too young to be thinking about kissing boys. Did I want to grow up to be a whore? In yet another teachable moment, I learned from Glen that everything, every shred of myself must be hidden in order to be kept safe.

I used the money I earned working at the Cody Cafeteria over the summer to upgrade my wardrobe before the start of the eighth grade. The aesthetic enhancement wasn't sufficient to catapult me to popularity, but it eliminated clothing from the list of things that made me self-conscious. When the restaurant closed for the season I was able to find another part-time job at Skip's Drive In. Having sworn off sports for good, I decided I might as well work after school. It was the only outside activity that I was permitted to engage in, and the year-round income stream was something I had missed since giving up my paper route.

Soon after I started at Skip's I met Chris. He was already in the ninth-grade, one year ahead of me, and was on the swim team. He had blond hair and a stocky build and was most definitely cute. He seemed to be friends with everyone who worked at Skip's. He and I both worked in the kitchen. I made milkshakes and fulfilled soft drink and food orders for the car hops. Chris was a fry cook. He and the other cooks were always goofing around and poking fun at one another. Their practical jokes and good-natured banter were infectious. I found myself stealing glances at him, hoping he would look my way.

I began finding excuses to go into the walk-in cooler when he was inside replenishing his supply of frozen fries. He always paid attention to me. My self-consciousness seemed to melt away in his presence. Our flirtation turned to romance when he asked me to "go with him," My affirmative response elevated our status officially to the level of boyfriend and girlfriend.

Our mutual infatuation infected us with an insatiable desire to be together. We took advantage of every opportunity, meeting in between classes at school and stealing a few extra minutes together after a shift at Skip's. Eventually I began sneaking telephone calls with him at night, carefully choosing times when I knew Glen was engrossed in a TV program or the current issue of *Playboy*. Before classes started each day I would sneak into the natatorium and watch him practice. Beholding his athletic prowess filled me with a giddy sense of pride. I couldn't believe that he was my boyfriend.

I knew better than to ask to go on a date with him or meet him at a football game, but I was smitten with young love. Kids at school were already jockeying for dates to the upcoming dance. The image of Chris and me slow dancing planted itself in my mind and began putting down roots. Despite the strict boundaries that governed my life, I could not shake the longing I felt to go to the dance with Chris. I had yet to be permitted to attend a social gathering with friends, but my newfound infatuation created an optimism within me that made me believe anything was possible. *It wouldn't hurt to ask, would it?*

I decided to broach the topic with Glen one night while I worked on his feet. I despised rubbing his feet. When he summoned me for the task I ran through a well-rehearsed list of excuses as to why I could not possibly spend the time. These were centered around homework or a school project. I found myself lingering in the kitchen, looking for more dishes to wash in order to avoid being recruited for the loathsome task. The problem was, if I were to be excused, the deed would fall to Jay. As much as I loved getting out of it, I hated knowing that my little brother was left to pick up my slack. There were also plenty of times when Jay and I were simultaneously commandeered to massage his fat sweaty feet. It was just one of the many inappropriate indulgences that Glen had convinced himself was acceptable. On this particular night I didn't resist his request for a foot rub. I plopped myself onto the floor at the end of his recliner, peeled his damp white socks off and went to work. I squeezed hard, pushing my thumb into the fleshy and innermost part of his foot. When my hands started cramping I kept going, believing I was priming him for approval of the proposal I was about to make. He remained engrossed in his magazine, seeming indifferent to what I deemed to be a premier foot massage. I worked diligently and waited patiently for some affirmation that I was doing a good job. That would be my cue to make the ask. My focus on the task at hand thankfully dulled my senses. I barely noticed the odor of his feet, or their clammy stickiness. or felt the need to counter my typical obsessive desire to run into the bathroom and wash my hands before I finished.

Finally, I became impatient, the tension surrounding my need for an answer getting the best of me, and I blurted out, "I want to go to the eighth-grade dance."

At first he seemed not to hear me, so I repeated my request. Without looking up from his magazine, he said, "We'll see."

I sat in stunned silence. Had I heard him right? I watched his face a moment longer and saw that he was still consumed by whatever article he was reading in his magazine. His head nodded almost imperceptibly, even as his eyes remained firmly fixed on the page before him.

I was shocked and thrilled at the same time. I had never gotten this far before. I worked his feet until he dismissed me. After washing my hands extra thoroughly, I practically sprinted down the hall to my bedroom. In spite of my excitement, I still feared he would call me back and tell me that he had changed his mind.

Long after I got into bed, I imagined Chris and me at the dance. He would look at me with that smile of his. We would hold hands, maybe even kiss. I had no idea when Glen would deliver his final answer. I was sustained by the fact that, at least for now, he hadn't said no. I wanted to believe it was possible.

At last, I gave into my fatigue and drifted into a hopeful sleep, only to be awakened a few hours later.

It was Glen.

I knew the sounds he made, the click of the door opening as he turned the knob slowly, the rustling of air as it swished past his fat body. I was immediately and fully awake, but I faked sleep. While I couldn't see him, I knew that having just come from his own bed, the one he shared with my mother, he would be wearing nothing more than his white briefs and a t-shirt. The image this created in my mind made me want to vomit.

I felt his weight as he sat on the edge of my bed. He put his hand on my shoulder and shook me. I continued my fake slumber. He shook me again, this time more vigorously.

"Come on, I know you're awake. I want to talk to you."

I knew all too well how this scene would end if I gave him an inch of opportunity. I scooted to the far side of my bed, the one that butted up to the wall. I had trained myself to awaken at even the slightest noise and had come to despise the sound of his entry into my room, him shaking me, whispering in a voice I never heard him use any other time than when he wanted to act out his sick, perverted fantasies on me.

I felt my anger rising as he shook me the third time.

"Get away from me," I demanded, my back facing him.

"Oh, come on," he said, "I just want to talk to you."

He moved closer. I instinctively stiffened and pushed myself tighter against the wall.

"So, you want to go to this dance?"

Even before the next words came out of his mouth I began to comprehend where he was going. My pulse quickened, a sick feeling growing in my stomach. I should have known better than to expect anything good from him. I had allowed my crush on Chris to cloud my judgment, my feelings for him to make me weak, believing that good was possible, even from Glen.

"I know you have a boyfriend now," he said. "Your mother told me she has heard you on the phone with him."

My heart sank. Why had she told him? Was there nothing that could be kept from him? My hurt and irritation gave way to curiosity. If he knew about it why hadn't he tried to catch me and punish me?

"And you're going to want to have sex with him before too long."

What?

"What? No, I'm not! You're disgusting," I whisper-shouted at him, my back still facing him.

"Maybe not now, but before long you will. I know how these things work. I have a lot of experience. Sometimes the first time isn't so great for the girl. Most young guys don't know what they're doing or how to please a girl. All I'm saying is that you should let me show you how. Before you decide to do it with him. That way you will know what to do when the time comes."

He paused briefly.

"And if you let me have sex with you, I will let you go to the dance."

I could barely control the combination of nausea and rage rising within me. Suddenly, my fear of him became secondary to my fear of the disgusting proposal he had just made.

First of all, I hadn't even contemplated the notion of having sex with Chris. Second, to place in the same category what Glen did to me, what I endured from him, and the physical interaction with someone I truly cared for, was incomprehensible.

The realization that he believed such an idea was acceptable, and that I would agree to it created a new terror in me.

I decided right then and there that I would die first, die at his hands if necessary, but I wouldn't go down without a fight. I would claw his eyes, kick his balls, and punch him with my fists. I would make a weapon to defend myself against him and stash it underneath my bed. A stick, a hammer, or maybe a cast iron skillet from our kitchen. So help me, I would come up with something I could use on him.

"Get out of here and leave me alone or I'm going to scream," I said in the most even, forceful and controlled voice I could muster.

"Well, if you do that you definitely won't be going to any dances. Ever," he responded.

"I don't care. I hate you. You make me sick. You will never touch me again and the only way you will ever have sex with me is if you kill me trying. Now get the fuck away from me," I said, surprising myself with the conviction in my voice.

"OK, calm down," he said, somehow finding a soothing quiet tone. "I was just trying to find a compromise that would give both of us something that we want."

"And I am telling you to get out of my room right now or I am going to go get Mom," I said, my back still facing him.

"OK, suit yourself," he said, rolling away from me at last.

"Just remember, you will be here when all of the other kids are having fun at that dance. And don't think you are ever going to go anywhere with your pussy boyfriend. Tell him he is not allowed here and not to ever call you again. You can see him at work, but that's it. If I find out about anything funny between the two of you, you won't be working there anymore."

As he left, closing my door behind him, I thought about how much I had wanted to go to that dance 20 minutes ago. How masterful he was at taking something that represented happiness, fun and joy, and turning it into something disgusting and perverted. I knew I wasn't going to go to the dance, and not only did I not care, I no longer wanted to go. He had ruined it, making the idea seem dirty and me feel violated in a whole new way.

But that is what he always did. He infected everything beautiful with his ugliness. That is why our lives were so dark and lonely. Nothing beautiful or happy could survive around him. He was like a cancer that turned perfectly healthy functioning bodies into sick, crippled messes.

I had tried for the past four years to avoid being alone with him. Our house was so tiny it seemed impossible to think that he could leave his own bed and come to mine completely unnoticed. But I knew my mother was a heavy sleeper, she also often worked in the evenings, giving him another window of opportunity. I always locked the bathroom door, but if he wanted to come in the lock was easy enough for him to pick.

There would often be long stretches of time between his offenses, enough to permit me to believe he had curbed his unseemly urges. But there was no motivation to make him stop. There was no one to hold him in check. He was keeper of the keys to the kingdom known as our house. He could do as he pleased. Go where he wanted. And not a single one of the four of us, not even my mother, presented an impediment to him.

I asked myself many times, why?

Why didn't I protect myself that very first time? Run from my room back to the safety of the living room where my mother sat? Part of it was the incomprehensibility of what was happening. A grown man touching a nine-year old girl that way was something I never contemplated. But I knew what he was doing was wrong within the first few seconds.

Why didn't I fight back?

He was bigger than me. He took advantage of my innocence and lack of preparation for what he did to me. He was stronger than me, bigger than me.

But I could have screamed. I could have done something.

But I had done nothing. Just like he expected. When I didn't fight back or tell on him after that first time, we both knew I never would. He sniffed out my reluctance to engage in confrontation. My need to please. My unwillingness to make waves -- even to my own detriment. I had passed my first test with flying colors, allowing him to maneuver me into the judge's office. My vulnerability was ripe for the picking and he exploited it shamelessly. Add to my list of weaknesses stupidity and my belief in the idiotic notion that he would somehow grow a conscience and stop on his own accord.

I was determined to find the courage to do the thing he smugly believed I would never do. I would tell my mother. I tried to imagine how such an admission from a future child of mine would make me feel. I envisioned rage. It was hard to see past my own strong desire for her to vindicate me, but I knew the confession would also hurt her. Since the onset of his abuse, concern about her feelings had posed the biggest deterrent to telling her. He was her husband, for God's sake. I had convinced myself I had no right to take away her happiness. Even though I had pretty much always hated him I knew that she loved him. She had struggled mightily all those years with my dad and had found someone she could love. I couldn't understand what she saw in him, but I didn't have the heart to be the one to ruin it.

While I couldn't settle on the exact nature of her reaction, I was certain of one thing -- she wouldn't be able to look past something this big. She would have no choice but to demand a divorce. She had put up with a lot from him. She had given up her house and the ties to all things familiar in order to move halfway across the country with him and live in a rented house next to a cemetery. Glen's verbal tirades were typically directed at her children, but she was far from exempt. I had seen him shove her, slap her, and I had a strong suspicion that the time back in Ohio when we came home from school to find her eyes blackened, the culprit was not a fall down the stairs, as she had told us at the time.

Maybe she was so in love with him that she allowed herself to believe things would improve, that she could change him. Or maybe she chose to accept the trade-off of his abuse for the monogamy he self-righteously bragged about providing. Except he wasn't monogamous. The news that he was dallying with her daughter, I told myself, would be the final straw.

My resolve strengthened as the weeks passed. I rehearsed my conversation with my mother over and over in my mind. Depending on my mood and the events of the day, the outcome varied. One scenario had my mistreatment being rewarded with vindication, but another nagging version ended much less positively. As I worked through different iterations of the actual words I would use I struggled to find the combination that didn't make it sound like it was my fault.

What if she blamed me? What if she became angry that I didn't tell her sooner? Guilt seeped through me as I thought about what my confession would force her to do. As awful as life was with him she hadn't given even the slightest indication of wanting to divorce him. Instead, she seemed to be trying to make the best of it. Like the rest of us, she walked lightly, talked quietly and tried to stay under his radar in an effort to keep the peace. As the weeks passed by I knew I needed to buck up. The bomb I was preparing to drop was certain to bring war.

Chapter 39

Revelations

The eighth-grade dance came and went without my attendance.
I barely noticed. My attention was laser-focused on the
dilemma that faced me. I knew it was only a matter of time
until Glen found an opportunity to advance his agenda.

I continued to contrast the unpleasant consequences
of outing him with the even more unpleasant prospect of
maintaining my silence. I had enough experience with him
to know that telling on him would bring repercussions. I
envisioned outcomes ranging from physical retaliation to being
kicked out of the house. The more I pondered my situation the
less I cared about the ramifications. After countless debates
with myself I finally concluded that there was really no choice.
I had to tell my mother.

The next challenge I faced was how to do it. My initial
plan involved interjecting my revelation into one of our
conversations. The problem was my mother's work schedule
permitted us little time alone. And even if I succeeded in
commandeering a private moment with her, how would I
broach the topic? Pedophilia wasn't a subject that you could
just tag on to a conversation about school or the weather. The
anxiety I felt escalated with the passage of time. Weeks had

passed, and yet I had made no progress toward my goal. I needed to come up with a better plan.

In the midst of my struggle to come up with Plan B an inspiration appeared in the form of a magazine article I stumbled across at the dentist's office. My mother dropped me off and had gone to run an errand. I sifted through the stacks of magazines while I waited to be called, gravitating to the latest issue of *Cosmopolitan*, a known source of intelligence about all things pertaining to the independent, modern woman. I eagerly thumbed through the pages, trying to decide which article I wanted to focus on, knowing I would not have time to digest the entire issue before being called to the examination room.

My vision of living independently in my wonderful big-city apartment remained alive in my mind. It was what sustained me. Each time I imagined it I would color in more detail, picturing each piece of my off-white furniture, the toss pillows with purple tassels, the fluffy mauve comforter on my bed, and the tasteful beige curtains framing the window that overlooked a beautiful park with a duck pond set on the backdrop of a city skyline. I would also imagine myself dressed in stylish clothes, my hair cut in a contemporary and flattering style, and my fingernails neatly filed and polished a pale pink. I pictured myself hurrying out the door, briefcase in hand, sliding behind the wheel of my red convertible and heading to my high-rise office.

As my search for articles continued, I would stop and briefly linger over photos that mimicked the imagery of the apartment in my mind, or a hairstyle or outfit that fit the future picture of me that I envisioned. I became so engrossed in my fantasy that I rolled right past an article about sexual abuse. My hand froze in mid-air as I digested the title. I slowly paged backwards until I landed on the page that had caught my subconscious eye just moments before.

The article profiled a girl named Mary, whose uncle had sexually abused her over the course of her childhood -- right under the noses of both of her parents. My pulse rate quickened as I read on. She described how she felt guilty, like it was her fault, and how these feelings kept her from ever telling anyone. Later, as an adult, she experienced difficulty sustaining a relationship with boyfriend after boyfriend. Eventually the burden of her secret became too much, and she sought psychiatric help. Through her psychotherapy process, she discovered that the shame she experienced from what her uncle had done to her made her feel unworthy of being loved by her boyfriends. The article went on to describe how she overcame this through working with her psychiatrist. Mary ended by saying how important it is for anyone experiencing sexual abuse to tell a trusted family member.

I continued staring at the page, no longer seeing the print. Mary's story changed my life in an instant. I was no longer the only girl I knew who had endured unwanted and inappropriate attention from a pervert who was part of my own family. And like me, Mary didn't tell anyone. Until now.

Hope trickled over me like a gentle spring rain, the potential for salvation refreshing me in that instant. Learning I wasn't alone in my struggle strengthened my resolve to carry out the difficult challenge I had issued myself. I finally had a model to follow. Mary was living proof that I could succeed. She not only told a friend and her psychiatrist, she told the world by allowing her story to be published in a magazine. I reread the article, making sure I didn't gloss over any important parts in the excitement of my first reading.

Moments ago, I was a lone warrior heading into battle, now I had an army behind me. I discreetly slipped the magazine inside my jacket. It was critical evidence, something I could point to when I told my story to my mother. She would have no choice but to believe me if I showed her the article.

I planned my conversation carefully, going over and over the words in my mind. I wanted to write it down but did not dare. Glen had established himself as a snoop and I couldn't risk him finding my draft confession. Eventually I got the message straight in my mind, I would begin by talking about the magazine article. I would extract it from its hiding place under my mattress and have it on hand, critical evidence that I hoped would help me convict Glen.

One of my greatest concerns was that my mother might not believe my accusations. Starting with Mary's experience would, in my mind, validate the existence of such behavior in today's world. This was an important premise to establish assuming that she, like me, had never before contemplated the notion of a grown man carrying out such acts on a little girl. I would then segue into my own experience. How detailed did my account need to be? That was a delicate question. I shuddered at the thought of having to describe the nitty-gritty of what he had done to me. That was the other benefit of having the article on hand. I could just say something like, "Glen was doing stuff just like this to me," and hand her the magazine so she could read what my newfound heroine had written about her own experience.

The problem with planning a conversation about such an emotion-ridden topic is that the stress builds with each passing moment, creating the opportunity for a knee-jerk reaction. And that is exactly what happened.

I wanted to have the conversation in person, but gaining private access to my mother became a seemingly insurmountable challenge. I reached the point where I felt like I was going to burst from the pressure of the burden I carried and I ended up spewing the contents of my carefully rehearsed narrative to my mother over the telephone while she was at work. I omitted the majority of my deliberately selected words, and worst of all, squandered the weapon I had found in the magazine article.

It went something like this.

"Mom, um you know, I was reading this article at the dentist's office the other day and it was about a girl whose uncle was having incest with her and, well, I have been wanting to tell you for so long, that Glen has been doing that to me."

Long pause.

I was preparing to launch into more detail about the article, having resurrected some of my planned words in an effort to fill the uncomfortable silence that transcended the phone line between us, when she finally said, "You know, I wondered about that."

I exhaled the breath that had stalled in my lungs.

Had I heard her right?

Did she just say she wondered about that? As in, she wondered if her husband was molesting me?

She wondered?

Wondering was something people did when they were mildly curious about something that they had experienced or witnessed, but not interested enough to find the answer. Wondering was something people did idly when they were bored or waiting for something more exciting to focus on. Wondering was never a verb I would have associated with a mother's suspicion that her husband was doing disgusting things to her daughter.

As I labored to digest her reaction, she went on.

"There were so many times I would wake up in the middle of the night and he would be gone, and I thought at least a few of those times he was in your room," she said.

I absorbed her words, thinking back to a night when she actually came into my room and found him there in the dark, next to my bed. She accepted his lame answer that he just stopped in to say goodnight to me one more time and they left together, her intervention saving me from him that one night.

Her words came at me like little pellets, each one stinging upon impact. But it wasn't until I comprehended their collective meaning that I felt the hit to my gut. All the time I had spent worrying about her believing me, or worse yet, blaming me. All the agony I endured at the possibility of ruining her marriage.

It never once occurred to me that she already knew the awful truth I had finally found the courage to speak out loud.

As I slowly comprehended my new reality, my mind turned to the consequences I had thought so long and hard about. I was pretty sure I could rule out the notion of divorce. Not only did the news I just delivered to her not constitute headline material, I doubted it would make her newspaper at all. My mother had always been a pretty cool cucumber. Like my brother Kirk, she held on tightly to her emotions, rarely offering the world a glimpse of what was really going on inside her. In spite of this, I was amazed at her calm. She simply acknowledged my confession, the one I had agonized over for months, and then told me she would talk to him.

I hadn't expected a tearful outburst, or even an angry tirade about what a nasty, worthless, son-of-a-bitch he was. She seemed to have used up all her emotive reactions years ago on my father. I had never seen her unleash like that on Glen, even though in my mind he was far more deserving. At the same time, I had expected some reserved display of anger or disgust and dared to hope for a pledge of protection from her. Maybe my mind confused my deeply rooted desire for her to defend me with a realistic expectation of her behavior.

I lacked the wisdom to comprehend it at the time, but my revelation marked the beginning of the divide that grew between us and eventually swallowed us up. I had broken through her wall of denial. She could no longer look the other way and pretend that what she suspected wasn't really happening. I forced her to face the truth -- by speaking his transgressions out loud -- and in the process dragging forth the ugly reality from that vault deep within her where she shoved everything unpleasant in her life.

I broke with her that day by daring to put myself first. I rocked the boat, something I had never before done. In contrast to the thunderous downpour I had foreseen, my confession had the impact of a single bolt of lightning far off in the distance. Its glimmer was so brief that you might question whether you had actually seen the flash at all. The battle I had envisioned didn't even rise to the level of a skirmish.

Not one single element of the numerous scenarios I had envisioned came to fruition as a result of me unburdening myself on her. I was momentarily angry with myself for shooting my wad over the phone, but then I realized that even the most ideal of settings would have had no impact on the outcome. She knew the punch line before I told the joke. Her reaction was predestined.

Now, I had no choice but to move on. I didn't witness the confrontation between my mother and Glen, but I imagined that her words were civil and void of emotion, sounding similar to the tone she assumed while affirming her suspicions of his behavior to me during our phone call. I further imagined that she delivered him no ultimatum. She had no power with which to wield such a threat, and not even something this huge and awful could make her believe that she did.

She talked to him that very afternoon when he made his routine stop by the Mini Mart on his way home. Right there at the counter, in between customers shuffling in and out, paying for gas or buying a bag of chips or a Coke. She phoned me after they talked and said that everything was OK and that he had told her it was all a big misunderstanding. He wanted to have a chance to explain all of this to me and was on his way home to talk to me.

Chapter 40

Deserted

He was on his way home and I was alone. The earlier scene I imagined with him hurting me in an angry retaliatory rant flashed before my eyes.

"What! He's coming here? Now? Without you?"

The words framing my rejection of her ill-formed plan spilled forth, as I tried to get my mind around how she could possibly think it was a good idea for him to explain our "misunderstanding" to me without the protection of a third party.

I paced back and forth across the kitchen floor, dragging the long white phone cord behind me, trying to gain command of my escalating fear.

How long would it be before he got here? Twenty minutes, 15? Less maybe?

She assured me he wasn't angry when he left, and that he just wanted to talk to me. There was no reason to be afraid, she said.

"Mom," I finally responded, "I am not going to be here when he gets here. I don't trust him, and I think he's going to want to hurt me. I don't care that you don't think he was angry.

You know him. Don't you?" I paused, trying to get a grip on my frustration.

"Don't you?" I practically pleaded with her.

Somehow my words, or maybe my emotion, succeeded in breaking through the thick wall of her denial. She agreed to try to find someone to cover her shift so she could leave early. But it could take an hour or more. In the meantime, she told me to go to the neighbor's house.

The calm, almost offhand way in which she reported the results of their conversation to me confirmed that she believed whatever bullshit he had fed her in response to my accusations. In spite of the fact that she wasn't the least bit surprised about what I had told her, I still couldn't believe she allowed him to minimize it to the level of a misunderstanding.

Now it was my turn to wonder.

I wondered how his actions toward me could possibly be misunderstood.

Did she think it was normal, healthy behavior for a step-parent to pick a bathroom lock so that he could watch his step-child in the bathtub while he gratified himself in front of her?

Was she comfortable with her husband showing me her vibrator, a device whose purpose I couldn't comprehend -- until he explained to me in full detail how the two of them used it to pleasure themselves.

Was it acceptable for this same step-parent to perform oral sex on her daughter?

And finally, was she OK with him offering to let same daughter attend the eighth-grade dance in return for having sex with him?

But there was one thing I didn't have to wonder about, and that is how he had gotten away with it for so long. Because he could. Because there was no one to stop him.

My heart thudded like a hammer in my chest as I raced to find my coat and boots, zipping my coat as I pushed my way out the front door and slammed it behind me. I raced across the snowy field behind our house to the Langford's, looking nervously behind me all the way. Our neighbors, Dan and Carol Langford, were a kindly couple who had horses but no children. They seemed to be close in age to my mother, but I wasn't certain. Carol went out of her way to welcome us soon after we moved in, introducing herself and bringing a homemade casserole. She was friendly, either waving or stopping briefly to chat if anyone from our house happened to be in the yard when she drove past our house on her way to the main highway.

I saw Glen's truck slowing in front of our house as I glanced back one last time before reaching our neighbor's doorstep. He had made it home in record time. *Damn him.* I forced my shaking hand to bang on the door, praying someone was home to answer it. My prayer was answered when Carol opened the door with a smile and invited me in. The smile never left her face, but her eyes bore an expression somewhere between surprise and mild concern. She ushered me in and took my coat. I followed her into her kitchen after stealing another look out of her front window. Our driveway was not visible, but I imagined he was in the house by now. Looking for me. She invited me into the kitchen and set about retrieving cookies from a cupboard and putting them on a plate.

"How's school?" she asked.

"Fine," I said.

She sat down across from me, after placing the plate of cookies between us, and looked me directly in the eyes.

"Is everything OK?"

"Oh yes, everything's fine," I said, avoiding her gaze.

"OK, well, this is a nice surprise," she said, watching me closely.

We chit-chatted for a bit. She often subbed for teachers at school, so we talked about junior high subjects, which teachers I liked and which ones were difficult. It became increasingly difficult to hide my nervousness. I had the sensation of hundreds of tiny live wires coursing just beneath the surface of my skin, threatening to break through any minute.

Carol leveled another look at me and asked, "Amber, are you sure everything is OK?"

"Yes, my mom just thought it would be a good idea for me to come to your house for a while. She will be on her way home as soon as she finds someone to cover her shift."

"Is anyone at home in trouble?" she asked. "Is anyone hurt?"

I looked at this kind, concerned woman sitting across the table from me. My mind flashed back to my experiences with Vivienne when she cut my hair, and Coach Samuel after my outburst at basketball practice. For the third time since moving to Cody, someone who knew virtually nothing about me sensed that there was something very wrong in my world.

Certainly, my behavior in each situation had tipped each of them off, but their reactions went beyond simply noticing. They could just as easily have brushed my tears or nervousness aside, telling themselves I was behaving like any other hormone-ridden teenage girl. They could have chosen to ignore the signs right in front of them, believing it was none of their business and having no desire to take up for a girl they barely knew. But each of them in their own way had acknowledged my struggle, and two of them expressed what seemed to be a genuine desire to help.

Why couldn't one of them be my mother?

"No, no, of course not. No one is hurt and no one is in trouble."

I paused, trying to come up with something else I could add that didn't sound like a blatant lie. I had nothing. My mind was unable to focus on anything other than the confrontation I knew was coming. I tried to relax my facial expression, forcing the corners of my mouth upward. Just then the phone rang, its unexpected and loud invasion of my thoughts causing me to jump.

Carol turned briefly toward the noise, which was coming from a room beyond the kitchen, "Dan's in there. He'll get it."

Her statement was confirmed when Dan appeared in the doorway. He saw me and said, "Oh, I didn't know you were here. Glad I checked first. Your father is calling for you."

I froze. The only words that came forth were, "He's actually my step-father."

Not knowing what else to do, I stood up and forced my wooden legs to move forward as I followed Dan into his office. He retrieved the receiver from the desk where he had left it. I took it from him, and as I put it to my ear he said quietly, "I'll let you talk to him." Then he walked out.

"Hello."

"Amber?"

"Yes?" I said, bracing for the storm of expletives I knew was about to follow.

"Your mother told me what you said to her, and I want you to come home so I can talk to you," he said.

"Is Mom there?" I asked.

"No, but that doesn't mean you can't come home. "I'm not going to do anything to you."

The calmness in his voice stilled a few of what felt like the hundreds of butterflies flitting about in my stomach, but I knew better than to trust him. Of course he wanted me to come home without my mother being there, so he could say and do as he pleased.

At the same time, I knew that my mother wasn't going to offer much, if anything, toward my defense, but her presence was something. He would be outnumbered. I had to believe if he tried something really awful she would stop him. I hoped she would.

"She said she was coming home, I'll wait until she gets there."

I put the receiver back in its cradle before I could hear his response. I was astounded at my own behavior. My wooden legs suddenly turned to jelly. What was I thinking? Not only did I defy him, I hung up on him. When I made my way back to the kitchen I found Dan and Carol standing near the kitchen table, facing one another and talking quietly. Hearing me enter, they both turned. Dan took a run at finding out what was going on.

I gave him no more information than I had given Carol but let him know that my mother should be home soon, and I was sorry to be a bother. Dan fell all over himself after that, telling me I wasn't being a bother, they were just concerned. They wanted to be sure no one was in danger of being hurt.

My mind began to piece together their concerns and I smiled inwardly. Their suspicions could only be focused on one potential perpetrator, and that was Glen. I felt a brief moment of satisfaction at the notion of someone else seeing him, even if only speculatively, for the person he really was.

I jumped when the phone rang a second time. This time it was my mother calling to tell me she was home. I thanked Dan and Carol, pulled on my coat and trudged across the field, forcing my once-again wooden legs to deliver me.

I dreaded the unknown nature of the situation that awaited me and had already resigned myself to the acceptance of a far less than ideal outcome. I found my mother and Glen in the kitchen. Glen wasted no time before launching into his explanation of how his affections had been completely misunderstood by me. He was still using that calm and quiet voice, the one I never heard him use unless he was working up to molesting me, or like now, trying to lie his ass out of a situation in which he knew he was guilty. He had the balls to go on, saying I wasn't used to physical contact because my own father hadn't loved me.

My mother stood quietly next to him, saying nothing. I could have upped the ante, bringing forth detailed descriptions of his acts, none of which any sane adult would place in the fatherly love category.

But if there was one thing I recognized at that point in my life, it was defeat. And I was defeated. It was pointless to continue. There was no one who could or would defend me. And he knew it.

He had always known it.

Chapter 41

Hearse-Side Hissy

I awakened, feeling troubled but unable to pinpoint the reason. It was 6:30 a.m., half an hour before the alarm was set to go off. Reality seeped into my consciousness, and before I opened my eyes I knew today was the day, the last day I would feel his earthly presence. Of course, his spirit was already long gone, having exited his body the moment his heart stopped beating almost a week ago. I knew this, and yet I had allowed myself the indulgence of hanging onto him these past five days.

I clung to those last words he said to me, "I'll see you later this week," treating them as an omen, one I could not forsake. I kept him alive all week, telling myself I would be ready by Friday. I just needed those five days to get me there. I sat up in bed and began ticking off the order of the morning's events. I would get ready first. The kids could be herded through the cleaning, dressing, and breakfasting process relatively quickly, but we would need to stay on top of them and keep them moving. Getting our entire clan up and out of the house was a challenge on any occasion. We weren't known for being early risers. Austin, in particular, could require three, if not four attempts to get him out from under the covers.

The funeral was scheduled for 10:30, but we needed to arrive by 10:00. Matt and I had agreed on 9:45 just to be safe.

If I was going to see my father one last time we had to arrive well in advance of everyone else.

On Monday, when we had met to finalize the funeral arrangements, Rob had posed the question of whether we wanted to view my father's body. It went without saying that the casket would be closed for the service, but he explained that arrangements could be made for a private viewing by the family. The thought immediately repulsed me, bringing forth gory images of my father's head and the gaping hole that had surely ruined him for viewing by the living. I felt my face crinkling into a wince as Rob quickly explained that, depending on the location of the fatal wound, it might be possible to disguise it or remove it from view.

Doris wanted no part of it, but I found myself surprisingly open to the idea. I had no interest in imprinting onto my brain a gruesome final image of my father, but Rob assured me that he would give me his opinion once he'd had a chance to assess the condition of the corpse. He promised to tell me if the damage was beyond his cosmetic capabilities.

Rob reported to me later in the week that the shot had penetrated my father's neck and there was absolutely no impact to his head. By placing him with his left side to the back of the casket the wound would not be visible at all. He assured me my father would look completely unmarred -- as if he had died in his sleep. The news was bittersweet. I was relieved to learn that seeing him one last time was feasible, and as the week progressed I became increasingly committed to the notion of bidding my father a final farewell, face-to-face.

Even so, Rob's account of my father's condition haunted me. I had no choice but to imagine the damage the 12-gauge had done to his neck. He went on to tell me that my father died from blood loss, not the impact of the shot. His assault on himself was almost unbearable to picture, and yet I was compelled to play the reel of his final act once again in my mind's theatre, layering in the additional morbid details I had just learned.

My resolve to view my father mystified me. Even now, just hours before his funeral, my nerve remained intact. I had never relished the business of viewing a dead body. Instead, I would hang back at a funeral home, shying away from the box, gaping and exposed in the front of the room. I broke this rule only once, for my Gramma. Having just graduated from college and coming off the whirlwind of finals, celebrations, and starting a new internship, too much time had passed since I had seen her. I couldn't bear to let go of her without gazing upon her face one last time and bidding her a proper goodbye.

I looked at the stranger who lay still and cold, eyes forever closed, unable to see the woman I loved so much. It took time afterward for my mind to replace the vision of her framed up in that crate with the warm and vibrant image that pervaded my memories. The letdown of my parting moment with her posed the singular challenge to my current decision, but it was not enough to change my course.

Entering the funeral home with Matt at my side, I was once more grateful for his presence. He steered me through the door of the dimly lit parlor furnished with nothing more than my father's open casket.

My knees felt weak. I sensed sweat beading in the crevices of my clenched palms as we made our way to the center of the room. When at last my legs delivered me to the side of his coffin, a wave of relief washed over me. I expelled the balloon of air from my chest and felt the tension exit my shoulders as I looked upon the face of the man who had given me life.

The vision before me was every inch my father, from his silky white hair and smooth cheeks to his broad, big-knuckled hands folded across his midsection. My lip quivered, ushering in the tears that followed. The likeness was nothing short of astounding. Had I not known the cause of his death I couldn't have guessed it. I looked longingly at him, unable to stop myself from wishing that he was resting, that I could nudge him and he would wake up.

At last I willed myself to move. I reached into my purse and extracted the letter I had written to him that morning, tucking it carefully into the satiny folds of the box that would serve as his bed for the ages. I knew the words and the paper they were written on would disintegrate with time. I didn't care. I was certain he had already felt my words through the cosmos when I wrote them earlier that morning.

Almost involuntarily, I reached for his hand, gently placing mine upon his. I let it rest there as I let my mind's film-reel play, one after another, scenes that he and I had shared. I pictured our garage in Grand Rapids. My father was wearing his blue coveralls and smiling at me from across the open hood of the '57. I saw him and Jennie waving to me from the ground as my brothers and I rode a roller coaster at Cedar Point. I felt the warmth of his cheek on mine when he kissed me after I received my college diploma, and again when he delivered me to Matt at the altar on my wedding day. I watched him look lovingly upon the bundled newborn forms of Cameron, Rachel, and Austin as he held them in his arms for the first time.

I was completely absorbed in my time travel when I felt Matt gently squeeze my arm. It was time to go. I took one last look at my hand perched on top of his. Although smaller, I could not deny its resemblance to my father's hands. As I retracted it, I acknowledged the notion I had held for years that my hands were too squared, my fingers too short, and that overall, they were just plain unattractive. Why had I thought that, I mused inwardly as Matt ushered me out of the parlor.

I squinted into the sun as we walked outside again. The weather had been hopelessly cheerful all week, standing in sharp contrast to how I felt inside. Shading my eyes with my hand, I scanned the parking lot and spotted Kirk standing next to his truck, the driver's side door cocked open. Doris' former son-in-law, Ray, stood next to him, his wide grin visible even from across the parking lot. I had never seen "Brother Raymond" without the backdrop of the ornery grin that eased into a smile as he brought to bear the colorful and often suggestive banter that was his trademark. As I approached, I couldn't help but think how handsome my brother looked as I tried to recall the last time I had seen him in a suit. *My wedding, perhaps?* I caught the eyes of both of them before I reached the truck. Kirk turned to pull me into a hug.

"I'm so glad you're here," I said, feeling the need to reinforce his decision to show up. Eyeing the open door of his truck suspiciously, I went on, "You are staying, right?"

"Yes, I'm staying, I have to," he said, staring off into the distance, "for Dad. But I hate this. Every minute of this is going to suck, but I gotta do it," he said, suddenly unleashing a big grin. My brother had a way of doing that. When the conversation became too intense or too dark, he'd usher in a sarcastic or self-deprecating comment, or simply grin to alleviate the heaviness.

"You here to drink with us?" Ray asked, reaching into the space under the seat and extracting what else, but a bottle of Jack, and handing it to me with a bigger-than-ever grin.

"Of course," I said, huddling a little closer behind the open door to shield what I was about to do from view of the mourners filing into the funeral home. I tipped the bottle, welcoming the burning assault to the back of my throat.

"Thanks, I think I needed that."

"Hell, yes, you did! I know we're standing around in the parking lot drinking whiskey before a funeral, but in all seriousness, I want to say how much I loved your dad. He was a helluva man, and I'm really sorry for your loss. I know how much he meant to you. He's going to be missed," Ray said.

The tears welled up again the moment he expressed his love for my father. The water works were in full force now. I grabbed the wad of tissues from my purse and caught a stream on the left side before it dripped off my chin. I nodded fiercely, unable to speak. The bottle made its way around again and I welcomed one more hit from the fountain of fire.

Trying to refocus and stop the flow of tears, I thought about Ray and how he had hung onto my father even after his divorce from Doris' daughter. He, my brother, and my father were of the same ilk. There was no pretense, no apologies, no fanfare. They didn't need anyone. The three of them are the kind of men who measure your worth by what you do, not what you say or what you have. Brother Raymond was no longer invited to family events, but he managed to maintain contact with my father. My father, having redrawn the boundaries of his own family map numerous times in his life, had no compunction about maintaining a friendship with worthy people who found themselves on the other side of the border due to divorce. Dad would be happy that he came. On the other hand, I suspected Doris would be none too pleased.

Having now composed myself, I turned to the two of them, "It's probably time to head inside."

"Matt and the kids already inside?" Kirk asked.

"Yep, we got here early. I saw him," I said.

"Yeah?" Kirk asked.

"It was really good. He looked … amazing. I'm really glad I did it."

I looked Kirk straight in the eyes, "It's really him in there. It's weird, but I'm not sure I could have believed it if I didn't see it for myself."

Kirk nodded slightly, the smile completely gone from his face.

I turned to Ray.

"You're going to make sure he gets inside, right?" I pointed to my brother.

"I will," he promised, with a smile that paled in comparison to his signature grin, but affirmed his commitment.

I found Matt and the kids, and we filed into seats in the second row, directly behind Doris. I listened, unmoved, as Pastor Lewis went on about my father, a man he had never once spoken with. I mean him no disrespect; he seemed kind and full of good intentions.

The highlight of the service for me was the portion dedicated to personal memorials. Will Ryan, a long-time friend of Dad's, described his long friendship with Dad and how my father had helped him launch his own electrician business. There were tears in his eyes as he paid his heartfelt and final tribute to my father, a true and trusted friend of his. Matt's sister Jill spoke on my behalf, describing our infamous cross-country drive from Denver to Toledo after I made the decision to leave Wyoming. I made good use of the big wad of tissues I had brought.

As Kirk had aptly summed up the ordeal, "It sucked, but it was necessary."

It was a relief to make my way outside. This time, the brightness of the day refreshed me. I willed that big yellow orb to fill me with warmth and relieve the heaviness I felt in my heart. Matt, Rachel, Austin, and I made our way toward the hearse that was backed up and ready to receive its solitary passenger. Cam was already standing near the doorway with the other pallbearers.

I found comfort in the strangest things during the week following my father's death, one of which was the knowledge that my son, Cam, would help to deliver his grandfather's coffin. Similar to the act of gently laying a newborn into the warmth and safety of his bassinet, my son would lay his grandfather lovingly into the car that would take him to his final resting place, and then deliver him to the edge of his grave in the garden that would be his home for eternity. I had never given a second thought to this funeral ritual until this week. I now saw it as a sacred and beautiful act. It had become a crucial piece of the "letting go" plan I had constructed for myself.

Most of the mourners made their way immediately to their cars in order to line up for the processional. Only a small group of us clustered around the back of the hearse. I waited patiently as the group of pallbearers that included my two brothers and my son disappeared inside. I watched intently as I awaited their return. First, two appeared, next my brothers came into view, then Cam and his counterpart on the opposite side. They walked slowly, taking great care with their precious cargo. The final two carriers emerged, bringing the coffin into full view. They positioned themselves, preparing to lower my father and place him in the back of the hearse, when the sanctity of the moment was pierced.

"What's this? Where's Billy?" a voice, unmistakably Doris,' demanded.

She had made her way in front of me and was now obstructing my view. When her demands went unanswered by the pallbearers in front of her, she turned and faced my direction. Her face was red and her tiny, dark eyes shot angry darts into the inconspicuous audience that had gathered near me. I had seen this transformation countless times that week. One minute she was wailing and bemoaning the loss of her husband, and in the next, almost as if she flipped a switch, she seemed indifferent to the fact that she had sustained the loss of her beloved spouse just days before.

I fought the irritation that was mounting within me. I had no idea what had undone her. I only knew that she, like the incessant talker sitting next to you in the theatre, was completely ruining my moment. Her demand still not satisfied, she next queried the crowd.

"Who changed the pallbearers?"

When none of us chose to divert their focus from the deceased to answer her, she went on.

"You want changes, I'll show you fucking changes!" and stormed away, demonstrating no regard for the scene she had just interrupted.

I later learned that her son, Billy, a designated pallbearer, couldn't be located to man his post when the time came. Jay, who had been assigned the responsibility for handling the recruitment of the pallbearers, asked Brother Raymond to stand in at the last minute. Ray readily agreed. Doris was irritated enough that Ray had shown up. To add insult to her injury, he had been given a job he was not worthy of performing in her mind. Except, I thought, for the fact that my father would have been happy to have Brother Ray carry him. But, I observed, her lack of concern regarding what Dad might have wanted was fast becoming a trend. From locking Jay out of the barn to refusing to share my father's final words with his children, she seemed to be sending us all a clear message that there was a new sheriff in town.

I realized I had overestimated Doris. Her husband had been dead for less than a week, yet she had already shifted her focus from the loss of him to the activities that would assure her complete control over all that he had left behind. What I found strange was that I knew that my father had left her in control. I was designated as a co-executor of their joint estate in the event of their simultaneous deaths. In the event of their individual deaths, the entire estate was designated to the surviving spouse. She stood to inherit all my father's worldly goods without contest, so there was no reason for her adversarial behavior, no reason to draw lines in the sand.

Yet the more I thought about it, the more I saw that her behavior this past week was consistent with her true nature. As Matt pointed out, she was tough as nails, the kind of person you might characterize as a real street-fighter. Her harsh characteristics were part of what had put me off when she and my father started dating. A memory of our first meeting flashed in my mind. Dad had brought Doris over to our house for Cam's birthday; he could not have been more than two or three. She was friendly enough, laughing and telling stories the whole time we visited. The problem was the way she peppered profanity into her narrative. From "shit" to "fuck," she seemed completely oblivious to the fact that my young son was hearing her every word.

She showed a different side of herself to us when we became family. She and my father routinely took care of the kids and they loved her. She was a caring grandmother, demonstrating patience and a true sense of fun. She always had their favorite juice and snacks on hand, took them on regular trips to the Dollar Store and generally spoiled them the way most grandmothers do.

But now, as I reflected on her rage at learning that Ray stood in as a substitute pallbearer, I understood that not only did she not classify him as family, he was now the enemy. It seemed she drew firm boundary lines around blood and marriage. I suddenly understood on which side of that boundary my brothers, my family, and I now stood.

Chapter 42

Makeshift Memorial

I could see the long, tree-shaped shadows imposing their forms on the ground outside of Kirk's workshop. My father's last day was coming to an end.

I recounted the day's earlier events. After Doris' outburst in front of the hearse, I had still somehow found the stomach to dutifully pile my family into the back of the black stretch limo she had chartered for the ride to the cemetery. By this point my disgust with her was at its peak, and yet I complied.

Why? What, I asked myself, compelled me to make nice with someone I had lost every ounce of respect for? My brothers skirted the invitation and drove themselves to the cemetery. The air inside the limo was too thick for conversation, so the 20-minute ride was carried out in silence. The sun continued its gaudy demonstration, aided by a cloudless sky, its enthusiasm marginalized only slightly by the dark-tinted windows.

We stood behind the rows of chairs and listened to Pastor Lewis' brief words, committing my father's soul for all of eternity. Jim, he said, was with the Heavenly Father now.

He was free. We, his surviving loved ones, could find hope in the knowledge that he was in good and loving care. It was a fairly routine gravesite service, but for one unusual and beautiful touch. Rob orchestrated the release of a single white dove at the conclusion of the service. I watched as it spread its eager wings and flew full tilt into the expansive blue sky above, swiftly putting distance between it and the confines of its former cage.

My eyes never left the dove. I was determined to follow it until it was no longer visible. It soared farther and higher, becoming a mere speck in the distance. Just as I was about to drop my gaze, it flew sideways, and as I watched, circled and turned back toward us. After a half-dozen or so flaps of its wings it turned again, resuming its former course, and gradually disappeared into the distance.

I couldn't help but relate the bird's display of indecision to my father. Had he felt that way before he pulled the trigger? Did he reconsider, if only for a few seconds, before resuming his course of action?

Forgoing the lunch Doris planned at the American Legion had been an easy decision for my brothers and me, serving as our final act of defiance to her self-imposed authority over all that remained of him. Her actions throughout the week, and earlier that day, were collective segments of a line drawn in the sand. The stubbornness we all shared, and the bad taste that our former, particularly nasty step-parent, Glen, had left in our mouths, made it impossible for us to pander to her. The picture was clear enough. We could expect that anything we might hope to receive from our father's estate, no matter how small or value-less, would become a bargaining chip the moment we expressed interest in it. Wife number four was giving every indication that she was posturing for a conflict that we wanted no part of.

Instead we retreated to Kirk's. Tonight was for the three of us to resurrect stories that would incite both tears and laughter against a backdrop of excessive alcohol. Matt and the kids dropped me off on their way to the lake with his family. I would join them the next day in an effort to salvage a few days of true vacation from our week before returning to Houston.

I sighed involuntarily. The last of the rituals were complete. There were no remaining ceremonial acts to facilitate my letting go. He was gone. I needed to accept it. Except, I reminded myself, for the private memorial service that the three of us were currently engaged in.

Scanning the room, I noticed the car first, neatly covered with a tarp. The red '68 Camaro convertible was without a doubt one of my brother's most prized possessions. My eyes moved next to the weight bench, the beer fridge, and finally the drawing table and cabinets Kirk used as a workspace for his construction business. The three of us were seated at the card table, its centerpiece a bottle of Crown Royal, now less than half full. Maggie and Mannie were sprawled out on the couch. The NASCAR channel played in the background, providing its own contribution to our makeshift memorial.

My eyes returned to the Camaro and settled on its bulky shape. The building of that car was the project that bonded father and son after a near decade-long struggle of testosterone and ego. I smiled at the memory of the time Kirk had let me drive it.

"Remember the maiden voyage I took her on?" I asked, motioning toward it with my head.

"Yeah ..." he said, cocking his head sideways with a grin, "how could I forget?"

"I really thought I'd ruined the hood. I felt awful, and I could tell you were pissed," I said, smiling.

"I remember watching you take off, and seeing the hood fly up and thinking, *holy shit, what is she doing?"*

"How was I supposed to know the hood wasn't latched?"

"I know. Dad lectured me. Told me I should never let anyone drive it without checking everything first," he replied.

"Well, thanks to Dad for saving my ass that day," I said. As I thought about it, that was a pretty characteristic thing for him to have done. Despite his involvement in countless conflicts throughout his life, when it came to the inner-workings of his family, he was ever the peacemaker. He was happiest when everyone was getting along.

I thought back to that day. It was not long after Dad and Kirk had finished the Camaro. Dad and Doris were hosting a barbeque. It was summer, maybe Memorial Day weekend or July Fourth? Both of my brothers were in attendance, Matt and I had all three kids in tow, and there were hordes of other family members and friends milling about. Matt and I meandered into the barn along with other guests to see the finished product. Similar to the process I had witnessed with the '57 so many years before, I had watched the Camaro transform over countless months of my father and brother's ministrations. I had seen plenty of my father's creations, but I found this one particularly impressive. Its red paint glistened and the chrome exhaust pipes sparkled despite the dim interior lighting. Taking notice of my admiration, Kirk asked if I wanted to take it for a spin. Of course I did!

He threw me the keys and I opened the driver's side door, noting how much heavier it felt than the door of my Nissan Maxima. Matt got into the passenger side as I acclimated myself to the control panel, noting how much had changed in the 30-plus years that had passed since this car first rolled off the assembly line. I pressed my foot to the brake and turned the ignition. The loud, throaty roar that followed startled me. I shifted in my seat in an effort to disguise the involuntary jump of my body at the sound.

Maneuvering out of the barn, I made my way down the long driveway and turned onto the quiet rural highway that ran in front of my father's house. I let it idle for a few seconds, feeling the power of the engine vibrating throughout my entire body. I looked over at Matt.

"Ready?"

When he grinned and nodded, I floored it.

The power of the acceleration slammed my body backward into my seat and simultaneously plunged the car forward. In that instant I got it. I suddenly understood what all the fuss was about with these muscle machines. The combination of the deafening noise and the raw power was nothing short of exhilarating. I had no sooner adjusted to the adrenaline high I was experiencing when the view in front of me was completely obstructed by the hood of the car that had spontaneously flown up.

Reacting as quickly as possible without slamming the brakes, I slowed and stopped. Matt jumped out and closed the hood while I looked nervously behind me. I was amazed at how much distance our little sprint had placed between the car and my father's house. *This is one helluva fast car!* I wondered if my brother saw what had happened, and more importantly, I worried I had broken something.

Seeing the look on my brother's face on my return, I immediately knew he had seen the whole thing. I apologized profusely as he popped the hood and began a careful inspection. To my great relief, Dad had already coached him, having witnessed the scene alongside my brother. He reminded him that lots of people had milled around his car that day, admiring it and more than likely looking under the hood. One of them, unbeknownst to my brother, had failed to securely latch the hood. In my eagerness to take the beautiful beast for a spin, I simply jumped behind the wheel, having no reason to think the hood wouldn't be secure. I didn't witness their conversation, but I imagined my father struck an amenable balance when making his point, protecting me and at the same time not offending Kirk.

My father's absence from our early lives, and Glen's influence, soured my brother on the notion of deferring to any fatherly figure. Dad had to earn his right to reclaim the role of father that Kirk believed he had given up years before. The two of them walked a careful line, stepping carefully around their differences. Inevitably Kirk's frustrations bubbled up and spilled out, the friction between them sometimes lasting for months on end. Fatherly patience, the natural maturation process, and time eventually brought them to common ground, first, in the form of my brother's construction business, and later in the building of something unique to the two of them. The Camaro offered a platform from which my father could share his beloved hobby and my brother could create a lasting treasure.

The process involved numerous phases, the first of which was sourcing parts. This required weekend meanderings across the northwestern quadrant of the state of Ohio, attending swap meets, visiting junkyards and chasing down obscure ads in trade magazines. Next was the assembly phase. According to my father there were always unexpected obstacles. Parts didn't fit, or the mechanics didn't integrate. I came to learn that while these issues frustrated him, it was solving them that offered some of the greatest satisfaction he derived from his hobby. He would grin from ear to ear, arms crossed in front of him as he described the unique fix he'd come up with to solve his most recent perplexing roadblock. Bringing his son into this process bonded them to a common and righteous cause. The prize for success was so much more than a one-of-a-kind trophy car, it created a base upon which they could build a future.

I thought back to my own reunion with my father, which took place during a 20-plus-hour road trip from Colorado to Ohio. My car was packed with my clothes and a few personal belongings. I was leaving Wyoming for good. When I was a senior in high school he had extended me an invitation to live with him and attend classes at the University of Toledo. That had been my original post-graduation plan. Plan B kicked in when I couldn't find the will to separate from my boyfriend of two-years. Instead, I chose to sit out of college for a year and wait for him to accumulate enough money to join me at the University of Wyoming. A born and raised Cody-ite, he wasn't open to a move to Ohio, but Laramie, Wyoming was an option.

It turned out that college life wasn't enough to prop up our already shaky relationship. After my freshman year I was ready to call it quits and eagerly picked up the threads of my original plan. Meanwhile, Dad remained steadfastly in the background, ever encouraging and ever patient. Not wanting me to make the cross-country drive alone, he flew to Denver where I picked him up in my '67 Mercury Cougar, the very first car I ever owned. We decided to spend that first night outside of Denver and begin the long drive the next morning. We found a Mexican restaurant, a favorite of both of ours, and devoured chimichangas, drank margaritas, and began a dialogue that lasted the entire trip.

I was still hurting over my failed relationship and told him all about it. Really, we had never gotten along, and in the end, I was more committed to college than he, I explained. Dad reinforced me, telling me how smart I was to focus on getting a degree so I would always be able to support myself. The sharing of my relationship woes prompted him to talk about his regrets over how badly his marriage to my mother ended. They were a complete mismatch, marrying out of necessity, but, he admitted, he could have handled it better. We had missed out on a lot of years together and he was so happy I had made the decision to come and live with him and Jennie. He wanted me to have opportunities that weren't available to him when he was my age. College wasn't an option for him, especially after marrying so young.

In those few hours, I learned more about my father than I'd ever known about him before. As time passed we touched on more difficult topics, including Glen. He admitted he hated him and yes, he had come looking for him that night at our house, sawed-off shotgun in tow. By this point his admission didn't faze me. I had finally found someone other than my brothers who shared my hatred of Glen, and that only made me love my father more in that moment.

With the aid of the tequila, one story after another spilled forth, filling in the void that the years away from each other had created

I described Glen's strict command over all our lives, how nothing we did ever seemed to be enough to stifle his mean nature. My father listened in silence, his expression solemn. Sensing his mood change, I shifted away from that topic. There was no point in divulging details that would only make him feel guilty, or worse, incite him to embark on a second assault mission. It was over. It was in the past. I was drinking margaritas with my father, having one of the best nights of my life, and my future had never felt more promising.

Our mother initiated Jay's reunion with our father. The woman who just a few years earlier had stolen us away from my father, fearing that he would fight her for us, became suddenly eager to unburden herself. My decision to live at home for the year between high school and college was met with strong opposition from her. It was during the conflict that arose when she challenged me to pay rent that I had ended up on the ground in our front yard. My brother's transgression was different. After being caught for the second time at a party in his senior year of high school, Mom had had enough. She decided he could finish his last semester and get his diploma in

Ohio, under my father's supervision. It was time, she said, that he dealt with his children.

While not the most ideal of circumstances, my father looked upon my mother's dictate as an opportunity. Jay had enjoyed pretty much complete freedom under my mother's laissez-faire parenting approach. My father, new to the role of parenting a minor, believed in structure and rules, making clashes between the two of them inevitable.

Jay's new high school refused to accept the credits for certain classes he had already completed. Equivalent courses weren't offered in the spring semester, Jay's last remaining before completing his senior year. In order to graduate on time, he supplemented his classroom time with correspondence courses. Immersion into a senior class of students who had spent the last four years together, some having spent their entire educational history together, posed another set of challenges Jay had to overcome. It took quite a bit of heavy lifting by both Dad and Jay, but he graduated with his adoptive senior class the following June. The father we had all been told was worthless had vindicated himself once and for all.

Chapter 43

Shifting Gears

As I looked at my two brothers in the fading afternoon light, I had to admit that in spite of the tremendous strides we had made, we were still far apart. Like the three legs of a stool, we had learned to bear the weight of our shared burden at a safe distance from one other. To adopt a model different from the one we grew up with required a paradigm shift that we had yet to master. Without the aid of alcohol, casual conversation between us was a chore. We led different lives. For the last 20 years my attention had been focused on my career and my kids, and I had to admit I had a bias toward spending time with my husband's family.

I found the act of describing my work, even to others in the business world, a challenging task. I couldn't imagine the boredom my brothers would feel if I droned on about the latest bonus program I developed, or the inner workings of stock options, or the basic tenets of employee benefit plan design. My brothers had both been childless for years until Jay married Glynis and became a step-father to her two children. This awareness prompted me to keep the kid talk in check, having spent my own childless years avoiding people who had nothing more to offer to a conversation than tedious accounts of "accomplishments" that amounted to little more than normal bodily functions.

I had studied friends who shared close bonds with their adult siblings. Many, like Matt's sisters, enjoyed similarities in both their interests and lifestyles. But I also knew plenty of others who had virtually nothing in common with their siblings other than their shared parentage, and still they considered their siblings to be among their best friends. I pondered the reasons for that, and finally determined that it was their shared experiences that bound them closely throughout their lives. Even those from families who experienced significant losses found ways to cleave to one another. The challenge we faced in conversing as adults was that we had not done it as children. Verbalizations regarding both happy and traumatic events remained enmeshed in our young minds, mere drafts of feelings and observations that would never become fully formed through the act of speaking them out loud. Fighting the monsters of our past individually had deprived us of the opportunity to rally as a team.

We had poked and prodded the beast of our past over the years, taming it in the process. Our deepest discussions took place with the encouragement of alcohol. Many of these talks had taken place in the presence of our father. He seemed to share our need to reconcile with the past and willingly entered into hours of reflective dialogue with us. Why did our mother fall for Glen? How could she not have seen him for the monster he was? Why was she so distant now? My father listened and offered his perspective, but refrained from making disparaging comments about her. It was during these conversations that I felt closest to my brothers. We gained a deep respect for one another as we relived our hurts, seeing them through each other's eyes.

I thought I knew the full extent of Glen's malevolence, but my brothers managed to surprise me with accounts of his deeds that I was either not aware of or had blocked from my memory. I shocked them equally by sharing Glen's sexual abuse of me. It was on the heels of this admission that Jay confessed to also being a victim of Glen's perversion. I sat stunned, repeating his words over and over in my head.

Glen did to Jay the same stuff he did to me? My brother? *A boy who was six years younger than me?*

Jay was just four years old at the time. It started right after Glen moved in with us. *He initiated both of us at the same time.* The level of my disgust for him reached a new high.

I paged back through the years, recounting my little brother's nature. He had always been fun-loving and easygoing, and for a brief period was somewhat of a ham. By the age of two he had developed a love of rock and roll music, playing along to his favorite songs on his air guitar -- long before the term had been coined. Everyone egged him on and he loved the attention. Eventually he added dancing to his routines, shaking his body from head to toe so fast that photographing him produced nothing more than a blurred image. As his vocabulary increased, he started singing along, copping anything that resembled the shape of a microphone and displaying a surprising grasp of the lyrics. He was sensitive, picking up on the moods and feelings of others. When my mother developed an ulcer during her second divorce, Jay engaged in what appeared to be a sympathetic reaction, refusing to eat anything but baloney and cheese, developing anemia in the process.

When Glen entered the picture, the three of us began tucking away all of the things that made us happy. We learned early on that anything that pleased us would eventually become either a bargaining chip or the focus of one of his absurd punishments. It was at that time the fun-loving attributes of Jay's personality receded into the background. The singing, dancing, and guitar-playing all but disappeared as he fell into quiet obedience. Unlike me, Jay never smarted off after being pushed beyond the brink of self-control by Glen's taunts and insults. And when Glen exited our lives, Jay seemed to undergo the most visible change, noticeably relaxing, his former lighthearted happiness making a reappearance. Now I knew why.

How could I not have known?

If he had been born a girl I would have guarded her with my life, fearing that Glen would impart upon her the same perverse attention he did on me. My imagination was incapable of conceiving such a scenario between Glen and a preschool boy. Our tiny house, whose bedrooms practically sat on top of one another, provided little opportunity for true privacy -- and yet he had succeeded in getting my little brother alone, out of earshot and eye sight. But why did that surprise me? He had achieved the same outcome with me. He didn't need complete privacy. He had the keys to the kingdom. Watching eyes wouldn't have helped my brother. After all, my mother's "wondering suspicions" had done nothing to help me.

By now we knew all there was to know about the ills each of us had suffered. We just hadn't figured out how to put it all behind us, how to heave the beast once and for all off our stool. But today that changed. We spent the better part of 10 hours recounting stories from our young lives, our recent lives, and even our "Glen lives," but the focus shifted.

The long week had worn on us, exhausting our tolerance for the negative. We were inspired to dig deep and find the happiness in our shared past. The obvious starting point was our grandparents. Kirk and I recounted our favorite memories in the care of Bernard and Thelma and their quirky but loveable traits. From there, one recollection sparked another, and in between the passing of the bottle we found ourselves smiling, even laughing. Before we knew it, the sun had set. Like magic, at the moment when we most needed to find some beauty in our collective pasts, we had somehow managed to do it.

Hugging my brothers goodbye the next morning, I felt again the shift in energy between us. Ironically, Dad's departure seemed to have created a base upon which the three of us could build. He would never again act as the buffer or be the facilitator. It was up to us to shape ourselves into a family, a family who could fill the void his loss left within us as its realities continued to trickle into our lives with the passage of time. How many times would Jay, out of habit, point his car in the direction of my father's house before the memory of his death surfaced? How many times would Kirk look at his phone, wondering why Dad hadn't called lately to check in? How many times would I pick up my phone, search for "Dad" in my contact list and push the button, before reminding myself that he was in a place beyond the reach of AT&T's cell towers?

He would be absent for every Christmas, birthday and summer vacation for the remainder of my life, as well as all of the significant moments that had yet to occur. High school and college graduations, weddings, the births of great-grandchildren. His smile, the touch of his hands, his laughter, would live on only in our memories. It was up to us to keep him alive in our hearts, and for that we would need each other.

Chapter 44

A Door Closes

The weeks following my return home had me anxiously sifting through the mail every day in search of an envelope with my father's handwriting. I clung to a tiny shred of hope that in anticipation of Doris' behavior he had chosen to issue me a direct farewell, rather than through her. I knew it was a long shot, but I wasn't ready to abandon hope. Having cut all ties to Doris, the final words she alleged he had left behind remained a mystery to me.

There were days I simply could not make my heart believe that my father had willingly, in his right mind, put a shotgun to his head and pulled the trigger. I vacillated between the extremes of accepting his final decision, to calling complete and utter bullshit on the whole notion of suicide, convincing myself that he had to have had help. The unanswered questions surrounding his death compelled me into long debates with my brothers, who confirmed that they, too, questioned how Dad could have made the decision to off himself. The sheriff had yet to issue the final investigative summary, but we held little hope for an answer other than the obvious conclusion that had been drawn when his body was found.

When my frustrations became unbearable I did what I had done since I was old enough to read: I turned to books. I stood in the self-help section of Barnes and Noble, thumbing through title after title on the topic of suicide. The first handful I scanned focused on prevention, pointing to a pervasive history of failed suicide attempts as a common thread among those who ultimately succeed. Another indication, I read, is depression, both diagnosed and undiagnosed. These attributes weren't consistent with my father's profile. I searched further, and eventually found a title that discussed victims whose families never saw it coming. I bought the book and read it from cover to cover that very day. A short section was dedicated to men in their sixties, who as a group, experience a higher than average rate of suicide. I sat digesting what I had read, trying to superimpose its tenets upon the characteristics of my father's life and behavior at the time of his death.

The book pinpointed feelings of isolation and a lack of belonging as the factors that ultimately tipped the scale toward taking action. I couldn't imagine my father feeling isolated. Beyond his family, who after years of fixing up had finally shed the majority of its outward dysfunction, he also had friends. In particular Dave, the guy who accompanied him on his beer-pitching revenge ride in East Toledo, who he worked with throughout his entire life and who remained a close and trusted friend. Not only that, he had his car hobby, a deep love that he had nurtured his whole life.

A further argument against suicide being my father's actual cause of death was the fact that the book stated that nearly all victims talk about their inclinations before acting. I thought of the universe of people to which my father would have chosen to disclose such thoughts: his three children, his best friend, and his wife. I knew with complete certainty that my father had never uttered a word about wanting to end his life to my brothers or to his best friend. Doris had maintained complete shock over his death, so I had to believe he had not shared such feelings with her either.

The book described how victims experienced intense emotional pain and feelings of helplessness. I had to admit I had noticed a change in my father that had begun a good six months before. My thoughts turned to a conversation I had with Rob the week before my father's funeral. As a funeral director, he had considerable experience in dealing with families who had lost loved ones to suicide, and had done a fair amount of research on the topic himself. He described the victims as being in an altered state of mind, their hope so far gone that they lose all concept of how to solve whatever problems they faced. All the aspects of their lives that once gave comfort and happiness are replaced with a single, unshakable focus on all that is wrong. Death becomes a solution, the only option that will assure complete freedom from the victim's anguish.

I thought about Dad's life. Both of my brothers alluded to his frustrations with working contract jobs that took him out of town for weeks on end. I, too, had heard him lament the need to supplement his income and the limited options that existed for doing so. His retirement from Ford had occurred a good two years ahead of schedule, when he was fired based on an accusation of sexual harassment from a female coworker. I remembered that time well, as he sought my advice as a human-resources professional. I knew the odds that he faced; companies did not take such actions lightly.

Regardless of the truth, someone had clearly built a convincing case against him. I encouraged him to get an attorney and fight, which he did. After months of appeals he was unable to compel a reversal of the company's decision. The income he would have earned in those two years was paltry compared with the increased value of his pension had it been permitted to fully vest. He watched the financially comfortable retirement he had spent his whole life working for evaporate before his eyes.

The retirement income issue was not new. I thought back to the timing and I estimated he had lost his job some 12 years before. And then there was the DUI. My dad had just returned from a two-week job, the bad taste of it still in his mouth. The very day he gets back he gets a DUI, ushering in feelings of embarrassment, shame, and the recognition that its consequences would result in a further strain on what he already deemed to be inadequate finances. The foregoing facts began to compel me, but the final piece of the puzzle came several months later, when I learned that my father had told his best friend Dave, just weeks before his death, that he wanted to divorce Doris.

The picture was now complete. At the age of 66 he already had four divorces under his belt. He was no longer earning the six-figure salary he had earned since I was in college, and he no longer, I guessed, had the stomach for an all-out brawl with another ex-wife. I was privy to a side of Doris in the week following the funeral that my father had to have been well acquainted with. Divorce would have no doubt been ugly.

My father was staunchly independent. I thought back to our long-ago conversation about caring for him in his elder years, and how he had so strongly asserted that he wanted no part of being dependent upon anyone else, not even his children. He didn't want to endure the turmoil of a divorce, and yet, I surmised, at the same time he could no longer abide the conflict and unhappiness of a failing marriage. He wasn't the kind of man who was capable of living a lie. On the other hand, he would have concluded that divorce would result in the division of his dwindling assets, issuing a further challenge to his need to supplement his income.

The DUI laser-focused his thoughts on the negative, on his mistakes, and in the process erased all hope that he would find happiness in the future. It did him in. I had to admit I didn't like the picture I'd just painted, but it became harder and harder

to deny that there was probably more truth to my theory than
fallacy.

At long last some closure arrived in the form of documents
released by the sheriff's department. Jay ran through the
details with me over the phone and pledged to send me copies
of everything. The report confirmed the initial conclusion of
suicide and summarized the recovery the body, the nature and
location of the fatal wound, my father's attire and reported the
officer's interactions with Doris on the morning of his death.

When I received my copy of the investigation documents
I read every word, looking for a deeper explanation hidden
somewhere within the generic facts before me. I noticed that
his birthday was incorrect in the report and that his hair was
indicated as being gray instead of white. The errors irritated
me. An event that had loomed so large in my mind for so
many months was reduced to less than three full pages that
cited incorrect facts. My careful review yielded no additional
facts that Jay had not already shared with me during our phone
conversation.

I put the sheriff's report aside and focused on the remaining
two pages, copies of the letters my father had left behind.
The "note" Doris had so elusively referred to was actually
two notes. One outlined a list of keepsakes that he wished to
bequeath his children and grandchildren. Tears welled in my
eyes as I read the third line that awarded the Nova he had just
completed to me. He and I had talked many times about the
car he would build for me, but never settled on a model or a
plan. *One more thing I had taken for granted that his future
would permit*, I thought, as I tried to picture the Nova. My
heart fluttered at the realization that in his final dedication
he had remembered, and that he wanted me to have the last
mechanical masterpiece he would ever create. I dragged my
focus back to the present and read on. He had also designated
special items for each of my three children.

I knew that the intentions outlined in his letter were not legally binding, having not been witnessed, nor having been incorporated into his official will. I also knew that Doris had already sold the Nova. My brothers heard through the local car-enthusiast network that this transaction had been completed within weeks of the funeral. There was no question in my mind that the items designated for my children would never find their way into their possession. I felt a brief sense of disappointment at not having anything of his to pass on to my children, to help keep his memory alive in their young minds. I quickly got over it. No material item was ever going to bring him back. I had taken a different approach to keeping him present in their lives. Following the funeral, I encouraged them to tell stories about their Poppie and to write down their memories. I knew that the passage of time and their youth would slowly erode them otherwise.

The second letter was essentially an apology to Doris. He stated his love for her, at the same time lamenting the days when they enjoyed a fun-loving relationship. He wanted those days back, but acknowledged that he didn't know how to reclaim them; their communications seeming to always turn to arguments. He admitted failure as a provider, husband, father, and grandfather. He spoke of the last two weeks being, "more than he could handle," and compared himself to a time bomb of emotion. I put the letter aside, its contents leaving me deeply saddened.

I couldn't fathom how he had so easily overlooked the positives of his life that far overshadowed his failures -- becoming an electrician in his early twenties, achieving a promotion into management after years of working on the shop floor, earning a college degree while working full-time, and taking the initiative and committing to the difficult and often thankless work that reuniting his family required.

He was real. He gave a damn. He took full ownership, never wasting effort on making excuses. He loved my brothers and me. He loved my children and they adored him. As I continued to add to the list, I couldn't imagine anyone seeing my father's life as anything less than successful. The fact that he lost all appreciation for how much he mattered tore at my heart.

If only … but I knew there was no point in thinking of what could have been, what might have been. He was gone. He had always lived by his own rules, and in the end, he died by them.

Chapter 45

And Another One Opens

I lay in bed trying to recall my dream, anxiety surfacing as the veil of sleep lifted. I rarely remembered the subjects of my dreams unless I awakened in a panic, desperate to escape from whatever creature or villain was chasing me. My occasional frightening dreams typically occurred after watching a scary or disturbing movie just before I went to bed.

Other than the fearing-for-my-life variety, there was only one other theme that regularly patterned my dreams. It had to do with taking a college exam. The scene always opened at the start of the semester. As I made my way toward my classroom, my path became cluttered with one deterrent after another.

Hills and random stairways sprang up in front of me, creating an obstacle course between me and the lecture hall I sought. Corridors led me to room after room, none of which housed the class in which I was enrolled. People appeared out of nowhere, diverting my focus by chatting with me or asking me questions. When I finally returned my attention to the mission before me, new and different impediments inevitably appeared.

By the time I reached the classroom the entire semester was finished. I had missed every single lecture and did not even own the textbook yet, and still I was faced with taking the final exam.

At that point, the stress that accumulated over the course of my quest would reach its climax. I always awakened before completing the exam, filled with anxiety over the failing grade that would have been a certainty if my dream had reached its conclusion. The feeling I was experiencing right now was similar to how I felt after one of those exam dreams. I tried to relax, hoping its content would resurface.

Slowly, the images recreated themselves in my mind. I was in the garden of my childhood, in the back yard of our house in Grand Rapids. It was nighttime. The moon was full and bright, illuminating not only the garden but all that surrounded it. The apple and willow trees were bathed in a soft light, leaves whispering to each other at the encouragement of the warm breeze that danced among them. The scene was beautiful and peaceful.

I turned my attention to the garden. Each of its rows belonged to a different family member. I stood in the middle of my father's row. It was hoed to perfection, the neat indentations in the soil from the metal prongs of the hoe still visible in the light of the moon. The middle of our garden was always dedicated to vegetables, and yet this row, in the very center, was full of nothing but flowers: yellow snapdragons, white petunias, orange marigolds, pink peonies, and purple iris flaunted their vibrancy, which even the pale light could not camouflage.

My attention turned next to the rows of vegetables to my right. These, I somehow knew, belonged to my brothers. The corn tassels waved to me as the light breeze caught them. Pepper plants contained themselves within their wire cages, despite the weight of their bulbous, ripe and ready-to-harvest fruit. While I could not see the plants, the sharp, herby scent of tomato leaves filled my nose, bringing forth an image of my favorite garden treat.

My eye was drawn to a row at the edge of the right side of the garden. The variety of plants was difficult to discern from my vantage point. I carefully stepped across my brothers' rows to get a better look. Closer inspection revealed the broad, five-pointed leaves of a cucumber plant. A tangle of gangly shooters spilled into the soil that separated this row from the one adjacent to it. Some of the vines were dotted with blossoms, squash or pumpkin, I guessed. The rest of whatever grew in that row was almost completely overgrown with weeds, some as high as my knees.

Why hadn't I hoed that row? I couldn't abide that row being unkempt when everything else looked so pristine. I set about trying to locate the trusted tool of my childhood gardening days. Making my way to the edge of the garden and onto the grass, soft and damp, I nearly tripped over something long and hard.

"Ah, the hoe," I thought.

Stooping to pick it up, I realized it was not the hoe at all, but a shotgun. Horrified, I threw it away from me and moved myself quickly in the opposite direction.

My search took me to the four corners of the garden, but the hoe stubbornly eluded me. Seeing no other alternative, I began to pull the weeds by hand. I didn't feel the sting of the prickers until I extracted my second fistful. Holding my hand up to my face, I counted dozens of tiny splinters poking out of my fingers.

I sat down and began extracting them, my frustration mounting. I didn't like the interruption this task posed to my overall mission, but I still felt compelled to complete it. I quickly realized the spikes were too tiny and too numerous. Removing them would be a long and tedious task.

Driven to liberate that row from the invasive freeloaders, I decided to push through the weeding exercise and extract the thorny residue from my hands after I finished. Bending to resume my task, I saw that fresh weeds had already replaced the ones I had just pulled. I extracted another handful and waited. Within seconds, tiny green shoots poked through the soil and grew upwards at a freakishly fast rate. It was as if I was watching time-lapse photography. My task, I acknowledged, just turned from difficult to impossible. As my frustration reached its pinnacle, my subconscious rescued me from further distress by rousing me from my dream.

Why, I pondered, *did I seem to be incapable of having a dream with a satisfying conclusion?*

In the coming weeks, I found myself revisiting the scene my subconscious mind had created in that dream. I finally concluded that the dream symbolized the unresolved void between my mother and me. Tricky how the mind works. My stalemate with my mother had occupied a good bit of my attention in the past months. There was nothing I wanted more than to feel strongly bound to her. The fact that I no longer believed it to be possible held me back.

Were I to initiate contact with her, I felt there was a decent chance she would capitulate. That was not my concern. The issue was that I knew it would only be a matter of time before she cut me off again. I wouldn't be made aware of my transgression or be given the opportunity to make it right, she would simply blacklist me without warning.

For years I had tried to convince myself that I could accept the one-sided nature of our relationship. I taught myself to expect her to randomly withdraw from me without warning or explanation, but I had not yet learned how not to feel hurt by it. Her last exit was no less painful than the countless others that preceded it. I could no longer justify the disappointment and hurt I would sustain by resurrecting an accord she clearly wanted no part of.

The thorny, overgrown weeds in my dream took root many years ago. I no longer indulged the belief that my actions alone could eradicate them. Perhaps my dream was a means of solidifying my commitment to put my feelings first where she was concerned. I eventually stopped obsessing about what I had done to motivate her rejection, and found that abolishing my expectations helped to relieve some of the failure I felt at my inability to sustain a meaningful connection with her.

In time, I came to regard my garden dream as my moment of truth. The loss of my father could not be disputed. He was gone from this world, and my life, for good. Despite our long period of estrangement, I still had moments when I wondered if there was hope for my mother and me to shape a future that included one another. But try as I might, I could not come up with a credible strategy to resuscitate the corpse of our relationship.

I was, in effect, an orphan. As I swallowed and slowly digested the bitter pill of my new reality, I eventually concluded that I had lost her a long time ago. The change was not in our circumstances, but my acceptance of them. This reality brought me no joy. But happiness and peace are two different animals. Sometimes peace is the best you can hope for.

The year that followed my father's funeral saw me preoccupied with the different, yet real losses, of both him and my mother. The bulk of my mental energy was focused on reconciling these two weighty chapters in the book of my life. In those months I had little capacity to devote to the chapter on my marriage. I welcomed the mental vacation, at times telling myself things were fine and believing that I had finally accepted my situation. As the first anniversary of my father's death approached, the old familiar doubts resurfaced, and I found myself once again with more questions than answers when it came to my husband and me.

As advertised, the expectations of my new employer continued to be reasonable, freeing up time that had eluded me for the past four years. I reengaged with my family, helping more with homework, and in general being more present in my children's lives. Despite my more relaxed schedule, life was still demanding. Football games, swim meets, and school activities continued to occupy the majority of our family's discretionary time. I expected to feel some relief in the workload associated with the kids now that Cam was in college, but the change was imperceptible.

Matt and I drifted back into our former, role-based patterns. Our time together as a couple was spent socializing with other couples rather than just the two of us. Even when we did engage in an occasional date night, the spark of romance continued to evade us.

I thought back to our early life together in an effort to understand what had changed. Our numerous shared interests formed the basis of our initial attraction, from exercise and cuisine to our college majors. We even worked for the same company in the early years of our marriage. Conversing was easy, we never lacked for something to talk about; companionship was a given.

I had to admit that burning passion was never the hallmark of our relationship. Our union began as a friendship that gradually turned to romance. I surmised that the flicker that sustained us in the beginning and led us to what we both expected to be a lifelong marriage, had completely burned out. I believed if we could rekindle even a small spark we would have something to build on, that there would be hope.

But I didn't know where to begin.

I remembered our first date. We talked for hours about life, God, our hopes and dreams; it felt like our souls touched in that moment. Now, I couldn't remember the last time we had an aspirational discussion. As I sat across from him at dinner one Saturday night, I tried to engage him in deep eye contact. He either failed to notice or didn't want to encourage me. I raised the topic of our life after kids. How did he envision our life? He brushed my probes aside with rote answers. It became clear that while I yearned for intimacy, he seemed content with being companions who shared a home, slept in the same bed, and otherwise lived completely separate existences.

Occasionally I was successful in enticing Matt to meet me for lunch, but our interaction was as bland and sterile as our Saturday night dates. As my hopes for a new beginning faded, the vacation incident returned to the forefront of my mind, painting the vivid picture of my husband in another man's embrace. Its reappearance, combined with the disappointment I felt at Matt's apathy, wore away at my patience. We rarely spoke during the day. I stopped calling him, knowing that if his phone went directly to voicemail my blood pressure would escalate and I would begin my obsessive analytics about where he might be and what he might be doing. Leaving a message was futile, as he rarely called back, preferring instead to address the reason for my call later that evening.

When I was inclined to leave a message and it went unacknowledged I couldn't let it go. By the time I got home that night I would be unable to contain my frustration.

"Why is it so much to ask for a simple return call?" I would ask.

First came the excuses of how busy he was. When I probed further, wanting to know what he had been busy doing, the mood always turned hostile. I was so out of touch I must have forgotten all that he had to do to keep the house humming, he'd say. When was the last time I had put dinner on the table?

I took him for granted. Just because he didn't go to an office every day didn't mean his days weren't busy. Was I saying he wasn't trustworthy? He didn't have to explain his daily whereabouts to me.

He was a master at diverting the focus of the conversation away from him and placing it firmly on to me. His deflection succeeded in either wearing me down or escalating the argument. Regardless of which tactic he chose, the outcome never yielded a satisfying response to the questions that plagued me.

It would only be four more years before our youngest son, Austin, went to college. Four years until Matt and I became empty nesters. Even in my most optimistic moments, I was unable to concoct a satisfying picture of our childless future. I could come up with nothing between now and then that would motivate Matt to change his habit of disappearing into the city each day, a practice he engaged in even on weekend days that were free of kid-centered activities. Despite all our conversations about his plans to find work in the face of my less demanding work schedule, he had yet to take any action. I completely abandoned the notion of him getting a job. He had no motivation to work -- he had me.

A sense of defeat seeped into my being. I began to relate staying in my marriage to settling for a subpar outcome. I inventoried my personality. I wasn't the settling type, I was the set-a-goal-and-get-it-done type. The problem was that despite the failure I felt, I couldn't seem to find the will to abandon the goal of sustaining my marriage. I couldn't, I told myself. That would be weak, I would be a quitter, I would be like my parents. Besides that, based on all external measures, I was a screaming success. Matt and I looked perfect to the outside world. But we weren't perfect -- far from it. In my moments of brutal self-reflection, I regarded our relationship as a shell that had not only been robbed of its pearl, it was also void the oyster.

Matt encouraged my internal vacillation by keeping his head down and pushing forward. On the rare occasion we were able to calmly breach the topic of our marital quality, he asserted that he was happy; our union and our family were all he had ever hoped for. But, I asked myself over and over, how could he be happy when I was so miserable? The truth, I decided, was that we were both settling. I wondered how long we could go on this way, and it became increasingly difficult to remember a time when I had felt differently. The fact that I had accepted our situation for so long posed a challenge to the notion of taking action at this point. How could I justify it?

I had always upheld a firm commitment to keeping my marital discontent to myself, believing that my first and highest allegiance was to my husband and my children. Plus, I saw no value in airing my dirty laundry. Speaking ill of Matt would only serve to diminish him in the eyes of my friends and family. The temporary relief I might feel from venting about our latest argument didn't seem to justify the long-term strain it would place on our relationship.

But things were different now. I felt more conflicted than ever. Our polar opposition had me questioning my own judgment. I felt an increasing urge to relay to an impartial third party all my fears and suspicions and ask them if I was crazy. I considered entering therapy, but it would be impossible to hide the expenditure from Matt. I wasn't ready to shine that bright a light on my growing doubts. The pressure of my escalating emotions percolated inside of me. I couldn't help but feel that it was only a matter of time until they bubbled to the surface and blew the lid off of our carefully pantomimed life.

Chapter 46

Mel

One evening I was sitting with my boss, Melanie (Mel, as we all knew her), debriefing a meeting. It was well past five o'clock and the corporate offices of Michaelson Industries had emptied out. We had worked together for almost a year now. Conversation was easy between us, and I often found myself sharing things with her I had never before shared with a boss. I confided in her all the details of my father's death and regularly talked to her about the kids. Having grown children and grandchildren of her own, she proved to be a great sounding board. She had a way of minimizing whatever concern was nagging me in the moment. She had lived through all the punishments that teenage girls inflict on one another and assured me that, like her own daughters, Rachel, too, would find her way into a solid group of friends. I knew Mel was going through a divorce, but knew none of the details.

That evening, after completing the list of action items from our meeting, the conversation turned personal. She opened up about her divorce, telling me that her husband had cheated on her, then forced her hand by refusing to give up the other woman. I listened, enthralled. I couldn't fathom someone being so brash that he would demand to have his cake and eat it too.

She asked about my marriage. My default response spilled forth like a well-rehearsed speech. I loved my family. I had achieved so much more than I had ever hoped for. Matt was a supportive husband, staying home with the kids so I could pursue my career. But, I continued, we would be empty nesters in a matter of four years. At that point, I said, I would likely pursue a divorce. The words literally fell out of my mouth. I sat silently for a moment, mentally playing back the sentence I had just spoken.

Did I just say out loud that I planned to divorce my husband?

Within seconds I confirmed that yep, I had just uttered the biggest Freudian slip in the history of my life. The solution to my deeply rooted doubts about my marriage rose up and shot out of me like a bullet. I sat in stunned silence for a few seconds, as if waiting for an imaginary hammer to drop or a cannon to fire. When neither occurred, I returned my focus to Mel. She was nodding and conveying understanding with her eyes. She remarked that if I had such thoughts now, she doubted I would last four years before making good on my intentions.

The words I spoke in that moment breathed life into a notion that had been flitting around inside my head for so long it had become innate. The combination of my spoken intention and Mel's reaction changed everything. It wasn't so much what she said, but what she didn't say. She demonstrated no judgment, no horror, no reaction at all, really. If anything, her response was one of complete empathy, her comment focused entirely on me. Not Matt. Not the kids. Not our families and friends. She said that *I* wouldn't last four more years. It was as if she somehow knew the difficulty I faced.

The impact of my spontaneous admission was profound. Something was different now. I hadn't realized how alone I was until that moment, when suddenly I wasn't. I had forged plenty of casual friendships with colleagues, and with parents of my children's friends since moving to Houston, but the handful of close friends, the ones in whom I could confide anything, lived miles away and faced the same demands of kids, husbands and jobs. Spontaneous as it was, my confession had the effect of forging a bond that I desperately needed, with someone who knew firsthand the perils of the journey for which I was preparing.

In the months that followed, a picture of my future began to form in my mind. The details I envisioned added color and form to a notion that for nearly 10 years had been a shapeless and intermittent urge, a hint of something so formidable I dared not imagine it more clearly. As the picture came into sharper focus I realized its attraction had little to do with additions to my life. My life had everything I ever wanted. The career I had built and being mother to my three children exceeded every expectation I had ever imagined as a child.

I realized the appeal of my new life was more about what would be *absent* from it. I would no longer care if Matt found a job. I would never again obsess over how he spent his days and debate myself as to whether I should hire a private detective to follow him, nor would I continue to challenge my own stupidity for believing his hapless explanations. The voice in my head that was always telling me to push onward and not to rock the boat would be forever silenced. There was nothing, not a thing I could think of, that I did not like about the future I imagined.

I felt my resolve building, but something still held me back. I told myself to be patient, that I just needed more time to adjust to the idea of initiating action. I found myself looking for a sign or an event that would push me to take the first step in making my spontaneous admission a reality. And then, three months after my conversation with Mel, it came.

Not surprisingly, the vacuum that existed between Matt and me extended to our sex life. I tried not to keep track, but I guessed it had been upwards of a year since we were last intimate with one another. Our habit of giving each other a quick peck on the cheek and then retreating to our respective sides of the bed was firmly entrenched. Most nights I was exhausted enough not to care, but as weeks turned to months, our platonic existence became yet another warning sign that I couldn't continue to ignore. It wasn't just his responsibility, I preached to myself. Unable to remember the last time I had invited an encounter, I couldn't hold myself blameless.

Some combination of the need to test my theory and my craving for human contact finally got the best of me. I resolved to initiate sex with my husband. One night, instead of following my usual routine, I hovered near the middle of the bed after we said goodnight. I reached over and touched his shoulder lightly. I waited, holding my breath.

Why was I so nervous, for God's sake?

When another five seconds of contact failed in achieving even the slightest reaction from him, I applied more pressure, moving my hand gently but firmly from his shoulder to his chest. I felt a tightening of the muscle beneath his t-shirt. Next came his response, but it was not the one I had hoped for. He rolled from his back onto his side and scooted himself to the far edge of his side of the bed. I maintained the tension in my arm for a moment, feeling nothing but the chilly air between us. Finally, I withdrew my arm, returning it to the confines of my side of the bed.

I was stunned. He rebuffed me without so much as a word. He wasn't even compelled to offer an excuse.

I soaked in what had just transpired like a dry sponge absorbs water, replaying the scene over and over in my mind,

AJ WOOTTON

steeping myself in it. To my surprise, I didn't feel sad, or even embarrassed, at being rejected by my own husband.

I felt relief.

I would never again be able to tell myself with a straight face that our defunct sex life was accidental. Matt's reaction sent a clear message. He was closed for business where I was concerned. My lack of emotion continued to confuse me, until I comprehended that the scene that had just played out was the confirmation I had been seeking. I now had something to act upon. Something tangible that could not be refuted. Matt could continue to assert that our life was perfect, and that he was happy, but he couldn't brush aside the fact that he had just ignored, no he blatantly rejected, an overture that came on the heels of nearly a year of celibacy. He had either lost all interest in sex or he was getting it elsewhere.

The next day I made a beeline to Barnes and Noble on my lunch hour, once again in search of a book that would calm the turmoil churning inside me. The liberation I felt the night before in my newfound commitment to move forward was short-lived. The morning found me riddled with the same old fears I had been entertaining for years. What if Matt fought me for the kids? How would I afford an attorney? How long would it take to finalize the divorce? How would we handle living arrangements in the meantime? How ugly would he be? My doubts and fears succeeded in swinging the pendulum back to the side of keeping my mouth shut and carrying on. No, I told myself. You have got to find the courage.

You have come farther than ever before, even if it's still mental progress. Push onward and stop looking behind you.

I sat in my car, poring through the pages of *Can Your Relationship be Saved?* The book provided assessment criteria in the form of a quiz as well as advice to readers who were troubled enough by their current relationship to pose the title's fateful question. The fact that it was written by a psychologist on the heels of his own divorce added tremendous credibility to its power to help me. I scanned the first few chapters and then zeroed in on the relationship-assessment quiz. My hope for salvation peaked as I read the first questions. I was convinced that the author, Dr. Michael S. Brody, would lead me to the answer I had sought for so long.

My pulse was racing. I had a flashback to the dentist's office some 30 years before. On that day, an article in *Cosmopolitan* gave me the courage to overcome a fear that had been five years in the making. Now, I looked to this book to instill in me the courage to conquer my fear of divorce, a fear that had lived inside of me for as long as I could remember. I devoured the book the way a refugee would eat a chicken leg. I sat, immobile and engrossed, my attention never diverting from the pages before me. It wasn't until I closed the cover that I noticed the tingling sensation in my right thigh and rear end. I extended my leg in an effort to reintroduce blood flow to the area. Glancing at my watch I realized I had been sitting there for over an hour. I needed to get back to work.

The book delivered, as I hoped it would. By the time I turned the ignition on, I felt my previous night's resolve returning. My responses to the questions posed in the book returned a nearly unanimous indictment against my marriage. The author cautioned that one's ultimate decision about his or her relationship should not be based entirely on the mathematical score. I resolved to review in more detail the guidance for each of my affirmative responses to what he deemed to be high-risk issues when I had more time, but I doubted that a deeper analysis would yield a different result. I knew the outcome before I even opened the book. My marital concerns had spanned the better part of a decade.

I inventoried my emotions as I weaved in and out of traffic. Concluding that my relationship couldn't be salvaged gratified my intellectual self, but this, I decided, had never been my problem. My brain was already well-versed in the answer to the question it would have never posed had it not already known the answer. The problem was overcoming the tidal wave of emotion that overtook me every time I thought seriously about leaving. The tingling sensation that began in my stomach ramped up to a full-scale churn within seconds.

I thought back to my first long-term relationship in high school. Brett and I were far from a model couple. We fought. We were insecure and jealous of one another, and had no real interests in common. The cherry on top of it all was that he was unfaithful. Those facts were undeniable, yet I still managed to convince myself that he was *the one* for me, I just needed to stay the course and somehow, we would transform ourselves from dysfunctional to happily-ever-after. The possibility that a more mature and reciprocal relationship existed never entered my mind. When I finally cut the ties, I hung onto the dangling threads, entering into an on-again, off-again long-distance accord for another year before finally letting go.

The chapter dedicated to the topic of ambivalence spoke to me. I felt as if Dr. Brody had written it for me. He aptly described the seesaw of indecision I had been riding for so long. In addition to my unwillingness to face my dysfunctional fear of letting go, I acknowledged that there were other tangible benefits I continued to derive from staying put. Actually, I could boil it down to one benefit, the belief that my family-together-forever fantasy would prevail in the end. I wanted my offspring to enjoy the enviable pleasure of belonging to a family bound by blood, and void of the complications presented by step-relatives whom they had no part in choosing.

I wanted this so badly I had convinced myself that Matt and I could be fixed. As this hope slowly dissolved, I next tried to convince myself that I could bear it, and that the benefits of keeping my family together outweighed my growing unhappiness. But today was a new day. Sucking it up was no longer an option for me. *Finally, I have exhausted my ability to tolerate my rationalization of the problems between us.* I smiled to myself. I was actually going to go through with this.

My internal pronouncement to move forward gave rise to the need for a plan. Similar to the difficult conversation with my mother I had planned so many years ago, I knew that the topic I wished to talk with Matt about was not going to come up naturally. I would have to force it.

The weeks that followed had me flip-flopping back-and-forth at least a half-dozen or more times. I seemed to have an endless capacity for changing my mind. But when I felt my resolve fading I would return to the book or seek Mel out for a pep talk. There were other times when my fears crept from the dark corners to the center of my being. Anxiety and near panic would overtake me as visions of losing the kids flashed through my mind. A milder version of paralysis would grip me at the thought of paying spousal support to Matt for the rest of my life.

Chapter 47

No Going Back

One day at work I was so overcome with emotion I couldn't stop crying, my eyes leaking a seemingly endless stream of tears. I left my office, got into my car, drove to a nearby parking lot and called a college friend, Chloe, with whom I hadn't spoken in almost a year. I spilled my guts to her.

Was I crazy to want to throw away all that was good about my marriage, I asked her?

Her kind, non-judgmental nature reassured me that no, I wasn't crazy. A voice deep inside of me was telling me something and I needed to listen to it, she said. It was neither normal, nor healthy to feel this way. I needed to try and let go of my self-judgment. If divorce turned out to be the only means of achieving that, then so be it. The universe, God, and the world would not punish me, she reassured me.

At her suggestion, I turned to a regular regimen of journaling, meditation, and exercise. I still found myself with a surplus of anxiety, but my practice did wonders to help me manage it. I came to regard those weeks between reading the book and my confrontation with Matt as boot camp. I was undergoing a mental-training program and testing my mettle in the process. When at last I initiated the conversation, I was shocked at the calm and non-emotional manner in which he received the news.

"I understand," he said, "but really, do you want to do this before my 50th birthday?"

His milestone birthday would take place in less than three months. We were planning a weekend getaway with some friends, coincidentally the ones that were on hand when I blackened his eye almost two years before.

I stared at him, having no idea how to respond. He knew me so well. All he had to do was interject a vision of the outside world looking in on my dastardly decision and I was all but shut down. As I attempted to push away the vision of our friends whispering to each other about the bombshell of our divorce decision, I told him he should go without me. How could he, he asked? It wouldn't be the same.

Outing our decision in just three short months did not allow adequate time to plan our communications to the kids, our families, and friends. In the meantime, we needed to keep up appearances. Besides, he challenged me, was it too much to ask that after more than 20 years together I spend his 50th birthday with him? Did I despise him that much? His response tugged at my guilt and slid me right back into my old seat on the bus headed nowhere. No, I thought, I didn't despise him, but in that moment, I despised myself. Then I reminded myself of Chloe's advice to stop judging myself. I just needed more time, I told myself, and reaffirmed my commitment to stay the course.

Six weeks later my resolve bubbled up again and compelled a second equally fruitless conversation. This time my desired outcome was thwarted by plans to host Matt's family over Christmas. We needed to get through the holidays, he said. We needed time to work on things. Our life wasn't so bad, was it? Then he launched into a long dissertation about all that was right with us. I listened and responded with two ultimatums

-- marriage counseling and an immediate reinstatement of our sex life. He agreed, and then we promptly returned to life as we knew it.

He brushed aside my suggestions for counselors, saying they were too expensive. Wasn't I the one, he reminded me, that was so focused on money? At the same time, no magic spark spontaneously appeared and breathed life into Matt's libido, thus our sexual stalemate continued. Despite those factors, the holidays seemed to lull us back into the state of tranquilized comfort we knew so well. The presence of extended family worked its ever-potent magic. We got along famously and to our guests, appeared to be the perfect, happy family.

The warm glow of the holidays faded as soon as I turned the page of the calendar to January. The trickling of divorce thinking returned, and by the end of January it had become a tsunami of emotion inside me. On the last Sunday morning in January, shortly after we awakened, I turned to him and said, "I'm moving forward. Nothing has changed, and nothing is ever going to change."

The irritation showed on his face as he replied, "Well, that's a selfish decision. I hope you have thought through how this will impact the kids."

It was as if we had never before conversed on this topic. Why, I wondered, had I expected anything different?

I replied that I had, and I did not for a moment underestimate the impact on our children. Divorce was the last thing I wanted. I wouldn't be doing this, I told him, if I felt there was an alternative.

"I can't stop you if this is what you really want," he said, "I just don't understand you."

"But you aren't happy, either. You can't possibly be. You just won't admit it," I said, trying not to sound as frustrated as I felt.

"No, we aren't perfect, but why don't you want to work on it?" he asked.

And so commenced the infinite loop of denial that had come to characterize the topic I was now broaching for the third time. I opted not to bite this time. I no longer believed I could persuade him to see my point of view. Instead, I turned the topic back to him.

"I understand your hesitation. This is going to be a big change for all of us. I'm not underestimating how hard it's going to be on you. You are going to have to find a job, but really, I don't see any issue with that. You have a solid resume and great skills. In spite of your time out of the workforce, I'm confident you can find something. I will help you in any way I can. The job market in Houston is booming," I said.

"Yeah, I know. You can't stop harping me about finding work. You've been nagging me since I quit and how many years ago was that? Seven? Eight? At least I won't have to listen to that anymore," he retorted.

"Fine. We won't talk about that. But there is one more thing I want to say. You won't admit it to me, but I know you are gay. You are either afraid to tell me, or you haven't yet admitted it to yourself. It doesn't matter. It's OK. I support you. If there is one thing that is obvious to me, it's that you and I are finished as a couple. Done. Can't be resuscitated. I want you to be happy, I really do. I want us to do this right, to put the kids first in this process and treat each other as civilly as possible," I said.

He rolled his eyes.

"Oh, now that topic again. I'm not gay, Amber. I've told you a hundred times. You just can't let anything go. You're like a broken record," he said.

"OK, fine. I'll let it go. I won't bring it up again. Let's move forward. Can we agree to cooperate and work through this divorce together?" I asked.

We talked for another 10 minutes, agreeing to take the lowest cost approach, which we both believed to be mediation. He too, wanted a civil ending to our marriage. Afterward, we got out of bed and made breakfast for the kids, acting as if it were any other ordinary Sunday morning.

A few hours later I noticed that his car was gone. I thought nothing of it, having become accustomed to his unannounced comings and goings. I couldn't help but congratulate myself on how well the whole exchange had gone. It had been more than four months since I had first raised the topic of divorce with him. The time in between was fraught with frustration, as I seemed to be making no progress towards achieving my goal. Maybe my unintentionally drawn out approach had been best, I told myself. Maybe he just needed time to get used to the idea.

I spent my day alternating between feelings of sadness and elation. Thoughts of dissolving our family tore at me. Today it felt more real than ever before. I knew the path ahead of me wouldn't be easy. Matt and I had so many milestones to achieve before it was over, telling the kids, our families, our friends, dividing our finances, and moving into separate homes. But once we got through all of that, I told myself, things would get better.

I had finally taken a step, a giant one. And the difference this time was that I wasn't going back.

My self-satisfaction evaporated the moment Matt walked through the door some five hours later, stinking, slurring drunk and loaded for bear. In response to several unanswered texts I had sent him regarding dinner plans, his first sarcastic words were, "Isn't dinner always my responsibility?"

He unloaded simultaneously the makings for dinner and a barrage of insults on me, telling me I was nothing more than a piece of ass (news to me) and a selfish bitch who thought only of herself. Desperate to resurrect the calm we had experienced earlier that morning, I willed myself not to engage, instead offering to help him with dinner.

My attempt at diffusion failed miserably.

"You can go sit on your ass like you always do. I don't need anything from you," he spat at me.

I left the kitchen and busied myself in the bedroom. Thankfully the kids were upstairs, well out of earshot of the scene that had just transpired. I kept my fingers crossed that Matt would get himself in check before we all sat down to dinner. I wanted a dignified break-up of our family, absent of screaming matches and theatrics. I pictured Matt and I sitting down and having a calm and rational conversation with them, availing us to their fears and concerns, not dumping our buckets in front of them.

By the time we gathered at the table he had calmed down considerably, his demeanor cool and distant, but not hostile. My seat felt like a pincushion as I chewed my food, tasting nothing. Despite the reprieve, I sensed the tension just beneath the surface like a wire pulled tight, threatening to break at any moment. We made it through the meal without a blow-up. Afterward we watched some television together with the kids, also without incident.

It wasn't until we retired to the bedroom that the mean and nasty Matt who had walked through the kitchen door several hours before reemerged.

"You want a fight?" he said, eyes narrowed and glaring. "Well, you got one!"

Chapter 48

Hoeing My Own Row

I buckled my seatbelt and glanced behind me. The kids were settling into their seats. Rachel was sending one last text, probably to her boyfriend. Austin was leaning back, already seeming to have melted into his seat. I gave it five minutes after takeoff before he fell asleep. Rachel would wait to see if our flight included a movie. Depending on what might be showing, she, too, might be asleep by the time we reached cruising altitude.

The mood in the car on the way to the airport was lighthearted; we were all excited about our weekend getaway. It was our first family trip without their dad. I imagined their thoughts had turned to him many times already. I knew the drive to the airport would have brought forth memories of past vacations and imagined they might have felt a pang of sadness at the notion that we would never again board a plane as our former unit of five. Such thoughts, if they had occurred, had not visibly dampened their spirits. They were adjusting to our new life.

It was a Friday night and we were on our way to visit Cam for the weekend. It would be my first time back to the Michigan State campus since delivering him as a freshman two years ago. By the time we landed, rented the car, and made the drive from Detroit, it would be late when we rolled into East Lansing. We planned to stop by Cam's apartment to say a quick hello on the way to the hotel. Tomorrow we would go out for breakfast together, then head to the grocery store to procure burgers, hot dogs, and all other necessary supplies for tailgating. Cam's girlfriend, Ann; his roommates; and a handful of other friends were planning to join the party. Kick-off for tomorrow night's game against Notre Dame was set for 7:30 p.m. The weather forecast predicted an 80-degree daytime temperature that dipped to a pleasing 68 in the evening, perfect for a September football game. I could already picture the stadium lights, the crisp evening air, and the deafening roar of the crowd. It was going to be a great weekend.

Something about boarding a plane always revitalized me, I felt the effect even more acutely today. Thoughts of work, Houston, and the divorce were already receding into the corners of my mind. By the time we landed I would be fully immersed in our packed agenda, the change of scenery working its magic of focusing me firmly in the present and away from the worries and responsibilities of daily life. Despite its short duration, I expected our weekend away to work wonders for all of us. The kids needed the break as much as I did.

I turned my focus to my own row, catching Wayne's eye in the process. He took my hand and squeezed it tight, kissing me at the same time. He smiled his big, happy smile and said, "I'm looking forward to my first live Big Ten football game."

I couldn't help but smile back; he had that effect on me. His enthusiasm was contagious.

"And I am looking forward to showing you around," I said. My childhood home of Grand Rapids was located a good two hours in the opposite direction of East Lansing. We wouldn't have time to go there, but the landscape of southeast Michigan served as a proxy for that of northwest Ohio. To me, it would feel like being home again.

It was still hard to believe I was dating someone. Everything about the relationship I was now in -- and I couldn't deny that it was a full-blown relationship -- violated the post-divorce rules I had established for myself. First of all, I wasn't even divorced yet. I thought back to my moments of frustration in my final years with Matt and how I had yearned for the simplicity of single-handedly steering my household. I had envisioned this occupying my full focus, believing that even if I had wanted to pursue a love interest I wouldn't have the time or emotional capacity. Instead, I pictured myself enjoying the benefits of casual dating, completely absent of any ties. I pictured this happening after some sufficiently extended amount of time had passed. And yet, here I was. In the less than four months we had been together, I hadn't given a second thought to seeing anyone else.

My feelings for Wayne both thrilled and terrified me. I thought back to our second date, the date that did me in. It was the middle of June and the evening weather hadn't yet become too oppressively hot and humid. We were seated in the restaurant's outdoor area, talking non-stop between bites of steak and sips of wine. At one point he put his hand on my arm and squeezed it, that big smile illuminating his whole face as he said, "I love you, Amber."

His declaration washed over me like a warm tide. My experience with him, limited as it was, registered the words he spoke as sincere, and motivated by nothing more than a need he felt in that moment to share his feelings. I felt the corners of my mouth involuntarily turning upward. Before I could respond, he said, "I'm sorry. I shouldn't have said that, I know it's only our second date, but I've admired you since the day I met you. I can't believe I'm on a date with you. I'm just the kind of guy who says what I feel. I can't help it." He was still smiling.

I was too overwhelmed to respond in kind; my life was still mired in complexity. His apology graciously released me from any form of reciprocation. My brain immediately began sending out warning sensors, subliminal flashes designed to keep me from tumbling over the edge on which I was teetering.

Keep your distance, the voice in my head told me.

How could he possibly love me? He barely knows me!

For the rest of that night, and in the days that followed, I replayed his spontaneous admission and reminded myself of another time in my life when I allowed attention and flattery to lure me across a line I thought I would never cross. I renewed my vow to remain vigilant in protecting myself from potential hurt.

The source of my feelings for Wayne extended far beyond his words. It was the way he treated me, which quite simply, was like I was the most important person in the universe. He opened doors for me, carried my bags, and saw to it that I was seated at a table before he went to order our coffee at Starbucks. His gold-flecked, startling green eyes never left mine when we talked. His manner gave me the sensation that at all times he was availing his entire self to me. He spoke openly about his own first marriage, his childhood, and his belief in good old-fashioned true love. The kind, that once discovered, seals one's heart to the possibility of ever loving another.

Before I met Wayne, I would have mocked the notion of true love. I, who spent a fair amount of time analyzing people, had concluded that if in fact such a thing existed, it was ridiculously rare and would most likely never make an appearance in my own life. But the matter-of-fact way in which he imparted this belief compelled me to give the possibility some serious consideration.

But still, I tread cautiously. The platonic existence I had lived for so long rendered me a classic case of vulnerability.

The contrast between Wayne and Matt could not have been more pronounced. It would be natural to overcompensate for all that was missing from my marriage by seeking someone at the opposite end of the spectrum. I contemplated the possibility that this relationship could end in an equally disastrous fashion, but for very different reasons. At 6-feet-2, he stood a good four inches taller than me. I couldn't remember the last time that kissing required me to tilt my face upward. This had me combing my memory bank for an inkling of a past beau that stood taller than me, but my inward search returned no results. I was in my high analytics mode, questioning why, all of a sudden, I was attracted to someone with such a large and imposing frame. What did it mean? Why had my ideal profile suddenly changed?

I had met Wayne for the first time two years before, during my panel interview with Michaelson Industries. In recent months I found myself thinking back to that day over and over again. Interviews were not overly stressful for me, but at the same time knowing that I had 60 minutes to prove myself to four people simultaneously did plant a few seeds of angst within me. Wayne's manner had put me immediately at ease. He also impressed me with his preparation, demonstrating that he had clearly put some thought into his questions.

Many who sit on the hiring side of the desk feel it's your job to wow them, and don't bother even reviewing your resume before you walk through the door for the interview. The fact that I ended up getting the job probably also accrued some points in his plus column. The intervention he staged when Dave asked me how I felt about working with men was another feather in his cap, cementing the notion that he was someone who could be trusted to speak the truth, a trait that had recently catapulted itself to the top of my list of critical human attributes.

From my first day on the job I considered Wayne a friend. The more I interacted with him the more I felt the alignment in our thinking. I knew I could count on him to give me a candid opinion, regardless of the topic. Learning the difference between friend and foe takes time and careful study. Watching how people behave, not just in front of the boss but how they treat you, provides valuable insight that can only be gained through experience. Honesty was his hallmark, a trait that I quickly learned occasionally got him in to trouble. He had no use for sugar-coating the truth, and if something got him really riled him up he had no compunction about letting loose a stream of expletives.

I came to respect and appreciate his style, even though it was completely opposite mine. He was the first person outside of my family that I told of my father's suicide. I didn't plan on confiding in him; in fact, I had no intention of sharing that detail with anyone from my workplace. Two summers ago, he came into my office the morning after I returned from the vacation that began with my father's death, and asked how my trip was. It was just three weeks after I'd joined the company.

When I told him that my father passed away during my visit he immediately reached out and pulled me into a hug. My surprise at his unconventional response was more than offset by the comfort that his spontaneous expression of concern delivered to me. He sat down in the chair opposite my desk and gave me his full attention. I ended up spilling forth the whole story to him.

While we knew virtually nothing about one another, I felt a kinship with him that I could not explain. When I unexpectedly transferred to the corporate office four months later we saw each other intermittently at company leadership events or during an occasional happy hour or retirement party. It was I who sought him out after Matt left. I suggested that a group of us get together for drinks after work, as it had been a while since our former team had connected.

When none of the others showed up, Wayne and I ended up talking for hours about all that had transpired in my life and my pending divorce. He told me that when I was ready he would like to take me on a date. We went out the following Saturday. That was four months ago. Since then we had been discreetly inseparable.

Ever cautious where the kids were concerned, and uncertain of where Wayne and I were headed, I shielded them from him. When Cam was hired into Michaelson Industries' internship program earlier in the summer, he was assigned to Wayne's team. For the entire summer, Wayne and I kept our secret from him, as well as from the other two children. It wasn't until a few weeks ago that I owned up to dating him. Rachel, who I often joked had eyes in the back of her head, already knew something was up and suspected I was dating someone. She was magnetically drawn to my iPhone and its capabilities, which were far more advanced than those offered by her flip phone. In between Internet and YouTube sessions she managed to monitor my texts.

Knowing her highly inquisitive nature, I had anticipated the potential for her surveillance. Instead of listing Wayne under his real name in my contacts, I used an alias, a woman, whose name was Jessica, believing that Rachel wouldn't bother to inspect exchanges between myself and a woman I had described as being a friend from work.

I clearly underestimated her. When she learned that Wayne and I were dating, she confessed she had been reading my texts and suspected that either she now had two gay parents, or that I had disguised the true identity of my romantic interest. My attempt at disguising Wayne as Jessica became a source of humor for all of us and provided some levity for what had initially been a pretty tense subject. I knew that even more than curiosity, concern for my wellbeing motivated her to spy on my texts.

Chapter 49

The Outing

The mature and well-orchestrated family reorganization I so desperately wished for turned out to be anything but. Matt delivered on his promise of a fight. It would take me years to understand that while I bore the brunt of his full-frontal attack, his battle was not with me. I was all he had, the only tangible target upon which he could unload the aggression that accompanied inner Matt's journey from the shadows into the light. His secret inevitably bubbled up to where it hovered just beneath the surface. Despite the increasing will it required to repress it, he held firm, preferring the emotional torture of living a double life over coming clean.

How long, I often wondered?

At what point had he first acknowledged to himself that he found the male form more attractive than mine? For how many years had he squeezed my image out through closed eyes and played some homosexual reel in his mind while we made love? Had he already acted on his urges? Or was his source of frustration the fact that he yearned for something he would not allow himself to indulge in?

It was at this point in my ponderings that my thoughts turned inward. Why had I endured it for so long? What was wrong with me? I would then tick through the list of female friends and family members and confirm that nope, none of them would have sat there for 10 years, feeding on the steady diet of bullshit I had willingly lapped up.

Matt spent our last four months together as a family in a vodka-fueled haze. I chalked the first few weeks of his binge up to the fact that he was processing my decision while he continued his refusal to own any part of it. I told myself he would return to his normal self within a few months, but instead, drunk became his new normal. When the cable repairman came for a scheduled appointment during the week of spring break, Rachel called to tell me that Dad refused to get out of bed to answer the door. She, who had been counseled since she was old enough to understand to never open the door for a stranger, wanted to know what she should do.

I left the office and rushed home in a panic. The events of that day deteriorated to a showdown between Matt and me over his car keys, which I refused to give him until he sobered up. He managed to grab my purse and threatened to throw it in the pool if I didn't hand over the keys. I responded by calling the police, only to learn that unless Matt had hurt me or the kids, which he had not, there was nothing that could be done.

I took a few impromptu vacation days and drove Rachel and Austin to Galveston for the weekend, stopping first at a nearby hospital where I parked the car and we got out and sat together in the grass while I told them that their father and I had decided to divorce. The anger inside of me seethed in his direction. His behavior had left me no choice but to tell them. There was no way I could simply write off the scene they had just witnessed to "Dad having a bad day," or some fight between us that in the entirety of our marriage, had seen no rival.

I could barely stomach the fear I saw in their eyes and my own childhood memories that it resurrected. They deserved to know the truth, with or without Matt's participation. He, who had prohibited me from telling them anything until we had spent months crafting the messaging, had not only added to the complexity of the explanation through his erratic behavior, he had also rendered himself incapable of participating in the conversation.

Yes, Rachel and Austin admitted to me, they figured something was up. Matt and I had had plenty of arguments over the course of our marriage, but we always conducted them in private. Yet, in the past few months, Matt had completely abandoned his filter, demonstrating no care for who may be within earshot as he vented his anger and sent insults hurtling my way. Of course, this had not gone unnoticed. Add to that their father's volatile behavior, and both had already constructed the perfect recipe for our family's dissolution. Austin told me he had planned for the worst, his 14-year-old wisdom postulating that this would help prepare him for the news I had just reported to him, and at the same time would leave him delighted and somehow more appreciative if that news never came.

The following two months would see little change in Matt's behavior. In his occasional lucid moments, I talked to him about going to an Alcoholics Anonymous meeting and suggested we bring his mother down for a visit. The power of his family's disapproval at his behavior was the last lever I could think of that, if pulled, might snap him out of his altered state. I yearned for the calm that a visit from Matt's mother, my children's beloved Grandma, would impart. I found myself praying for his acceptance. But Matt refused on both accounts. He was not an alcoholic and had no need to sit around a circle commiserating with a bunch of losers who were. He was simply processing the selfish decision I had inflicted on our family. He was not yet ready to tell his family about our divorce.

I was immobilized by guilt. I needed to maintain my allegiance to him, I owed him that much. As the weeks turned to months, I began to feel a sense of being suspended in time. Matt refused to budge from his inert stance. My belief that he would come around was a testament to my own denial. I clung to our jointly conceived plan of mediating the end of our divorce, in spite of the fact that he had stopped participating in our appointments and generally refused to discuss the subject.

My silent plea for him to nudge me over my cliff of reticence finally came. Cam had been home from college just short of one week. Sadness settled over his eyes like the closing of a window shade when Matt and I delivered our news to him. We had seemed so happy, he said. When did things change? We responded individually with our neat, pat answers about how marriage is complicated and that we kept our troubles to ourselves, hoping we could make things work, but now realized that wasn't possible.

I wrung my hands under the kitchen table and cracked each knuckle that would cooperate. For what would be the last time, I told myself that Matt would get a grip, that we could land the plane of our divorce on a smooth and unencumbered runway, and there was no point in relaying to Cam the details of the downright scary flight we had flown during his spring semester.

The following weekend we went out to dinner as a family to celebrate Mother's Day. Matt was on his best behavior, conversation was easy, the mood was lighthearted, and we shared some laughs. I watched Matt carefully out of the corners of my eyes. Might he be sober? I held hope. That night as I got ready for bed I took notice of how relaxed I felt, a rare occurrence in life as I had come to know it.

I had moved out of our bedroom several months earlier when Matt refused to uproot himself. I was the one who wanted a divorce, he snidely rationalized, I could find somewhere else to sleep. I took refuge in our guesthouse, a detached structure that stood across the driveway, opposite our kitchen door. Our home's appointment with this self-contained suite that included a kitchenette ended up being the attribute that tipped our decision to purchase our house. It was perfect for accommodating the steady stream of northern visitors we anticipated. I reflected on the irony of that premise as I crawled into the bed that had been intended to host guests outside of our immediate family.

Surprisingly, I never struggled to sleep in those months. My mind cooperated every night in releasing me from its incessant planning for the next crisis. This night was no different. I was nearly asleep when my cell phone rang. Cam's name glowed in the dark as I answered the call, my panic instinctively rising. Cam was sorry to wake me up, but this was the second time this had happened. He thought I should know.

"What? What happened?" I rasped into the phone as I hurtled myself out of bed and began moving to the door.

Someone had come over and was in the bedroom with Dad. Cam was worried.

"Might Dad be doing drugs?"

Cam paused.

"Or else, um, is Dad gay?"

I was through the guesthouse door and standing outside my former bedroom door at what felt like *Wonder Woman* speed. Every cell of my body was wired for action. I tried the bedroom door and felt his weight on the other side of it.

"Get him out of here," I said through the door, "Now! Before I do something crazy."

Options ticker-taped through my head, fueled by the adrenaline that was coursing through me. The image of the car in our driveway registered as I stood waiting for a response from the other side of our bedroom door – *what nerve!* My mind instinctively began inventorying a list of blunt objects I might use to smash its windshield. The sledge hammer in our garage or one of our heavier frying pans would do the trick. Alternatively, I could launch an assault on the tires with one of our larger, kitchen carving knives. I felt the nerves jumping in my fingertips that were itching to mobilize.

At last Matt opened the door, saving me from the destructive multiple choice of actions that each vied for its bubble to be penciled in. I stood frozen in place as a stocky *and incredibly homely* man of indiscernible age filed first past me, and then past our three children. I forced myself to follow him into the foyer and then close and lock the door after he exited. The scene reminded me of a perp walk in which the criminal makes his way into the squad car while bystanders step aside to allow passage. In spite of the surreal quality of the moment I could not stop focusing on the physical characteristics of my husband's guest. *Could he not have found someone more attractive?*

By the time I returned to the bedroom to confront Matt, he was passed out.

"Get up," I told him, "so I can kick you in the balls."

I raised my voice and commanded him twice more. His response was an uninterrupted stream of snores. Relaxed snores, the kind that accompanies deep, peaceful sleep.

I felt my fury mounting. My body was a livewire. I needed a grounding source. Mechanically, I propelled myself to the kitchen, where I fumbled through the cabinets for the biggest glass I could find. I ran the tap to its rim and then returned to the bedroom and proceeded to empty its contents on his limp body. Slurred responses erupted from the depths of his drunken slumber.

"What are you doing? What the hell?"

I unloaded a round of acid vent on him. Be damned the eggshells I had been tiptoeing on for the past four months. I had officially reached my limit.

Fuck mediation.

Fuck playing nice.

He who had called for a fair fight seemed to have misplaced his gloves. Mine were coming off too, by God. Feeling some relief from my rant, I turned and left the bedroom, slamming the door behind me.

Now I needed to find the kids.

Chapter 50

Extracting the Prickers

In the span of a few months, Matt's speedometer had gone from zero to 120. Tonight, he had taken it to the limit by inviting a random sex partner into his bedroom while his kids watched TV and played video games upstairs.

Cam's words rang in my ear.

"It was the second time it happened."

The change Matt had undergone was astonishing. He seemed to have lost all control, all sense of the person he once was. I felt as if I was a spectator in some make-believe world, so bizarre it rivaled the most sensational of dreams that my mind had concocted over the years.

Except it wasn't a dream, I reminded myself as I stood in the front hallway contemplating my options. I knew I needed to pull myself together and develop a plan, but my brain wouldn't cooperate.

The scene I had just witnessed was stuck on replay in my mind. Like witnessing a bloody crime scene or walking in on your parents having sex, I didn't want to keep gaping at it, but I couldn't force my mind to change channels. The look on Matt's face, vacant and void of any expression, haunted me. The vision of the pint-sized, stubby man walking calmly out the front door would remain forever etched in my mind.

I dragged my focus back to the moment and to my children, who had co-witnessed the spectacle of Matt's un-ceremonial outing of himself. I couldn't imagine what was going through their minds. There was nothing, no event from their collective lives that could have prepared them for this. I felt the need to take some extraordinary action, but at the same time I knew there was no way to undo, to help them un-see or forget what had just played out in front of them. I conducted a flash inventory of the numerous dysfunctional scenes from my own past. Nothing compared. Even my father had had the decency to conduct his marital transgressions off-site. I gave up on the notion of a plan. I would just have to wing it.

I willed my legs to move toward the living room, where I found Austin, sitting alone on the couch. I vaguely remembered Cam and Rachel exiting the front door. Had it been a few minutes or a few hours ago?

I sat next to Austin, gently pulled him into me and said the only thing I could think of.

"I'm so sorry."

We sat there together, silently processing, until I heard the digital female voice from our security system announce, "front door open." As if obeying some invisible commanding officer, I rose, pulling Austin with me and went to gather Cam and Rachel into my arms.

I herded them upstairs to our game room, thinking about the many carefree and happy moments that had been spent here -- sleepovers, rounds of *Guitar Hero,* and endless hours of *X-Box* -- and how the discussion I was about to have with them would stand in such stark contrast. The conversation I had envisioned dozens of times that involved Matt gently explaining to our children that he had discovered a hidden truth about himself and had chosen to embrace it, was now left to me. I spent the remainder of that night talking to the three of them, striving to balance honesty and neutrality, a task I found incredibly difficult in that moment.

I felt an almost irrational need for justice. Matt's behavior violated every sense of what I believed to be right and fair. At a minimum, I needed an apology or an explanation. I couldn't imagine letting go of the rage I felt until he did one or the other. But, based on the one-sided exchange that had just transpired in the bedroom, I knew I had a better chance of being magically teleported to a tropical island than of him returning, even briefly, to the sane and rational person I once knew. His inability to meet my needs drove me to do the next best thing I could think of, which was to advance the undoing of my marriage to the next step.

I needed Matt out of our house.

Surprisingly, Jill didn't hang up on me. It was sometime between the hours of 1 and 2 a.m. when I called her and demanded that she come and remove her brother from our home. I suppose I had the advantage of catching her in the deepest stage of sleep, her senses dull and sluggish. Or maybe the intensity of the crazy she heard in my voice across the miles of cellular connection convinced her that I would in fact do something drastic if she didn't comply. I ranted about the limitations of my patience and his lack of morals. I told her with complete conviction that his ass would be on the curb the minute I could get a court order. She listened patiently and agreed to intervene. She would plan to fly down from Ohio next weekend.

The recent events of my life had me believing nothing could go right. In the following days I found myself fearing that either she wouldn't come, or he would refuse to go with her. I lamented my highly charged, impromptu spew I had dumped on her. But, the bucket that held my patience was dry as a bone, I was fresh out of "nice" and "rational" options.

As the sole breadwinner and the only sane adult in the family, I had to do something. I also knew that the content of my call had not come as a complete shock. Even though Matt had still not told his family about our divorce, I knew that Cam had called his Aunt Jill earlier that week and told her that we were divorcing, and that his father was drinking heavily. My call had just served to provide her with a few more graphic details.

To my great relief, Jill came the next Friday and somehow convinced him to leave with her the following Sunday morning, booking him on her return flight. The only feeling I could clearly identify in myself was relief. I felt as if I had finally been freed from confinement beneath an elephant-sized pile of bricks.

I could move.

I could breathe.

I felt lighter.

I returned to my bed in the guest house that night and slept peacefully for the first time in days. The next morning, I left for work free of worry about what drama might ensue in my absence. Something had finally gone right.

A few days later I learned that Matt landed himself in the emergency room on his first night in Ohio, after quitting the vodka cold turkey. He entered an alcohol-rehab program after his release from the hospital. I was happy he had finally found his way to people who could help him; even more so, I was grateful he was no longer my responsibility. Yes, I knew that alcoholism was a sickness. Yes, I knew that coming out in your fifties after being in a committed heterosexual relationship that produced three children had to be a challenge. I actually couldn't imagine it. But I had no more capacity for him.

What about me?

Was he sorry for all that I endured in the name of his midlife transformation? Did he even know what I endured? I doubted it. The unpredictability that pervaded our last months living under the same roof had ramped my anxiety level to a lifetime high from which I couldn't seem to come down. I envisioned soldiers in battle. With the enemy ever on the horizon you could never let your guard down. It felt like I was living a scene from my recurring college dream. I had a foreboding sense that some unforeseen obstacle would appear out of nowhere and impede my ability to reach the finish line of our divorce.

Finally, Matt and I began communicating, out of necessity. Until our assets were divided he was still financially dependent on me. Eventually he told me that he planned to stay in northwest Ohio. He had his eye on an historic home that needed tons of work in a transitional, mostly gay neighborhood. His offer to buy it was contingent upon the seller's agreement to schedule closing after our divorce was finalized and he had his half of our assets.

The picture my mind created of Matt restoring a circa-1800s home felt spot-on, but I was stunned by his decision. A part of me could see how this would be good for him. Within the first month of his return to Ohio he had reunited with Stephen, his gay "friend" from 10 years ago. What I couldn't comprehend was that his decision essentially granted me full custody of our children. For months I had entertained the terrifying notion that his threats to fight me for full custody would be realized. In an instant this fear was neutralized. My children were going to live with me.

Thrilled as I was with my end of the bargain, it felt less than ideal. I disliked the parallel between our co-parenting arrangement and the one I had experienced with my own father so many years ago. I knew firsthand the barrier that physical distance posed to cultivating relationships. Matt had always been an attentive and involved father. I couldn't imagine how he would be able to tolerate being so far away from them. But they are older than I was when I was separated from my father, I told myself. They had a lifetime of good memories with their father, in contrast to me barely knowing mine at the time. We would make the separation work.

I had to agree that being close to his family was the best thing for him. It would give him time to get back on his feet, get a job, and come to terms with his new reality. Living in Ohio did give him the advantage of being physically closer to Michigan and Cam for the duration of his remaining college years. Rachel and Austin were within a few years of legal adulthood; at that point they could choose to live with either parent. They could spend summers with Matt if they chose. If either of them expressed interest in such an arrangement now, I would encourage it, having no desire to influence their decisions about their father.

Despite all the drama that had played out in the past months, I had to admit there was some good that came out of the turmoil that our family experienced. The radar-like sense we developed to monitor each other's well-being gave me tremendous satisfaction. I felt my children begin to watch me, studying my facial expressions and scanning my body language in an effort to return a "situation normal" assessment. When they read concern or anxiety they hovered, asking if everything was OK. They teamed up to lighten my load, offering to help me with dinner or to clean and straighten before one of dozens of scheduled showings of our home, which was now on the market.

On those days, when I felt down, exhausted, or just plain alone, their demonstration of concern was all I needed to get me back on track. There was no better feeling than knowing that they had my back.

I leveled a similar focus on them. Learning that your parents are divorcing, your father is gay and has also picked up a serious drinking problem, is a lot to process in the span of a few months. Austin, in particular, became pensive. I sought opportunities to talk about his future, reassuring him that it would always include both of his parents. When he complained of a chronic stomach ache I took him to the doctor, who easily diagnosed the issue as stress-induced and recommended counseling. Despite my repeated attempts to convince Austin it may help to talk with someone, he refused. But I didn't give up on talking to him. Before long he began anticipating my prompts, responding with an eye roll or a shake of his head. How did he feel about our divorce? Did he have questions about his own sexual identity?

After the euphoria of Matt's departure faded I began to experience the harshest realities of divorce, those I had anticipated and feared for so long. Matt's family, who for 20 years had been the replacement for what I had classified as a subpar family of my own, was lost to me. And that was just the beginning. After a few months of showing up solo to athletic events or social gatherings, I finally had to confess. Our friends were universally shocked. Matt's fun-loving nature was infectious, especially at a party. Our companionship was easy and effortless in a crowd. From an outsider's perspective we were the perfect couple.

Chapter 51

The Future Unfolds

Despite the animosity that grew between us in the end, there were days when I missed Matt. These were the times when I harnessed the ability to recall his best traits, his wit, his cooking prowess, and sense of humor. I missed our time together as a family. Twenty years of happy memories that had encompassed Christmases, birthdays, and even all the long hours spent remodeling the old house in Whitehouse at a time when we had more energy than money, played through my mind. It was undeniable that our time together, especially in the early days, had comprised more good than bad.

During even the most turbulent of our years together, we had somehow managed to put our differences aside when it came to our kids. From the day each of them came into the world we dedicated ourselves to giving them the best childhood we could muster. We planned their extracurricular activities and jointly marveled at their every success. We encouraged them, loved them, and truly believed that each of them was a unique and special creation, superior specimens of humanity. Some of our most stressful marital moments were spent agonizing over how best to course-correct behavior. We didn't always agree, but in hindsight I realized it was one area of our marriage where we easily compromised. Later, as the divide between us grew, it was our mutual interest in our children that held us together.

I learned long ago that aside from your spouse and parents, few have the patience for the more mundane details regarding your children. Now, my parenting partner of almost 20 years was gone. I longed for our daily banter about the three we co-created, discussing how Rachel and her boyfriend were getting along, her breaststroke time at yesterday's swim meet, our shared pride in the glowing review Cam received at the end of his internship, or the great tackle Austin made at last night's football scrimmage. There were decisions to be made -- what to do with the latest creature Austin had brought home, a turtle he rescued from the bayou; analysis regarding personality traits; and which one of us they inherited it from.

I also missed the more practical aspects of having a man around the house. Throughout our life together Matt had taken sole responsibility for our household maintenance. Not only was he handy, he was a meticulous craftsman. He could paint a perfectly straight line without the aid of masking tape. He knew how to measure and cut trim pieces for a precise fit. He could diagnose and fix most functional failures around the house -- the dishwasher that wouldn't drain, an unresponsive light switch, or a leaky faucet. In contrast, my home maintenance skills topped out at turning a screwdriver and changing a light bulb. I learned about pool maintenance the hard way when ours became infected with a green fungus that took me weeks to eradicate. There was also the issue of time. After working all day, I had little patience for addressing home-repair nuisances. I made a list and began interviewing handy men.

But even in my lowest of moments, I didn't have to try very hard to find an equal number of benefits to the new life unfolding before me. My brothers were two of the first I told about my divorce. I broached the topic with some hesitation, worrying they would think I was a failure, and that I was an idiot for marrying someone who turned out to be gay in his fifties. They reacted neutrally at first, in spite of the one-sided spew I unloaded on them about my last months with Matt. Next came concern and compassion, not just for me, but also for Matt. I took pride in their unconditional support of him. Their wish for his full recovery was sincere. They both held him in high regard and were sorry to hear about his current struggles.

My miscalculation of their reactions showed how little I knew the men they had both become. I realized what an obstacle my marriage had posed to cultivating a closer relationship with my brothers in my adult years. It didn't have to be that way. I had made it that way, convinced that the family I grew up in and the one I married into couldn't possibly coexist in harmony. I had placed my bet on the ideal image that Matt's family projected, believing my life's greatest wish had been granted, pushing my own family into the background in the process. I now looked forward to the three of us being more present in each other's lives.

I was thrilled to have a friend again, a friend with whom I talked daily and who knew every last detail of my saga. Mel gave me a key to her house and assigned me a guest bedroom. I was welcome any time, day or night, when I needed sanctuary. I found myself driving to her house, which was a few miles from my office, at lunchtime or other random times when it became impossible to keep my emotions in check during the day. She was my lifeline during the four months of my pre-divorce cohabitation with Matt, making herself available to me at all hours of the day or night. She introduced me to Al-Anon and helped me find a therapist. I thought about the fortuitous change in my job that brought the two of us together. Her appearance in my life felt divinely inspired. I can't imagine those months without her.

Even as the news of our split became common knowledge, I remained tight-lipped about Matt being gay. I knew it wasn't anyone's business, but that wasn't the point. The more I thought about my motivation to guard this detail, the more I realized it had more to do with protecting me than him.

I was beyond feeling humiliated. What kind of woman marries a gay man? His mid-life decision posed a challenge to my already sagging feminine self-image.

On the one hand, it explained his recent lack of interest in me, but on the other hand, I couldn't help but wonder what attributes of mine had called out to his homosexual side when we met some 20 years before. I believed that being gay was always his truth, going all the way back to before we met in college. As much as my heart empathized with his mid-life decision to change teams, I still questioned whether there was anything I could have done to alter his course. Then I would remind myself that I was where I wanted to be. It didn't matter. It was done, and I had finally gotten my wish. The means to my end didn't matter. Time to move on.

I challenged myself to resist the power of the shame I felt when I pictured the reaction of our friends when they learned that Matt was gay. I knew I would never get over my self-consciousness until I became comfortable opening up about it. I tested the water by confiding in a few friends who knew both Matt and me. Their reactions were supportively non-reactive. They applied no judgment to either one of us, and instead sympathized with the difficulties I faced in light of learning this after so many years of marriage.

As I waded deeper into the pond of truth, taking a wider audience into my confidence, the responses began to vary, ranging from shock to a smug lack of shock. Some from the un-shocked camp went on to assert confidently that they had known all along, the implication being that I was either an idiot for not seeing it sooner or that I had for some reason intentionally married a gay man and proceeded to have three children with him.

In defense of those who had known all along, I had to admit that I too, had known the truth at some level. Matt's relationship with Stephen had tripped my concern sensor almost 10 years before. I ignored my instincts, choosing to believe that they were just friends, despite the signs that stood in sharp contradiction to that story. Even though I was the one who officially initiated the end of our marriage, the knowledge that Matt had de facto abandoned our relationship years ago and didn't bother to tell me, still hurt. Being reminded of how blatant the signs of his emerging reality were, burned like alcohol on a fresh cut.

The 10 years it took me to find the courage to abandon my doomed marriage led me to face some important truths about myself. I couldn't help but acknowledge the voice that had been speaking to me for years. The one I routinely ignored in favor of the extraneous chorus that droned on about everyone else's needs and expectations, and how I appeared to the outside world. As I dissected my situation and asked myself over and over how I got *here* I began to appreciate the wisdom that the voice of my soul had offered. I couldn't help but question my motivation for tuning it out all of these years.

My second revelation was that at the age of 48, I was still cowering in the face of conflict, fearing that all hell would break loose if I acted in my own self-interests. The more I pondered the topic the more I had to admit that there were events that had transpired in my life that I had no control over. There was no amount of denial and self-sacrificing behavior that could have saved my mother's marriage to Glen, or that could have prevented Matt's implosion. I had been the classic ostrich with my head buried in the sand, telling myself that the storm would eventually pass if I just bought some time and sucked it up in the near-term.

But what had that gotten me?

Contrary to the logic my young mind had rendered more than 30 years before, talking to the judge about my father and silently enduring Glen's abuse had done nothing to avert my mother's pain. If my actions had had any effect at all, it was only to delay the inevitable. The notion that telling her about Glen would lead to the demise of their marriage seemed so ridiculous to me now. My instincts had told me that their marriage wasn't worth saving in the first place, but I chose to overrule my wiser subconscious. How could I possibly have righted a train that was so far off its tracks?

The folly of my naiveté came to light when Glen made the decision to divorce my mother. His departure from our lives took place less than a year after that cold February day when I took refuge at the neighbors' house after blurting out my secret over the phone to my mother. While I couldn't take credit for prompting his exit from our lives, I took great pride in the fact that my final days of living under the same roof with him were free of midnight visits to my bedroom. He never touched me again after that day. The revelation that felt like a complete failure at the time served its purpose after all. Glen left Cody and returned Ohio a few years later.

The euphoria I felt upon his exit from my life was unrivaled in the course of my 14-year life. Suddenly, my possibilities seemed endless, my future never loomed more brightly. My enthusiasm was only slightly dampened when I learned that his decision was prompted by an affair he was having with a woman he carpooled to work with every day. Unbelievably, it was he who had tired of my mother. After all she had endured from him. She, who had every justification to kick his fat, sorry ass to the curb, was denied the satisfaction in the end. Putting myself in her place, I found it difficult to imagine a more humiliating insult.

Thoughts of my own inner struggles eventually shifted my focus to Matt. My notion of a post-divorce friendship with him was still alive and well, but I wasn't ready yet. Time needed to pass. We needed to replenish our well of shared experiences with some positive interactions. I needed to witness the reappearance of the lucid and rational Matt that I had known for so many years. Our final months together were seared into my memory. I would never be able to forget, but in time I would be able to forgive. The future stretched long and promising ahead. I was optimistic that our nearly 25 years together, and our shared concern for the best interests of our children, would provide the necessary motivation.

It might have taken me the better part of 40 years to learn how to tune into my inner radio channel and listen to my own God-given instincts, but I was ramping up the learning curve at the speed of light. I looked over at Wayne, thinking about how the old me would have never dared to entertain the feelings I had for him, and would never have introduced him to my children so soon. *Before I was even divorced from their father.* Visions of my own parents' conflicts and countless scenes from the Glen-era of my life would have been enough to squelch the idea before it could be formed into action.

But I am not my parents, and this is not their life.

Why not expose Wayne, with all of his happiness, generosity, and love of fun, to my children? I overcame my self-imposed potential step-parent fear within a matter of months. I invited him for dinner and like magic, he and my three kids bonded. My deep, dark fears had yet to materialize, and what's more, I was pretty sure they never would. My confidence in this belief surprised no one more than me.

I leaned my head back as the flight attendant announced our takeoff. I let the jet engines work their magic as they lifted the Airbus off the runway, thrusting my body backward into the seat in the process. I imagined the recent stresses of my life evaporating behind me like jet exhaust into the air as the plane ascended into the clouds. As if on cue, I turned my inward focus forward in time. I felt nothing but happy and hopeful as we gained altitude. I saw only upside. There was no limit. It was going to be a great weekend.

And I was going to have a great life.

THE END
<<<<>>>

Dedication

For Mom and Dad - in honor of the life you gave me and
the lessons you taught me – both the deliberate and the
unintended.

With Love and Gratitude

Wayne – my love, my protector, my best friend and most enthusiastic promoter. Without your encouragement and unwavering support, this book would still be an idea tickling the corners of my mind. Your fearless and unfiltered love is something I never knew to wish for. You have filled my life, and the lives of my children, in a way that makes it impossible to remember how it was before you.

Kirk and Jay – for standing beside me when I needed you most and rallying with me to put the fragmented pieces of our family back together. For long talks, for helping me fill in the blanks of our shared story, and for enduring the pain that reading my early drafts resurrected. For not judging me or anyone else. You are hands down, two of the finest men that I will ever know. I am proud to be your sister.

Cam, Rachel and Austin – for bringing to life my dream of building a family whose members find joy in belonging to one another, love each other unconditionally, and would put it all on the line for each other. For accepting all of my flaws and loving me anyway. I cannot imagine any greater accomplishment than my part in creating the three of you. My love for you is immeasurable.

Sis – you were the rainbow that came after a long storm. You are Glen's consummate achievement and the complete antithesis of him. Being your sister-mother taught me tons and I will always be grateful for your part in helping me learn to accept and forgive.

About the Author

AJ Wootton's early love of reading sparked a lifelong dream to become a writer. Lessons from her rocky childhood taught her the value of financial self-sufficiency. She opted for the solid foundation that a major in business offered in lieu of her heart's first choice, journalism. Her yearning to write resurfaces when in her forties, and on the heels of tragedy, she is driven to reconcile her past and present lives. In her authorial debut, AJ takes her readers on her own journey to overcome the past and face the realities surrounding her failing marriage. Her memoir validates both her calling to write and her gift as a story teller.

AJ is fascinated by the complexities of human relationships, and the beauty and peace that nurturing and healing them brings. Her 30-year career in human resources instilled within her a love of helping others realize their potential. She is thrilled to achieve a life-long goal of providing hope and encouragement through the written word. Her passion is bringing authentic characters to life in stories that inspire and entertain.

27410336R00236

Made in the USA
Lexington, KY
29 December 2018